Investigating Clinical Psychology

Investigating Clinical Psychology takes a deep dive into the field of clinical psychology through the lens of pseudoscience and fringe science. An expert panel of authors honors the role of science in the field while also exploring and guarding against the harms that pseudoscience can cause.

Clinicians have an ethical duty to provide the best available, evidence-based care. Engaging, accessible, and open-minded in approach, this book outlines the distinction between science and pseudoscience in order to prevent the false, and often quite harmful, effects that pseudoscientific practices can have on patients in need of mental health services. The book covers a variety of topics, including harmful therapies, purple hat therapies, animal-assisted therapies, hypnosis, and energy medicine. Featuring world-renowned voices from health care specialists to skeptics on the outside of the field gazing in, it equips readers with the skills needed to differentiate between pseudoscientific and evidence-based approaches in both study and practice.

Aligning with many major undergraduate textbooks for easy course integration, *Investigating Clinical Psychology* is valuable supplemental reading in undergraduate and graduate courses in clinical psychology. It is also a beneficial reference for clinicians in practice, as well as anyone interested in pseudoscience within the mental health sector.

Jonathan N. Stea, PhD, RPsych, is a practicing clinical psychologist and adjunct assistant professor at the University of Calgary (UofC) in Canada. He's a two-time winner of the UofC's Award for Excellence in Clinical Supervision and the 2022 recipient of the Psychologists' Association of Alberta's media and science communication award. His forthcoming book about mental health misinformation and pseudoscience will be published in 2025 by Penguin Random House Canada, Oxford University Press, and Audible.

Stephen Hupp, PhD, is a clinical psychologist and professor of psychology at Southern Illinois University Edwardsville (SIUE) in the United States. In 2015, he won the Great Teacher Award from the SIUE Alumni Association. He has published several books, including *Pseudoscience in Therapy* and *Science-Based Therapy*, and he is the editor of *Skeptical Inquirer: The Magazine for Science and Reason.*

Investigating Psychology Pseudoscience

The science of psychology has continued to grow exponentially over the last century. Unfortunately, pseudoscience in psychology has grown at an even faster pace, and yet very few texts have a primary emphasis on pseudoscience, fringe science, or other controversial topics in psychology.

The *Investigating Psychology Pseudoscience* series offers a fresh look into topics that have commonly been characterized as pseudoscience. The series considers early research while also incorporating the latest investigations into controversial topics. Scientific investigations into the fringe aspects of psychology can often reveal scientific principles, identify alternative explanations, and highlight the many ways the human brain can be deceived. These books are designed to help students, academics, professionals, and everyone else consider the full range of investigations that contribute to psychological science, pseudoscience, and everything in between.

Series Editor

Stephen Hupp, PhD, is a clinical psychologist and professor of psychology at Southern Illinois University Edwardsville (SIUE) in the United States. In 2015, he won the Great Teacher Award from the SIUE Alumni Association. He has published several books including *Pseudoscience in Therapy* and *Dr. Huckleberry's True or Malarkey? Superhuman Abilities.* He is also editor of *Skeptical Inquirer: The Magazine for Science and Reason.*

Books in the Series

Investigating School Psychology
edited by Michael I. Axelrod

Investigating Pop Psychology
edited by Richard Wiseman & Stephen Hupp

For more information, please refer to www.routledge.com/Series+Investigating+Psychology/book-series/IPP

Investigating Clinical Psychology

Pseudoscience, Fringe Science, and Controversies

Edited by Jonathan N. Stea and Stephen Hupp

Routledge
Taylor & Francis Group

NEW YORK AND LONDON

Designed cover image: © Getty Images

First published 2024
by Routledge
605 Third Avenue, New York, NY 10158

and by Routledge
4 Park Square, Milton Park, Abingdon, Oxon, OX14 4RN

Routledge is an imprint of the Taylor & Francis Group, an informa business

© 2024 selection and editorial matter, Jonathan N. Stea and
Stephen Hupp; individual chapters, the contributors

The right of Jonathan N. Stea and Stephen Hupp to be identified as the
authors of the editorial material, and of the authors for their
individual chapters, has been asserted in accordance with sections 77
and 78 of the Copyright, Designs and Patents Act 1988.

Library of Congress Cataloguing-in-Publication Data
Names: Stea, Jonathan N., editor. | Hupp, Stephen, editor.
Title: Investigating clinical psychology : pseudoscience, fringe science,
and controversies / edited by Jonathan N. Stea and Stephen Hupp.
Description: New York, NY : Routledge, 2024. | Series: Investigating
psychology pseudoscience | Includes bibliographical references and
index.
Identifiers: LCCN 2023019095 (print) | LCCN 2023019096 (ebook) |
ISBN 9781032195049 (paperback) | ISBN 9781032195056
(hardback) | ISBN 9781003259510 (ebook)
Subjects: LCSH: Clinical psychology. | Clinical psychology--
Methodology. | Pseudoscience.
Classification: LCC RC467 .I58 2024 (print) | LCC RC467 (ebook) |
DDC 616.001/9--dc23/eng/20230710
LC record available at https://lccn.loc.gov/2023019095
LC ebook record available at https://lccn.loc.gov/2023019096

ISBN: 978-1-032-19505-6 (hbk)
ISBN: 978-1-032-19504-9 (pbk)
ISBN: 978-1-003-25951-0 (ebk)

DOI: 10.4324/9781003259510

Typeset in Sabon
by MPS Limited, Dehradun

For my bubbie, Harriet Zaichick (J.N.S.)

For Pappas and Ila (S.H.)

Contents

Other Books

Other Books in this Series

- *Investigating Pop Psychology*
- *Investigating School Psychology*
- and more to come

Other Books by Stephen Hupp

- *Science-Based Therapy*
- *Pseudoscience in Therapy: A Skeptical Field Guide*
- *Child and Adolescent Psychotherapy: Components of Evidence-Based Treatments for Youth and their Parents*
- *Pseudoscience in Child and Adolescent Psychotherapy: A Skeptical Field Guide*
- *Great Myths of Child Development*
- *Great Myths of Adolescence*
- *Thinking Critically about Child Development: Examining Myths and Misunderstandings*
- *Dr. Huckleberry's True or Malarkey? Superhuman Abilities: Game Book for Skeptical Folk*

Contributors

Gordon J. G. Asmundson, PhD, is a professor of psychology at the University of Regina in Canada. He is also the Editor-in-Chief of *Clinical Psychology Review*.

Kitti Bessenyei, MA, is a clinical psychology doctoral student in the Department of Psychology and Neuroscience at Dalhousie University in Canada.

Blake A. E. Boehme, BA, is a graduate student in the Department of Psychology at the University of Regina in Canada.

Yevgeny Botanov, PhD, is a clinical psychologist and assistant professor at Pennsylvania State University - York.

Timothy Caulfield, BSc, LLB, LLM, CM, FRSC, FCAHS, is a professor in the Faculty of Law and the School of Public Health at the University of Alberta. He is author of the book *Relax, Dammit!: A User's Guide to the Age of Anxiety*.

Keaira Cox, BS, is a master's student in the Clinical Child and School Psychology program at Southern Illinois University Edwardsville.

Andres De Los Reyes, PhD, is a professor of psychology at the University of Maryland. He also serves as editor for the *Journal of Clinical Child and Adolescent Psychology*.

David J. A. Dozois, PhD, CPsych, is a professor of clinical psychology at The University of Western Ontario in Canada. He is also co-editor of the book *Treatment of Psychosocial Risk Factors in Depression*.

John F. Edens, PhD, is a clinical psychologist and professor in the Department of Psychological and Brain Sciences at Texas A&M University.

Edzard Ernst, MD, PhD, is an emeritus professor at the University of Exeter in the United Kingdom. He is author of the book, *Don't Believe What You Think: Arguments for and against SCAM.*

Howard N. Garb, PhD, is a clinical psychologist, the author of *Judging the Clinician: Judgment Research and Psychological Assessment,* and a retired research psychologist with the United States Air Force.

Jon Guy is an independent researcher and science communicator who writes about critical thinking, pseudoscience, logic, psychology, and related topics. He is the author of *Think Straight: An Owner's Manual for the Mind.*

Ruth Ann Harpur, PhD DClinPsych, is a clinical psychologist in independent practice in London, United Kingdom.

Isabella Hartley, BA, is a recent graduate of the University of San Francisco, where she majored in psychology and minored in neuroscience.

Owen Hicks, BSc, is a graduate student in the Department of Psychology at The University of Western Ontario in Canada.

Stephen Hupp, PhD, is a licensed clinical psychologist and professor of psychology at Southern Illinois University Edwardsville. He is also editor of *Skeptical Inquirer: The Magazine for Science and Reason.*

Vyla Hupp is a psychology student at the University of Illinois.

Robyn E. Kilshaw, MS, is a doctoral candidate in clinical psychology at the University of Utah.

Andrew (Hyounsoo) Kim, PhD, CPsych, is an assistant professor in the Department of Psychology at Toronto Metropolitan University in Canada. He is also an adjunct scientist at the University of Ottawa Institute of Mental Health Research at The Royal.

Gerald P. Koocher, PhD, ABPP, is faculty at the Harvard Medical School Bioethics Center, senior attending psychologist at Boston Children's Hospital, and the program director in Clinical and School Psychology at Capella University.

Daniel Machado, MSc, is a graduate student in the Department of Psychology at The University of Western Ontario in Canada.

David K. Marcus, PhD, is a clinical psychologist and professor and chair of the Department of Psychology at Washington State University.

Carmen P. McLean, PhD, is a licensed clinical psychologist at the National Center for PTSD, Dissemination and Training Division, at the VA Palo

Alto Healthcare System and a clinical associate professor (affiliated) at the Department of Psychiatry and Behavioral Sciences, Stanford University

M. Teresa Nezworski, PhD, is a clinical and developmental psychologist and a retired associate professor at the University of Texas at Dallas. She is also editor of the book *Clinical Implications of Attachment.*

Yilong Peng, BS, is a medical student at Harvard Medical School.

Montana L. Ploe, BA, is a doctoral student in the clinical psychology program at Washington State University.

Eve A. Rosenfeld, PhD, is an advanced postdoctoral fellow at the National Center for PTSD, Dissemination and Training Division, at the VA Palo Alto Health Care System and at the Department of Psychiatry and Behavioral Sciences, Stanford University.

John K. Sakaluk, PhD, is a social psychologist and assistant professor at Western University.

Jaden Sangoi, MS, is a doctoral student in the Clinical Science in Child and Adolescent Psychology program at Florida International University.

Lindsey Snaychuk, BA, is a clinical psychology master's student in the Department of Psychology at Toronto Metropolitan University in Canada.

Jonathan N. Stea, PhD, RPsych, is a registered clinical psychologist and adjunct assistant professor of psychology at the University of Calgary in Canada. He is currently writing another book about mental health misinformation and pseudoscience to be published in 2025 by Penguin Random House Canada, Oxford University Press, and Audible.

Miranda A.L. van Tilburg, PhD, is the research director at Cape Fear Valley Medical Center, Professor of medicine at Marshall University, adjunct professor of medicine at the University of North Carolina, and an affiliate professor of social work at the University of Washington.

Melanie Trecek-King, MA, is the creator of Thinking is Power and an associate professor of biology at Massasoit Community College.

Alexander J. Williams, PhD, is a clinical psychologist and assistant teaching professor at the University of Kansas.

Indre V. Viskontas, PhD, is an associate professor of psychology at the University of San Francisco, director of communications for the Sound Health Network, and president-elect of the Society for the Neuroscience of Creativity. She also co-hosts the *Inquiring Minds* podcast.

James M. Wood, PhD, is a clinical psychologist and professor emeritus at the University of Texas at El Paso. He is also author of the book *What's Wrong with the Rorschach? Science Confronts the Controversial Inkblot Test.*

Igor Yakovenko, PhD, RPsych, is an assistant professor of clinical psychology and psychiatry in the Department of Psychology and Neuroscience and the Department of Psychiatry at Dalhousie University in Canada.

Foreword

This is the age of health misinformation. It is everywhere. It is in our social media feeds, promoted by celebrities and influencers, and permeates the legacy news media. We are bombarded with advertisements pushing unsupported therapies and practices. Health misinformation has also worked its way into TV shows, movies, and books. And, increasingly, it is embraced and promoted by prominent politicians.

The harm done by this misinformation – particularly in the context of vaccines and public health – has received more attention over the past few years. Indeed, in 2022, FDA Commissioner Robert Califf suggested that "misinformation is now our leading cause of death." While that may sound a bit hyperbolic, there is no doubt that health misinformation is having a dramatic impact on the public's health and wellbeing. And this is why policymakers throughout the world are starting to consider how best to respond.

But one area that needs greater focus is the pseudoscience that surrounds psychology and mental health. There are, for example, many beliefs about psychology that have, despite a lack of supporting evidence, become normalized and are treated almost as truisms, such as the idea that we only use 10 percent of our brain, that all kids go through the "terrible twos," and that all adolescents are hormonal wrecks that can't stop themselves from undertaking high-risk behaviors. Pseudoscientific forensic psychology has become the basis of countless popular TV shows, novels, and movies. As concern about mental health issues has received increased (and much needed) attention in popular culture, we have seen a concomitant rise in the marketing of psychology pseudoscience products. There are, for instance, countless mental health apps, energy therapies, and allegedly mood-boosting supplements.

While it may seem like many of these examples of psychology pseudoscience are trivial or benign, we know that they can do real harm, including creating misconceptions about the field of psychology that can be used to legitimize unsupported alternative therapies, exploiting parental concerns to push books filled with science-free advice, and making it more difficult for those who need mental health services to navigate the chaotic information environment. And it shouldn't be forgotten that pseudoscientific forensic practices have led to false convictions.

This wonderful book – authored by a collection of stellar interdisciplinary scholars – sheds a much-needed light on these and many other critically important issues. In addition to debunking common psychology myths, the authors explore the nuances of what makes something pseudoscience (for example, is hypnotherapy an evidence-based practice, bunk, or a little of both?), provide practical advice how to spot pseudoscience, and illustrate the ways in which tolerating pseudoscience can do real harm. This book provides a reminder that we need to both seek to understand the foundations of psychology pseudoscience and do what we can do to constructively minimize the harm it can do.

Timothy Caulfield

Preface

This book has two primary audiences. First, it serves as a supplemental book for clinical psychology college courses. While the primary textbooks in these courses tend to focus on the science of clinical psychology, this book provides additional material that skews toward the other end of the science-pseudoscience continuum. However, if you aren't taking a clinical psychology course, fear not – this book was developed with you in mind as well. As you'll soon see, all the chapters, written by authorities in their fields, cover fascinating topics in an engaging way. Whether you'd like to learn more about clinical psychology for a class, for yourself, or for someone you love, this book contains several key messages that everyone should hear.

Clinical psychology has a lot to offer the world. In fact, most of us could benefit from therapy at some point, or maybe even many points, in our lives. Fortunately, the science of clinical psychology has advanced considerably over the last century. In the first wave of science-based practice, scientists such as John B. Watson and B. F. Skinner developed the theoretical groundwork – known as behaviorism – for conceptualizing human behavior. In the second wave, Aaron Beck's groundbreaking cognitive therapy expanded science-based clinical psychology by placing a greater emphasis on the role of thoughts on our psychological functioning. Combining these approaches yielded cognitive-behavioral therapy (CBT), an empirically supported treatment for several disorders. Clinical psychology continued to evolve with the "third wave" of science-based therapies – new variations of CBTs – developed by scientists such as Marsha Linehan (dialectical behavior therapy) and Steven Hayes (acceptance and commitment therapy). Surely, more waves are on the horizon, and if you'd like to read more about the past, present, and future of the science of clinical psychology, feel free to jump ahead to the last chapter of this book.

But now we must turn our attention to the less positive side of clinical psychology. Just as the science of clinical psychology has continued to flourish, so has the pseudoscience. Part I of this book opens with a chapter that defines and describes key topics related to pseudoscience in clinical psychology, and then Chapter 2 discusses the virtue of intellectual humility by providing historical examples of questionable claims. Indeed, one of the biggest problems of Sigmund Freud's theories is that most of his claims are untesticle.

Part II includes three chapters about questionable assessment practices. Specifically, Chapter 3 highlights the red flags of dubious diagnoses such as "chronic" Lyme disease. Chapter 4 provides a deep dive into Rorschach Inkblots, and Chapter 5 covers personality assessments including the Myers-Briggs Type Indicator.

Part III focuses on clinical psychology interventions. Chapters in this section tackle hypnosis myths; therapies that incorporate animals (from both land and sea); and energy medicine techniques such as therapeutic touch, chakra balancing, psychic healing, crystal therapy, and magnet therapy, to name a few. And while all ineffective therapies are harmful in indirect ways, wasting time and money, some therapies cause direct harm, and we have a chapter for that too. Furthermore, if you've never heard of purple hat therapies, you absolutely must use your eyes to read that fascinating chapter as well.

Part IV covers special topics in clinical psychology. The chapter on child and adolescent development critiques claims associated with the "terrible twos" as well as claims related to the "storm and stress" of adolescence. The chapter on alternative medicine provides a broad look at treatments by addressing over 25 dubious practices. Other chapters in this part of the book address controversies in neuropsychology and forensic psychology. Finally, Part V concludes with a chapter on science-based clinical psychology.

Experts wrote all of these chapters. Most of the authors are scientist-practitioners from the field of clinical psychology. Among the ranks, we also have a physician, a biologist, and a cognitive neuroscientist with a podcast (check out *Inquiring Minds*). These contributors have published peer-reviewed studies, authored books, and edited high-impact journals. For some chapters, graduate students – and even one undergraduate student – got in on the writing, thus assuring the next generation of scholars will continue to carry the critical thinking torch.

Investigating Clinical Psychology is the second book in a bigger series. The flagship book in the series, *Investigating Pop Psychology*, summarizes some of the key sources of false beliefs in an attempt to answer questions about *why* people believe strange claims. Adapted from the flagship book, the table below includes several sources of false beliefs – also called "The Faker's Dozen."

Table Sources of False Beliefs: The Faker's Dozen

Source of False Beliefs	Definition
Post Hoc Ergo Propter Hoc Reasoning	Believing that one variable caused another variable simply because the first variable occurred before the second variable.
Assuming Causation from Correlation	Believing that one variable caused the other just because they are correlated with each other.
Reasoning by Representativeness	Making a connection between two concepts based on a superficial similarity between them.
Argument from Authority	Arguing that something is true just because an "expert" claimed it to be so (claims made by celebrities are also included in this type of faulty thinking).
False Analogy	Explaining an idea by comparing it to a similar idea while ignoring key unsaid differences.
False Dichotomy	Depicting only two options when there are actually more than two.
Nirvana Fallacy	Assuming that something is completely bad simply because it's not perfect.
Grain of Truth Exaggeration	Making a grand claim based on the fact that only a small aspect of the claim is true.
Appeal to Nature	Arguing that a practice is safer because it's natural.
Appeal to Antiquity	Arguing that a practice is effective simply because it has been used for a long time.
Biased Sample Misperception	Believing we have a full picture of a phenomenon even though we've only been exposed to a specific portion of the phenomenon.
Selective Perception	Perceiving (and recalling) situations that conform to our ideas while failing to notice (or forgetting) situations that are contrary to our ideas.
Confirmation Bias	Seeking out only information that confirms our beliefs while ignoring information that contradicts our beliefs.

Note: This table was adapted from Hupp (2023) which was influenced by several other sources (Hupp & Jewell, 2015; Lilienfeld et al., 2010; Novella et al., 2018; Shermer, 1997).

As you read through the following chapters, think about how these sources influence the way you and others think about clinical psychology. Also, be on the lookout for other sources of false beliefs. *Investigating Pop Psychology* also identifies some of the hallmarks of false claims – called "The Mucky Seven." You can think of these hallmarks as red flags, indicating a claim might be questionable. The next table summarizes these red flags.

Table Hallmarks of False Claims: The Mucky Seven

Hallmark of False Claims	Definition
Meaningless Jargon	Incorporating scientific-sounding words that don't have any real connection to the proposed concept. For example, words like "quantum," have real meaning in certain situations, but these words are often used to make a pseudoscientific concept sound more scientific.
Untestable Idea Promotion	Endorsing statements that are not able to be studied through sound research designs. For example, there aren't research study designs that can test many of Freud's concepts.
Anecdote Overreliance	Putting anecdotes ahead of research studies. For example, testimonials are one type of anecdote that are often used to promote questionable treatments.
Placebo Exploitation	Relying on improvements that occur simply because people know they are getting a treatment. For example, people have the expectation that a treatment will help them get better so they start to feel better once the treatment starts regardless of which treatment is being provided.
Data Manipulation	Using problematic practices related to analyzing and reporting data. For example, when people make dubious claims, they often cherry-pick the data that favors their hypothesis and leave out the rest of the data.
Burden of Proof Shift	Offering a defense by suggesting that it's the skeptics that need to prove them wrong. For example, a psychic might suggest that a skeptic cannot point to research that disproves someone had lived a previous life.
Science Discreditation	Offering a defense by attacking different aspects of science. For example, those making dubious claims often harshly critique the peer-review process.

Note: This table was adapted from Hupp (2023) which was influenced by several other sources (Hupp, 2019; Lilienfeld et al., 2014; Novella et al., 2018; Sagan, 1996).

Keeping the hallmarks of false claims in mind will help you navigate each topic skeptically. But please also keep an open mind. That is, the goal with this book is to encourage the application of open-minded skepticism to all of the topics covered.

I'd like to end by sharing that the first book in this series was originally planned to be called *Investigating Pop Psychology Pseudoscience*, but during the book's development we shifted to another title – *Investigating Pop Psychology: Pseudoscience, Fringe Science, and Controversies*. And now all of the books in this series are following suit with this more open-minded title. The books in this series cover a broad range of claims; some are clearly pseudoscience-based, some are clearly science-based, and some fall somewhere in the middle. In this middle, we find well-done studies about *fringe* topics. As a prototypical case, there's a real science behind studying topics such as energy medicine or extrasensory perception (ESP). In fact, energy medicine research helped create the need for *dismantling studies* to investigate which components are the key ingredients to a treatment. Similarly, ESP research helped highlight the importance of *replication studies* which provide additional evidence from additional research teams. Dismantling studies and replication studies are now integral to understanding the science of clinical psychology.

Throughout this book, and with guidance from our experts, you can ultimately be the judge of where each claim falls on the science-pseudoscience continuum; and Chapter 1 will be the perfect way to set the stage for critical thinking about clinical psychology.

Stephen Hupp

Note: Did you catch the Freudian slip made earlier in this Preface? It was a tribute to Richard Wiseman, who first made the same slip in his book, *Quirkology: How We Discover the Big Truths in Small Things.*

References

Hupp, S. (2019). *Pseudoscience in Child and Adolescent Psychotherapy: A Skeptical Field Guide.* Cambridge University Press.

Hupp, S., & Jewell, J. (2015). *Great Myths of Child Development.* Wiley.

Hupp, S., & Wiseman, R. (2023). *Investigating Pop Psychology: Pseudoscience, Fringe Science, and Controversies.* Routledge Press.

Lilienfeld, S. O., In Lynn, S. J., & In Lohr, J. M. (2014). *Science and Pseudoscience in Clinical Psychology.* The Guildford Press.

Lilienfeld, S. O., Lynn, S. J., Ruscio, J., & Beyerstein, B. L. (2010). *50 Great Myths of Popular Psychology: Shattering Widespread Misconceptions about Human Behavior.* John Wiley & Sons Ltd.

Novella, S., Novella, B., Santa, M. C., Novella, J., & Bernstein, E. (2018). *The Skeptics' Guide to the Universe: How to Know What's Really Real in a World Increasingly Full of Fake.* Grand Central Publishing.

Sagan, C. (1996). *The Demon-Haunted World: Science as a Candle in the Dark.* Ballantine Books.

Shermer, M. (1997). *Why People Believe Weird Things.* W.H. Freeman and Co.

Acknowledgements

We are eternally grateful to Scott O. Lilienfeld, who inspired both of us to examine clinical psychology with a critical eye. We're also thankful for Richard Wiseman's role in the flagship book of this series and for Timothy Caulfield's willingness to support this project by voicing his wisdom in the Foreword. Perhaps most important of all, we are particularly thankful for all of the amazing contributors that wrote such thoughtful and engaging chapters!

Many people at Routledge also deserve considerable gratitude. Lucy McClune commissioned the first book in the series and helped expand the project beyond that first book. Danielle Dyal then contracted this book, and Adam Woods helped guide our work throughout much of the journey. Many thanks also to Zoe Thomson for seeing this book through to completion during the final stages of development. We are also grateful to Tarana Parveen for superb copyediting and Lauren Ellis for overlooking the final aspects of production. Many of the strengths of this book are due to all of their combined efforts.

Finally, we would like to thank our families who have supported us in many ways. This book is dedicated to Harriet Zaichick who is a beacon of unconditional love. The book is also dedicated to Pappas (Bernadine Connolly) and Ila Hupp, two amazing grandmas. Finally, we appreciate all of the support from Leslie, Heidi, and Lou (J.N.S.), as well as Farrah, Evan, Henry, Vyla, mom, and dad (S.H.).

Part I
Introduction

1 The Role of Science in Clinical Psychology

Jonathan N. Stea

We need to normalize not normalizing pseudoscience, especially in clinical psychology. The assessment and treatment of mental health concerns is a serious enterprise. Unfortunately, it is not uncommon to encounter patients who have received pseudoscientific health services. Many have asked, "So what? Why does that matter?" They further argue that such services do not jeopardize patient care. These assumptions are false and often quite harmful (McKay & Jensen-Doss, 2021).

The late and great Scott O. Lilienfeld delineated exactly why pseudo-scientific health services can be harmful: they can directly produce harm, they can indirectly tax time and financial resources from evidence-based services, and they can further erode the scientific foundations and trust of health professions (Lilienfeld et al., 2014). As the Canadian psychologist, Barry Beyerstein, so eloquently stated, "When people become sick, any promise of a cure is beguiling. Common sense and the demand for evidence are easily supplanted by false hope. In this vulnerable state, the need for critical appraisal of treatment options is more – rather than less – necessary" (Beyerstein, 2001; p. 236).

People who experience mental health concerns are at risk of encountering a myriad of pseudoscientific assessments and treatments both within and outside of the psychology profession. For example, a patient may present to a care provider with a cluster of mental health concerns and receive a dubious diagnosis, which could include those that are both medically recognized (e.g., dissociative identity disorder) and unrecognized (e.g., adrenal fatigue, parental alienation syndrome). The same patient may then receive further assessment using thoroughly debunked or precarious practices, such as the use of the *Myers-Briggs Type Indicator* (MBTI) or the Rorschach Inkblot to assess their personality. And equally worrisome, they may receive unsupported or pseudoscientific treatments. Patients, for example, who experience anxiety disorders and depressive disorders deserve first-line, evidence-based therapies such as cognitive-behavioral therapy, not

DOI: 10.4324/9781003259510-2

scientifically implausible treatments, such as many of those found in the domain of alternative medicine (e.g., naturopathy, energy medicine).

The potential negative consequences of mental health-related pseudoscience can mean continued suffering and in extreme cases, even death. One of the most famous tragic cases of such harm involved the death of Candace Newmaker, a 10 year-old girl who died during a 70-minute session of rebirthing therapy, whereby she was wrapped from head to toe and surrounded by pillows in an attempt to treat reactive attachment disorder (Josefson, 2001).

Clinicians in regulated health professions – and especially psychologists – have an ethical duty to provide the best available, evidence-based care. Indeed, this ethical imperative is baked into the fabric of our codes of ethics and standards of practice (American Psychological Association, 2002; Canadian Psychological Association, 2017). In order to provide such evidence-based care, the role of science in clinical psychology needs to be paramount.

Science versus Pseudoscience

An oft-quoted quip is the idea that to know happiness, one must experience sadness. This idea is predicated on the notion that a phenomenon can be helpfully conceptualized by understanding it from multiple angles and perspectives. This same idea might be true when it comes to understanding the nature of science. In order to maximize our understanding of science, it is important to understand the nature of its evil twin, so to speak: pseudoscience.

Granted, both science and pseudoscience are to some extent nebulous philosophical constructs. They are not one thing, but rather many things at once. Science might be most simply understood as both an accumulating body of knowledge as well as a method of inquiry. The scientific method works via an interplay between both bottom-up, data-driven processes, and top-down, theoretical applications. Scientists are skeptical – not cynical – and question everything by approaching claims with humility. If the scientific method were a person, they would be the most skeptical, humble, and likely annoying person you ever met. Indeed, "at its core, therefore, science is a form of arrogance control" (Tavris & Aronson, 2007, p. 108).

In contrast, pseudoscience is like a child that dresses as science for Halloween: It looks like science if you squint, thrives on magical thinking, and above all, wants to either trick you, take your resources, or both. In other words, in contrast to science, pseudoscience is an approach to evidence that avoids contradictory information and ultimately stifles the progress needed to sustain its evolution. Deciphering the difference between science and pseudoscience can sometimes be a difficult endeavor because science differs from pseudoscience in degree rather than in kind. However, as Lilienfeld and colleagues (2014) have brilliantly articulated, the distinction between science and pseudoscience is similar to the boundary between day and night: the fact that the precise boundary is unclear does not imply that the two cannot be meaningfully differentiated.

While philosophers of science have been debating the nature of pseudoscience for millennia in the context of an historical, complex, and rich literature on the topic (Curd & Cover, 1998), a cluster of warning signs have emerged that help to describe the features of pseudoscience. For example, Lilienfeld and colleagues (2014) have delineated several of these indicators, which can include:

- an overuse of ad hoc hypotheses designed to immunize claims from falsification;
- absence of self-correction;
- evasion of peer review;
- emphasis on confirmation rather than refutation;
- reversing the burden of proof on skeptics rather than proponents;
- absence of connectivity to the broader scientific literature;
- over-reliance on testimonials and elevation of anecdotal evidence;
- use of obscurantist and science-y sounding language; and
- absence of well-articulated limits under which predictions do and do not apply.

These indicators are by no means an exhaustive list (see also the Preface to this book; Hupp & Wiseman, 2023; and Ruscio, 2001) but they certainly target the core of what it means to identify pseudoscience. The more indicators that are present with respect to a particular discipline, treatment, or research program, the more likely it is the case that pseudoscience is afoot. While even excellent scientists are vulnerable to the trappings of pseudoscience, adherence to the scientific method and scientific processes – such as self-correction and peer-review – can help to protect against its lure.

Further, Lilienfeld (2005) has somewhat facetiously, albeit incisively, proposed 10 Commandments of helping students to distinguish between science and pseudoscience in psychology. Beyond becoming aware of pseudoscientific warning signs, there are other contextual factors that can add to a more complete understanding of how pseudoscience operates. For example, it is important to understand differences between skepticism and cynicism, methodological and philosophical skepticism, the scientific method and the scientists who use it, and pseudoscience versus metaphysics. It is also important to approach the topic of pseudoscience with care and sensitivity because pseudoscientific beliefs can appeal to deep-seated aspects of one's worldview and personal identity – it can therefore feel upsetting, threatening, and result in defensiveness when evidence is presented that suggests the way in which one understands the world or themselves is distorted. Nevertheless, it remains important to foster the critical thinking skills needed to distinguish science from pseudoscience, which in part also involves maintaining consistency in one's intellectual standards and raising awareness about potential fallacies and gaps in logic (Caulfield, 2020), cognitive biases (Kahneman, 2003), and motivated reasoning processes (Kunda, 1990) that can underpin and sustain pseudoscientific beliefs.

Notably, illusions of causality are very powerful anecdotal experiences that can trick many into believing that a treatment works (Matute et al., 2011). For instance, if a patient believes that they've found relief after receiving homeopathy, that's wonderful. But if their relief is used as evidence by clinicians to support the recommendations of other patients, then an ethical problem has emerged. Namely, the claim needs to be scientifically tested before it can be ethically recommended. Evidence-based treatment providers should be cognizant of the fact that the quality of scientific evidence exists in a hierarchy, broadly speaking, and that anecdotes offer low-quality evidence. Unfortunately, proponents of pseudoscientific treatments often unethically exploit anecdotes to their benefit. In this way, the hijacked use of anecdotal evidence may very well be the heart of pseudoscience.

The Scientist-Practitioner Model

Health care disciplines that are philosophically premised on evidence-based medicine (EBM; Wieten, 2018) and its more professionally inclusive variant, evidence-based practice (EBP; APA Presidential Task Force on Evidence-Based Practice, 2006) can rely on the scientific method to help guide patient care. EBP involves understanding and implementing patient care via an interactive and delicate balance between three pillars: the best available scientific evidence, clinical expertise, and patient characteristics (which include patient culture, values, and preferences).

The discipline of clinical psychology adopted science as an explicit value as early as 1947 when the idea that doctoral psychologists should be trained as both scientists and practitioners became American Psychological Association (APA) policy (Shakow et al., 1947). In 1949, the "scientist-practitioner model" (sometimes referred to as the "Boulder model") was born at the Conference on Graduate Education in Psychology in Boulder, Colorado to reflect the realization that future psychologists should be trained in both research and clinical practice – and that these elements of the profession should inform each other (Jones & Mehr, 2007). Today, the term "scientist-practitioner" refers to both a model of training and a model of practice. It involves "putting evidence into practice and practice into evidence" whereby clinical psychologists are expected to have expertise in the integration of research and clinical practice (Dozois, 2013). It means that clinical psychologists should be skilled consumers of the scientific literature and possess both the ability and willingness to incorporate that knowledge into their practice. It also means that psychologists have an ethical responsibility to promote and practice evidence-based patient care that is devoid of unequivocal pseudoscience and leery of its shades of gray.

Unfortunately, there exists a notorious gap between science and practice in clinical psychology. That is, we know that the empirical literature is often not utilized by practitioners for a variety of reasons, which can include variable attitudes in relation to EBP; concerns about the generalizability of research findings; and concerns about the importance of randomized controlled trials (RCTs) (Dozois, 2013). While it remains a tall order to implement the multi-pronged solutions that are needed to help close this gap, it is nevertheless vital to the sustainability of clinical psychology as a scientific discipline. Some of these solutions include better scientific knowledge translation by science communicators, better communication between scientists and practitioners, more effectiveness trials that evaluate treatments in real-world clinic settings as opposed to the laboratory, increased research on why and how treatments work (i.e., mechanisms of change and process research) rather than whether treatments work (i.e., outcome research), increased training in evidence-based thinking as well as health and science literacy, increased practitioner use of reliable and valid measures of patient functioning during practice, and increased collaborative data collection between scientists and practitioners (Dozois, 2013).

This gap between science and practice stretches to enormous proportions outside the domain of clinical psychology when it is extended to other allied mental health professions and beyond to unregulated health providers in alternative medicine circles and the wellness industry. Health care practitioners who purport to address mental health concerns in their practice but that do not value, respect, or understand the role of science in mental health care risk compromising the safety of patients and treatment effectiveness. Unfortunately, it can very much be a buyer-beware approach for patients in the unregulated space where mental health care is marketed and sold. And in the absence of science, opinion prevails (Nathan & Gorman, 1998).

Science and Mental Health Literacy in Clinical Psychology

It is important to understand that while the assessment and treatment of mental disorders falls under the purview of clinical psychology, the profession does not have a monopoly on these domains. For example, several other medical and allied mental health professions assess and address mental health concerns, such as educational psychology, counseling psychology, psychiatry, family medicine, nursing, occupational therapy, and social work, among others. Additionally, there are many other unregulated providers of mental health services in alternative medicine circles and the wellness industry who may identify with various titles, such as "life coach," "wellness consultant," and – depending on particular countries and jurisdictions – other non-legally protected titles, such as "therapist," "psychotherapist," "counselor," or "practitioner." Understanding the ways in which clinical psychology both competes and complements in these spaces is vital to understanding the nature of clinical psychology, its pseudoscientific variants, and where it fits into its larger health care context.

From the perspective of the psychology profession, there is an obligation to provide the best available, evidence-based care to patients, which is written into our ethical codes, regulated standards of practice, and clinical practice guidelines (American Psychological Association, 2002; Canadian Psychological Association, 2017). From the perspective of the general public and patients, mental health care is marketed and sold both within and outside of the psychology profession where there exists tremendous variation in quality of care. Unfortunately, this means that while it is incumbent upon regulatory bodies to safeguard the public – in part by ensuring that practitioners are practicing safely, competently, and ethically – it is also incumbent upon consumers and patients of mental health care to protect themselves from pseudoscientific and predatory practices. It is certainly no understatement to say that "the world of psychotherapy is bewildering," which was the claim of Meichenbaum and Lilienfeld (2018) when they estimated that there are at least 600 "brands" of psychotherapy that are growing on a monthly basis.

In order to maximize the incisiveness of clinical psychologists, patients, and the general public with a view towards ideal selection of mental health services, it would be prudent to improve the science and mental health literacy of all parties. While the construct of science literacy is multifaceted, it most generally refers to three aspects: knowing the basic facts established by science, understanding of scientific practices, and understanding of science as a social process (National Academies of Sciences, Engineering, and Medicine, 2016). The improvement of science literacy is one potentially important way to embolden the acumen of clinical psychologists, empower patients, reduce the spread of health misinformation, and prevent the proliferation of pseudoscientific health practices.

In a recent U.S. national survey, only 64% of American respondents understood the statistical concept of probability, only 51% correctly defined a scientific experiment, and only 23% were able to correctly describe the components of a scientific study (National Science Board, 2018). Although the relationship between science literacy and health-related behaviors is incredibly complex and influenced by myriad factors (e.g., cultural norms, self-efficacy, accessibility of services), science literacy may affect an individual's health in subtle and indirect ways. For example, lower science literacy has been associated with rejection of well-supported scientific theories and acceptance of viral and deceptive claims about health and science (Landrum & Olshansky, 2019); studies show that science knowledge can lead to increased self-efficacy, which is related to preventative health care behaviors (Bandura, 2010; Jayanti & Burns, 1998); and there is a developing research literature on the relationship between higher science literacy and better ability to evaluate and interpret online health-related information (Cavojova et al., 2022; Ellis et al., 2012).

One way to improve science literacy is to teach about the nature of science versus pseudoscience in the classroom and beyond. For example, Schmaltz and Lilienfeld (2014) advocate for dispelling examples of pseudoscience to teach scientific thinking in light of research literature demonstrating that it can be effective in countering pseudoscientific beliefs. Similarly, Wilson (2018) found that following an undergraduate science and critical thinking course, paranormal and pseudoscientific beliefs decreased. Beyond the classroom, the University of Alberta (2021) has been offering a free, online, well-received science literacy course to the general public, which is a brilliant way to increase the accessibility of science literacy concepts.

Relatedly, mental health literacy is an evolving construct that has arisen from the domain of health literacy and has been defined as: "understanding how to obtain and maintain positive mental health; understanding mental disorders and their treatments; decreasing stigma related to mental disorders; and, enhancing help-seeking efficacy (knowing when and where to seek help and developing competencies designed to improve one's mental health care and self-management capabilities)" (Kutcher et al., 2016; p. 165). While research has demonstrated that poor health literacy more generally is related to numerous negative health and social outcomes (e.g., increased rates of chronic illness, decreased use of health services, increased health care costs, early mortality), the evidence based on the relatively nascent mental health literacy construct has unfortunately been riddled with psychometric challenges (Kutcher et al., 2016). Nevertheless, the importance of mental health literacy in helping to improve health outcomes has increasingly been recognized and it remains imperative to enhance our understanding of its construct with a view towards the development of contextually and developmentally appropriate interventions, to be evaluated with better and validated measurements.

Summary and Conclusion

The primary purpose of this book is to increase the likelihood that students and the general public are able to differentiate between pseudoscientific and evidence-based approaches in clinical psychology and to provide a useful resource for clinicians to help them distinguish between science and pseudoscience in their practice. Our intention with this book is not to make sloppy claims about what is and what is not pseudoscience – rather, the intention is to educate about the nature of science versus pseudoscience and to help stimulate critical thinking about health decisions, especially with respect to mental health. In this vein, the word "investigating" in the title of our book – *Investigating Clinical Psychology: Pseudoscience, Fringe Science, and Controversies* – is purposefully apt.

Jonathan N. Stea, PhD, RPsych, is a registered clinical psychologist and adjunct assistant professor of psychology at the University of Calgary in Canada. He is currently writing another book about mental health misinformation and pseudoscience to be published in 2025 by Penguin Random House Canada, Oxford University Press, and Audible.

References

American Psychological Association. (2002, as amended 2010, 2016). *Ethical principles of psychologists and code of conduct*. Author.

APA Presidential Task Force on Evidence-Based Practice. (2006). Evidence-based practice in psychology. *American Psychologist, 61*(4), 271–285. 10.1037/0003-066X.61.4.271.

Bandura, A. (2010). Self-efficacy. In I.B. Weiner and W.E. Craighead (Eds.), *The Corsini Encyclopedia of Psychology* (4th ed., pp. 1534–1536). John Wiley & Sons.

Beyerstein B. L. (2001). Alternative medicine and common errors of reasoning. *Academic Medicine: Journal of the Association of American Medical Colleges, 76*, 230–237.

Caulfield, T. (2020). Does debunking work? Correcting COVID-19 misinformation on social media. In C. M. Flood, V. MacDonnell, J. Philpott et al., (Eds.), *Vulnerable: The Law, Policy and Ethics of COVID-19* (pp. 183–200). University of Ottawa Press.

Canadian Psychological Association. (2017). *Canadian Code of Ethics for Psychologists, Fourth Edition*. Author.

Cavojova, V., Srol, J., & Ballova Mikuskova, E. (2022). How scientific reasoning correlates with health-related beliefs and behaviors during the COVID-19 pandemic? *Journal of Health Psychology, 27*, 534–547. 10.1177/135910532 0962266

Curd, M., & Cover, J. A. (1998). *Philosophy of science: The central issues*. W.W. Norton & Co.

Dozois, D. (2013). Psychological treatments: Putting evidence into practice and practice into evidence. *Canadian Psychology, 54*, 1–11. 10.1037/n0031125.

Ellis, J., Mullan, J., Worsley, A., & Pai, N. (2012). The role of health literacy and social networks in arthritis patients' health information-seeking behavior: A qualitative study. *International Journal of Family Medicine, 1*, 1–6.

Hupp, S., & Wiseman, R. (2023). *Investigating pop psychology: Pseudoscience, fringe science, and controversies*. Routledge.

Jayanti, R., & Burns, A. (1998). The antecedents of preventive health care behavior: An empirical study. *Journal of the Academy of Marketing Science, 26*, 6–15.

Jones, J. L., & Mehr, S. L. (2007). Foundations and assumptions of the scientist-practitioner model. *American Behavioral Scientist, 50*, 766–771.

Josefson, D. (2001). Rebirthing therapy banded after girl died in 70 minute struggle. *BMJ, 322*, 1014.

Kahneman, D. (2003). Maps of bounded rationality: Psychology for behavioral economics. *American Economic Review, 93*, 1449–1475.

Kunda, Z. (1990). The case for motivated reasoning. *Psychological Bulletin, 108*, 480–498.

Kutcher, S., Wei, Y., & Coniglio, C. (2016). Mental health literacy: Past, present, and future. *The Canadian Journal of Psychiatry, 61*, 154–158.

Landrum, A. R., & Olshansky, A. (2019). The role of conspiracy mentality in denial of science and susceptibility to viral deception about science. *Politics and The Life Sciences, 38*, 193–209.

Lilienfeld, S. O., Lynn, S. J., & Lohr, J. M. (2014). *Science and pseudoscience in clinical psychology*. The Guilford Press.

Lilienfeld, S. O. (2005). The 10 commandments of helping students to distinguish science from pseudoscience in psychology. *Association for Psychological Science*. Retrieved from https://www.psychologicalscience.org/observer/the-10-commandments-of-helping-students-distinguish-science-from-pseudoscience-in-psychology

Matute, H., Yarritu, I., & Vadillo, M. A. (2011). Illusions of causality at the heart of pseudoscience. *British Journal of Psychology, 102*, 392–405.

McKay, D., & Jensen-Doss, A. (2021). Harmful treatments in psychotherapy. *Clinical Psychology: Science and Practice, 28*(1), 2–4. 10.1037/cps0000023

Meichenbaum, D., & Lilienfeld, S. O. (2018). How to spot hype in the field of psychotherapy: A 19-item checklist. *Professional Psychology: Research and Practice, 49*(1), 22–30. 10.1037/pro0000172

Nathan, P. E., & Gorman, J. M. (Eds.) (1998). *A guide to treatments that work*. Oxford University Press.

National Academies of Sciences, Engineering, and Medicine (2016). *Science Literacy: Concepts, Contexts, and Consequences (National Academies Press, Washington, DC)*, p 166. https://www.chemconnections.org/Reading/Scientific%20Literacy%20NAS%2023595.pdf

National Science Board. (2018). *Science and Engineering Indicators 2018*. NSB-2018-1. National Science Foundation. Retrieved from https://www.nsf.gov/statistics/indicators/.

Ruscio, J. (2001). *Clear thinking with psychology: Separating sense from nonsense*. Wadsworth.

Schmaltz, R., & Lilienfeld, S. O. (2014). Hauntings, homeopathy, and the Hopkinsville Goblins: Using pseudoscience to teach scientific thinking. *Frontiers in Psychology, 5*, 336.

Shakow, D., Hilgard, E. R., Kelly, E. L., Luckey, B., Sanford, R. N., & Shaffer, L. F. (1947). Recommended graduate training program in clinical psychology. *American Psychologist, 2*, 539–558.

Tavris, C., & Aronson, E. (2007). *Mistakes were made (but not by me): Why we justify foolish beliefs, bad decisions, and hurtful acts*. Harcourt.

University of Alberta. (2021). Science Literacy. Retrieved from https://www.ualberta.ca/admissions-programs/online-courses/science-literacy.html

Wieten, S. (2018). Expertise in evidence-based medicine: A tale of three models. *Philosophy, Ethics, and Humanities in Medicine, 13*(1), 2. 10.1186/s13010-018-0055-2.

Wilson, J. A. (2018). Reducing pseudoscientific and paranormal beliefs in university students through a course in science and critical thinking. *Science and Education, 27*, 183–210.

2 Intellectual Humility and Historical Roots in Pseudoscience

Daniel Machado, Owen Hicks, and David J. A. Dozois

The pace at which science has advanced over time is astounding, and our understanding of the factors that impact the quality of our scientific endeavours has grown alongside. Scientists and clinicians today benefit greatly from having access to this cumulative knowledge and may be tempted to consider themselves largely resistant to the errors that befell their predecessors. There is certainly good reason for such confidence. On a fundamental level, the presence of a protocol (i.e., the scientific method) that facilitates the collection of empirical evidence through controlled experiments is a boon that advances us far beyond the limitations of earlier eras. In the pursuit of knowledge, extracting a reasonable degree of certainty from a reality that can be quite relative is a formidable task – a task that requires a guiding framework to constrain and direct our impulses.

To this end, diligent and skillful application of the scientific method offers strong protection against error in and of itself (Dozois, 2013; Lilienfeld, 2010). Nonetheless, every twist and turn in the scientific process presents a critical decision point, and each requires some degree of judgement to be applied that affects the scope and limits of scientific objectivity. To combat this potential for error, the machinery that envelopes scientific inquiry has become more sophisticated over time. The systemic layers that detect and correct flawed work include rigorous training, peer review, institutional and professional codes, replication efforts, and, more recently, pre-registration and the broader open science movement. This support structure is a bulwark that mobilizes the expertise of the collective to assist the individual. In this manner, the system is designed such that all parts can work together to produce stronger, more reliable conclusions and limit the magnitude of errors.

This refinement across time has created a reputable structural framework that supports rigour, reproducibility, and consensus-building. However, it is important to remain vigilant; because, despite these safeguards, it is unrealistic to expect research to remain error-free. That is, although error

DOI: 10.4324/9781003259510-3

can be minimized, it is ultimately unavoidable. Further, error is not always obvious or deliberate, and may be partly a product of the protective system itself. For example, it is possible that we underestimate the extent to which modern science errs because flawed studies tend to be overshadowed by more interesting results. We are taught that science is iterative, provisional, and self-correcting, and yet researchers today are not easily exposed to clear examples of when science fails. The current incentive structure in the field is one of "publish or perish," which encourages the presentation of new and exciting results and discourages reporting of null or incorrect findings. These conditions contribute to publication bias, or the "file drawer problem" (Rosenthal, 1979). The file drawer problem refers to the many studies that are relegated to file drawers and deemed unworthy for publication because they contain "uninteresting" findings (e.g., cases in which one fails to reject the null hypothesis or in which effect sizes are small in magnitude). The absence of these studies from the literature base may then contribute to a skewed understanding of a given subject area; an understanding that is solely defined by studies with the most optimal outcomes and, in a worst-case scenario, high Type I error rates, also known as a false positive conclusion (Bakan, 1967; Hopewell et al., 2009; Scargle, 1999).

Science is an imperfect cycle of failure and progress. By discouraging openness about error and making it difficult to publish insignificant findings, we are avoiding exposure to real and comprehensive examples that we may learn from. Error detection, error acknowledgement, and the painstaking process of building robust theories are all critical to creating science that is reliable, valid, and replicable. It is imperative that we consistently practice looking for weaknesses in our own and others' work, and learn to accept unsatisfactory results as both necessary and largely helpful. Mistakes and dead ends are never useless; they are critically informative steps toward future success. When we take this approach, we will be better able to examine the many claims that are made within clinical psychology.

Examining the Claims

Cognitive Biases and Intellectual Humility

The history of clinical psychology provides rich opportunities to learn from the missteps of others. From a modern perspective, and with the benefit of decades of hindsight, some of these past errors may seem irrelevant to today. But even extreme examples of flawed science contain valuable lessons. For instance, it is easy to discard a practice such as trephination (see Dozois & Machado, 2021) as a barbaric example of pseudoscience that we have progressed far beyond. After all, what could we possibly have in common with ancient societies that used crude tools to perforate the craniums of live human beings to ward off evil spirits? Perhaps more than is apparent at first glance. Collective knowledge and the methods of acquiring it have undoubtedly advanced, but the fundamental "equipment" that we use to process and interact with the world remains subject to the same inherent limitations. Our brains are hardwired to produce numerous unconscious, systematic errors in thinking that lead us to misinterpret information (Kahneman et al., 1982; Kahneman, 2011), such as confirmation bias (Klayman, 1995; Nickerson, 1998), hindsight bias (Hawkins & Hastie, 1990), and over-confidence bias (Klayman et al., 1999). These biases can affect one's judgement at any stage of scientific inquiry, and research has also demonstrated their influence on clinical decision-making in healthcare settings (Featherston, 2020).

Most insidiously, cognitive biases tend to operate such that we remain blissfully unaware of their presence and effect. A large body of research demonstrates the existence of such a *bias blind spot*, in which people tend to think they are largely unaffected by cognitive biases, and that these biases are more commonplace in other people (Pronin, 2007, 2008; Pronin et al., 2002; 2004). Academics are not immune to this, as research has shown that susceptibility to blind spot bias correlates positively with cognitive sophistication (Pronin et al., 2002). It is discomforting to consider that one is not only susceptible to bias, but also may be completely unaware of it.

To combat ignorance, we must first be aware of its existence. Awareness, therefore, is a key component of the remedy to cognitive bias. In support of this process, numerous authors have discussed how researchers would benefit from practicing intellectual humility (e.g., Leary et al., 2017; Lilienfeld & Bowes, 2021; Lilienfeld et al., 2017). Intellectual humility is being curious about the existence of your own blind spots, and extending skepticism toward your own ideas, methods, and opinions (Leary et al., 2017; Lilienfeld & Bowes, 2021). This is a valuable trait because interrogating *why* one believes something can help build stronger claims. Importantly, it also cultivates the capacity for self-correction. Evaluating your practices with intellectual humility involves combing over previously tread ground with the motivation to find new information, which is a process that has myriad benefits when applied to research settings: it can help illuminate flaws, identify and discard false hypotheses, and, ultimately, move closer to the truth (Lilienfeld et al., 2017).

Scrutinizing our own beliefs and work in this manner may be uncomfortable, but it is also a professional and ethical responsibility. It is a responsibility because, when conducting research, it is crucial to always remain skeptical and to question if we are using the best available methods in pursuit of knowledge and progress. Further, we must embrace and openly engage with the bureaucratic structures that exist to facilitate this process of inquiry (i.e., the aforementioned protective frameworks of peer review, open science, ethics boards, etc.). Actively seeking critical feedback that challenges the work and ideas we have invested in heavily can be challenging, but will ultimately promote personal and professional growth and produce better science. Thus, intellectual humility helps us accept institutional barriers as necessary safeguards, and receive feedback – both positive and negative – with equanimity.

Intellectual humility is also useful when critically analyzing others' research. For example, it is intuitive to assume that all research is equally informative or meaningful, but it is necessary to challenge this intuition and evaluate research in terms of varying levels of importance. This concept of a "hierarchy of evidence" (Spring, 2007) refers to the notion that certain types of research (e.g., meta-analyses, systematic reviews) tend to provide more robust results than others (e.g., a single research study), which provide more reliable results than others still (e.g., professional opinion, case reports; Dozois et al., 2014). Conceptualizing research in this manner will inevitably place some work above others, which may initially seem unkind or judgemental. But when evaluated through a lens of intellectual humility, one is able to view individual work in each tier of the overall hierarchy as an important piece in an incremental puzzle that is contributing to pushing science forward. This evaluation also serves a greater purpose of inspiring pursuit of the highest level of evidence in one's own work, so as to make a meaningful contribution that is additive to existing research.

Many clinical psychologists are both researchers and clinicians, and intellectual humility has value in each role. For example, despite the substantial development of empirically supported treatments over the years, psychology remains a relatively young science, and much is unknown about the factors that impact the effectiveness of interventions. Thus, in the context of the interdependent relationship between evidence-based practice and practice-based evidence (Barkham & Mellor-Clark, 2003), it is undeniable that clinical judgement remains a useful and even essential skill. However, clinical judgement is certainly not paramount. In fact, as discussed by the influential Paul Meehl (1956), an essential tool in a reputable practitioner's skillset is the ability to recognize that actuarial (i.e., statistical) prediction is superior to clinical prediction. Acceptance of this reality may seem counterintuitive to the seasoned clinician who has necessarily used clinical judgment in other aspects of service delivery. By practicing intellectual humility, however, clinicians can recognize the limitations of their own viewpoints and acknowledge that robust data should usually supersede personal judgment at times when they contradict.

Using Intellectual Humility to Study History

Historical case studies are also a useful instrument for practicing intellectual humility. By resisting the urge to apply hindsight bias and instead choosing to examine past practices and events earnestly and in context, we remain open to learning from situations that we may have initially felt have little to teach us. In doing so, we build mental habits of being curious about what we do not know and being open to regularly testing and updating our theories, opinions, and beliefs. Further, recognizing that science has advanced in part by learning from error serves to normalize critical evaluation. This habit can be uncomfortable in practice but is essential for progress, and therefore must remain an established part of science.

To illustrate, we return to the earlier example of trephination and try to critically evaluate it without the "benefit" of hindsight. Although the premise of warding off evil spirits purportedly taking up residence in an individual's skull is incompatible with any provable reality, disregarding it as pseudoscience that we have nothing to learn from would be short-sighted. Societies that practiced trephination were archaic in their understanding of the nature of consciousness and its interaction with the physical world. However, it would be unreasonable to expect them to discard the spiritual framework they used to explain complex phenomena without first progressing through the intermediate steps that are necessary to adopt new methods and beliefs.

It is also insufficient to label something as pseudoscience based solely on it being proven incorrect later, as it is an innate feature of science to progress through falsification and rejection of prior theories to beget new and better ideas. It is perhaps more accurate to state that pseudoscience involves an element of willful obfuscation that gives the illusion of value, such as through the dismissal or exclusion of available scientific ideals and systematic practices. A theory such as trephination, which is simply not true when viewed through a modern lens, did not inherently avoid rigorous testing of its claims or comparisons with plausible alternative hypotheses; rather, the conditions through which this evaluative process could occur were not sufficiently advanced to permit it. A theory becomes obsolete when viable alternative explanations are presented and compete with the existing theory. But if the paradigm through which the alternative explanation is produced is not present in the cultural milieu of the time, then it is probably unreasonable to expect it to have been considered.

In many historical cases, there is no deliberate obfuscation of the truth, just a sincere attempt to describe and interpret reality using the tools available. In this sense, a claim can be wildly incorrect, but may not be considered pseudoscience when considering the conditions and context under which it was developed. When discussing scientific theories, it is easy to fall back on language such as "correct" or "incorrect." But theories are, at their most fundamental level, an attempt to describe the world and the matter within it; that is, they are merely approximations. A theory might be wholly incorrect for all functional purposes, yet it still might be possible to draw a faint line between it and a later but more accurate explanation. For example, purveyors of trephination were quite clearly mistaken in their belief that the practice released evil spirits from patients' skulls, but the procedure did reduce internal pressure following head trauma and therefore conferred some benefit to patients (at least to those who survived!). Further, trephination was the first known attempt at treating mental difficulties by cutting the skull. In fact, it is not wholly inaccurate to suggest that trephination was a very primitive precursor to neurosurgery (Liu & Apuzzo, 2003). Even though the processes and techniques of neurosurgery are more scientifically informed and sophisticated than those of trephination, the same basic procedure is still used: cut open the skull to access the brain. Thus, although speculative, the trials and errors of trephination, while certainly brutal, may have provided the necessary impetus for the eventual development of modern methods. At the very least, we can say with confidence that trephination was not a pseudoscience after placing it into proper historical perspective.

We must avoid categorizing a theory or practice as pseudoscience simply based on how foolish it appears from a modern lens or how wrong it proved to be. Otherwise, with enough passage of time, *any and all* incomplete or sub-optimal theories will become eligible for the "pseudoscience bin." For example, consider the Wright brothers, Orville and Wilbur, who are credited with flying the first motor-operated airplane. The Wright brothers' breakthrough three-axis control system remains standard today (Lawrence & Padfield, 2005), whereas other elements of their design quickly became obsolete and would be considered elementary, and even preposterous, by today's standards (e.g., designing wings with little consideration for inherent stability). However, it would be shortsighted to claim that the more fantastical aspects of the Wright brothers' design rendered their practices pseudoscientific. Rather, they reflected the limitations of research and design methods of the era. Moreover, over time, the weaker elements of their theory were outcompeted by the stronger elements. This is precisely how the scientific method is designed to promote progress and protect against the perpetuation of pseudoscientific ideas, and it should be celebrated.

Most historical cases (i.e., those that do not exhibit identifiable pseudoscientific qualities) are imperfect bodies of work through which valuable learning can occur. They help promote a view of failure as a potential opportunity, in which error provides space to build back better and stronger and with more certainty. Evaluating previous scientific efforts from a standpoint of intellectual humility promotes fairness and charity toward truth-seekers of the past, who were invariably constrained by the limitations of the collective body of knowledge existing at the time. While previous scientific pursuits undoubtedly vary in the degree to which they match the modern ideal of the scientific method, they nonetheless offer some present value – even if only as a sobering reminder of how *not* to seek truth. More substantially, science is an iterative process that grows in part through trial and error – or success and failure – and progress cannot be easily divorced from either component. Consequently, ridiculing or standing in judgement of the past while simultaneously benefiting from it is not a principled stance. If historians of the future were to evaluate present efforts solely through such a modern lens, with little consideration for context or nuance, our work would similarly appear to posterity as merely fossilized remnants of uncivilized orthodoxy.

Historical Examples of Pseudoscience

Thus far, we have provided the historical example of trephination: a practice that was not pseudoscience, but rather was a form of primitive – albeit mostly refuted – science. For the next part of this chapter, we discuss two more historical examples within the field of clinical psychology. The first example, primal scream therapy, is an obvious case of pseudoscience, whereas the second, psychoanalysis, is a more ambiguous case.

Primal Scream Therapy

Primal scream therapy, a form of trauma-based psychotherapy, was conceptualized by psychologist Arthur Janov in 1968. In 1970, Janov published his book *The Primal Scream*, which quickly became widely popular (Janov, 1970; Langer, 2017). In this text, Janov claims that mental illness is the result of repressed pain that usually stems from childhood trauma. The stated purpose of primal scream therapy, then, was to allow patients to re-experience this repressed pain and express any associated emotions (an experience known as the "primal"), which ostensibly resolves the trauma in the present (Janov, 1970). Celebrities such as John Lennon, Yoko Ono, and James Earl Jones have participated in primal scream therapy and have commented on its usefulness (Langer, 2017). Nonetheless, there is insufficient scientific evidence to support the effectiveness of primal scream therapy, and it has been largely rejected by the scientific community (Eisner, 2000). Indeed, by the early 1980s, the majority of practicing psychotherapists already considered it to be a "questionable" or "dangerous" practice (Ehebald & Werthmann, 1982). Janov's methods have also been criticized as pseudoscientific. For example, he evaluated his theory solely through clinical observation, at a time when the scientist-practitioner model was already well-established in the field. Most damningly, Janov had the required tools at his disposal to perform the studies needed to empirically evaluate the effectiveness of the modality, but he chose not to use them. In this manner, primal scream therapy was developed and practiced in almost complete isolation from the rest of the scientific literature on psychotherapy and received few opportunities for proper experimental testing or peer review. Janov also insisted, until his death in 2017, that the therapy had a 100% effectiveness rate, and claimed that it was "the most important dis-covery of the 20th century" (Langer, 2017, para 9).

Psychoanalysis

Psychoanalysis is an umbrella term used to describe a wide range of the-ories and therapeutic techniques predicated on the purported influence of the unconscious mind. It is a school of thought that was founded by Austrian neurologist Sigmund Freud in the 1890s. Psychoanalysis was the dominant theoretical and clinical orientation of psychiatrists in the Western world for a large part of the 20th century, and still maintains a moderate degree of popularity today (Bateman et al., 2021).

Dream interpretation is one example of the clinical application of psy-choanalytic theory. Freud (1899/1913) revolutionized the technique with the publication of his book *The Interpretation of Dreams*. In Freud's view, dreams are reflections of unconscious wishes that have been heavily dis-torted by repressive forces of the ego. Freud asserted that psychoanalytic techniques (e.g., free association; the expression of uncensored thoughts by the patient as a means of accessing unconscious processes) could be used to coherently interpret the true meaning(s) of dreams (Freud, 1899/1913). To develop this theory, Freud referenced his own and his patients' dreams, and used observational techniques to deduce recognizable patterns across cases. He was ultimately able to conceptualize and organize an impressively complicated web of meaning based on limited data. One might argue that Freud's initial method of using detailed observations to construct theory, which he undertook several decades before sophisticated data collection tools became available, is a clear example of a purposeful attempt at science.

Despite Freud's use of a commendable initial method of theory devel-opment in his work on dream interpretation, critics argue that he never engaged in experiments that directly tested his theories once they were established, and continually defended his theories despite a growing lack of evidence for them (Horgan, 2019). But it is important to note that, unlike Janov and his infamous primal scream therapy, Freud's pinnacle came decades before science was explicitly integrated into the field of clinical psychology (Benjamin & Baker, 2000). Critics also argue that recent supporters of Freud have adamantly fought to bolster the success of unempirical psychanalytic techniques (such as dream interpretation), in direct opposition to the dominant scientific framework of the modern era (Horgan, 2019). Thus, on the surface, it appears that Freud and many of his followers have engaged in behaviours indicative of pseudoscience. Notably, many prominent figures have labelled psychoanalysis as a pseudoscience. For example, famous psychologist Hans Eysenck described psychoanalytic theory as speculation that is not based on any concrete observation or experimentation (Eysenck, 1985). Eysenck claimed that all psychoanalytic theories are either (1) untestable or (2) testable and unsupported by existing evidence.

Indeed, the classical Freudian psychoanalysis appears to be a pseudo-science, as many of Lilienfeld's (2014) indicators of pseudoscience have been present in the theory for decades (e.g., overuse of ad hoc hypotheses, impossibility of falsification, reliance on anecdotal evidence, evasion of peer review). However, it is necessary to distinguish classical psychoanalysis from modern *psychodynamic* therapies: the offspring of psychoanalytic theory that utilize certain psychoanalytic concepts (see Prochaska & Norcross, 2018). There is no definitive date that identifies when empirically driven *psychodynamic* therapies differentiated from antiquated *psychoanalytic* therapies; it has been a gradual evolution over time (Fulmer, 2018). Today, most psychodynamic approaches are far removed from the more extreme Freudian viewpoints, and some are considered to be supported by evidence. For example, meta-analyses have shown large effect sizes for brief psycho-dynamic therapy, compared to wait-list controls, for a variety of presenting problems and age groups (e.g., Abbass et al., 2013; Crits-Christoph, 1992; Driessen et al., 2010; Leichsenring et al., 2004; Lilliengren et al., 2016; Scogen et al., 2005). Indeed, there appears to be a general acceptance in the field that certain psychodynamic therapies are sufficiently effective compared to no treatment or wait-list control groups (e.g., Prochaska & Norcross, 2018; Shedler, 2010). Additionally, some meta-analyses have found few differences between psychodynamic therapy and other psychotherapy ap-proaches (Cuijpers et al., 2021; Leichsenring et al., 2018; Steinert et al. 2017), although there is currently no substantial evidence to assert that psychodynamic therapies are *more* effective than other leading types of therapy. Moreover, there are inherent flaws with using wait-list control groups and no-treatment control groups as compared to comparison groups with a more active treatment component. For example, an active comparison group helps control for the nonspecific factors associated with therapy (e.g., therapeutic alliance) responsible for therapy gains to better isolate the effects of the specific psychodynamic techniques used. For a more detailed discus-sion of identifying science-based therapies, see Chapter 15 of this book.

Applying Intellectual Humility to a Particular Case

For the last part of this chapter, we will illustrate the principle of intellectual humility. Suppose you hold the common belief that all psychoanalytic methods are pseudoscientific because they cannot be directly tested. On the surface, this appears to be a justified opinion; but there are alternative arguments that challenge this notion.

First, it is important to consider that psychoanalysis may have become a pseudoscience over time. That is, perhaps it was not initially a pseudoscience, but later became one. To understand how this is possible, we will examine the context in which Freud operated. Freud developed his psychoanalytic theories from 1885 until his death in 1939. During this period, psychotherapy was not yet established as a legitimate branch of science. At the time psychoanalysis was conceived, it was frankly unclear whether the processes of the mind could be studied scientifically *in any way*. Despite this reason for doubt, Freud began theorizing what might be possible. He used the only tools he had at his disposal: his own experiences, his background in neurology, and stories from his patients (see Dozois, 2000). From there, he convincingly wove together an intricate story of the unconscious mind and provided the basic framework for modern talk therapy. And although Freud did not test his ideas using scientific procedures, it is perhaps unfair to label this choice as pseudoscientific, given the lack of established scientific methodology in psychology at the time.

What, then, is the argument for applying the pseudoscience label to classical psychoanalysis (and, in particular, untestable techniques) at a later date? Psychoanalysis was at its most popular in the 1950s and 1960s (Norcross et al., 2011), at which point it was widely accepted by psychiatrists and psychologists alike, despite an increasing shift toward the importance of implementing the scientific method. Therefore, perhaps it is fair to state that classical psychoanalysis *became* a pseudoscience after its proponents continued to vehemently support its bona fides during the second half of the 20th century.

Second, despite criticism that psychoanalytic techniques are unfalsifiable, the effectiveness of therapies that utilize them can be – and has been – viably tested. That is, even if the mechanisms by which psychoanalytic techniques operate cannot be individually verified, their overall effect on a patient's trajectory can. For example, if a patient's symptoms improve meaningfully after 20 sessions of psychodynamic therapy, or the individual endorses receiving valuable insight from the process, then the therapy can be said to be effective for that person. This conclusion can remain valid even if it is impossible to verify *how* or *why* each individual part of the therapy may have influenced this positive outcome.

What then are we to make of empirically supported psychodynamic therapies? And what if future studies support psychodynamic therapies as the best option for treating a particular clinical group? Should we still write off the constituent techniques as pseudoscientific, simply because we lack the tools to test them? Consider that the main goal of psychotherapy research is to determine the most effective treatment options for patients. This creates a predicament where we would have to acknowledge the usefulness of techniques that we do not – and may never – fully understand.

Famous scientists and historians alike (e.g., Richard Feynman, Henri Ellenberger) have claimed that psychoanalysis is a pseudoscientific cult. However, in viewing the subject through the lens of intellectual humility, we can recognize that not all psychoanalytic methods are pseudoscientific. We can use this same lens to recognize that Freud, who valiantly tried to develop complex theories of intangible phenomena at the turn of the 20th century, was not a pseudoscientist. We can safely assume that *some* of his theories were incorrect, because they were based solely on anecdotal evidence and whimsical thinking. But it is also fair to say that Freud laid the groundwork for many of the psychotherapeutic endeavours that have followed his death (including, but not limited to, psychodynamic approaches) and that he deserves credit for this feat.

Summary and Conclusion

In conclusion, we encourage the reader to practice intellectual humility when examining other examples of pseudoscience, fringe science, and controversies described in the remaining chapters of this book. Furthermore, we encourage the reader to use intellectual humility when considering other historical examples, consuming research, or embarking on your own scientific pursuits. Finally, we would like to emphasize that, in addition to practicing intellectual humility, we must always prioritize using the best scientific evidence that is currently available when selecting assessment and treatment options for psychological problems. By constantly striving to use the most evidence-based methods available, we are using science as it was meant to be used: as a safeguard against our tendency for subjective error.

Daniel Machado, MSc, is a graduate student in the Department of Psychology at The University of Western Ontario in Canada.

Owen Hicks, BSc, is a graduate student in the Department of Psychology at The University of Western Ontario in Canada.

David J. A. Dozois, PhD, CPsych, is a professor of clinical psychology at The University of Western Ontario in Canada. He is also co-editor of the book *Treatment of Psychosocial Risk Factors in Depression.*

References

Abbass, A. A., Rabung, S., Leichsenring, F., Refseth, J. S., & Midgley, N. (2013). Psychodynamic psychotherapy for children and adolescents: A meta-analysis of short-term psychodynamic models. *Journal of the American Academy of Child and Adolescent Psychiatry, 52,* 863–875.

Bakan, D. (1967). *On method: Toward a reconstruction of psychological investigation.* Jossey-Bass.

Barkham, M., & Mellor-Clark, J. (2003). Bridging evidence-based practice and practice-based evidence: Developing a rigorous and relevant knowledge for the psychological therapies. *Clinical Psychology & Psychotherapy: An International Journal of Theory & Practice, 10,* 319–327.

Bateman, A. W., Holmes, J., & Allison, E. (2021). *Introduction to psychoanalysis: Contemporary theory and practice.* Routledge.

Benjamin, L. T., Jr., & Baker, D. B. (2000). Boulder at 50: Introduction to the section. *American Psychologist, 55,* 233–236.

Crits-Christoph, P. (1992). The efficacy of brief dynamic psychotherapy: A meta-analysis. *American Journal of Psychiatry, 149,* 151–158.

Cuijpers, P., Quero, S., Noma, H., Ciharova, M., Miguel, C., Karyotaki, E., Cipriani, A., Cristea, I. A., & Furukawa, T. A. (2021). Psychotherapies for depression: A network meta-analysis covering efficacy, acceptability and long-term outcomes of all main treatment types. *World Psychiatry, 20,* 283–293.

Dozois, D. J. A. (2000). Influences on Freud's Mourning and Melancholia and its contextual validity. *Journal of Theoretical and Philosophical Psychology, 20,* 167–195.

Dozois, D. J. A. (2013). Presidential address – Psychological treatments: Putting evidence into practice and practice into evidence. *Canadian Psychology, 54,* 1–11.

Dozois, D. J. A., & Machado, D. (2021). Concepts of abnormality throughout history. In D. J. A. Dozois (Ed.), *Perspectives in psychopathology* (7th ed.). Toronto, Ontario: Pearson.

Dozois, D. J. A., Mikail, S., Alden, L. E., Bieling, P. J., Bourgon, G., Clark, D. A., Drapeau, M., Gallson, D., Greenberg, L., Hunsley, J., & Johnston, C. (2014). The CPA presidential task force on evidence-based practice of psychological treatments. *Canadian Psychology, 55,* 153–160.

Driessen, E., Cuijpers, P., de Maat, S. C., Abbass, A. A., de Jonghe, F., & Dekker, J. J. (2010). The efficacy of short-term psychodynamic psychotherapy for depression: A meta-analysis. *Clinical Psychology Review, 30,* 25–36.

Ehebald, U., & Werthmann, H. V. (1982). Primärtherapie--ein klinisch bewährtes Verfahren? [Primal therapy--a clinically confirmed procedure?]. *Zeitschrift fur Psychosomatische Medizin und Psychoanalyse, 28,* 407–421.

Eisner, D. A. (2000). *The death of psychotherapy: From Freud to alien abductions.* Praeger Publishers/Greenwood.

Eysenck, H. J. (1985). *Decline and fall of the Freudian empire.* Viking Press.

Featherston, R., Downie, L. E., Vogel, A. P., & Galvin, K. L. (2020). Decision making biases in the allied health professions: A systematic scoping review. *PloS One, 15,* e0240716.

Freud, S. (1899/1913). *The interpretation of dreams.* (A. A. Brill, Trans.). MacMillan Co.

Fulmer, R. (2018). The evolution of the psychodynamic approach and system. *International Journal of Psychological Studies,* 10(3).

Hawkins, S. A., & Hastie, R. (1990). Hindsight: Biased judgments of past events after the outcomes are known. *Psychological Bulletin, 107,* 311.

Hopewell, S., Loudon, K., Clarke, M. J., Oxman, A. D., & Dickersin, K. (2009). Publication bias in clinical trials due to statistical significance or direction of trial results. *The Cochrane Database of Systematic Reviews, 2009,* MR000006.

Horgan, J. (2019, May 13). Why we're still fighting over Freud. *Scientific American.* https://blogs.scientificamerican.com/cross-check/why-were-still-fighting-over-freud/

Janov, A. (1970). *The primal scream: Primal therapy: The cure for neurosis.* Dell Publishing.

Kahneman, D. (2011). *Thinking, fast and slow.* Macmillan.

Kahneman, D., Slovic, S. P., Slovic, P., & Tversky, A. (Eds.). (1982). *Judgment under uncertainty: Heuristics and biases.* Cambridge University Press.

Klayman, J. (1995). Varieties of confirmation bias. *Psychology of Learning and Motivation, 32,* 385–418.

Klayman, J., Soll, J. B., Gonzalez-Vallejo, C., & Barlas, S. (1999). Overconfidence: It depends on how, what, and whom you ask. *Organizational Behavior and Human Decision Processes, 79,* 216–247.

Langer, E. (2017, October 4). Arthur Janov, psychologist who created the 'primal scream', dies at 93. *The Washington Post.* https://www.washingtonpost.com/local/obituaries/arthur-janov-psychologist-who-created-the-primal-scream-dies-at-93/2017/10/04/03ab9f9e-a85e-11e7-b3aa-c0e2e1d41e38_story.html

Lawrence, B., & Padfield, G. D. (2005). Handling qualities analysis of the Wright Brothers' 1902 glider. *Journal of Aircraft, 42,* 224–236. 10.2514/1.6091.

Leary, M. R., Diebels, K. J., Davisson, E. K., Jongman-Sereno, K. P., Isherwood, J. C., Raimi, K. T., ... & Hoyle, R. H. (2017). Cognitive and interpersonal features of intellectual humility. *Personality and Social Psychology Bulletin, 43,* 793–813.

Leichsenring, F., Rabung, S., & Leibing, E. (2004). The efficacy of short-term psychodynamic psychotherapy in specific psychiatric disorders: A meta-analysis. *Archives of General Psychiatry, 61,* 1208–1216.

Leichsenring, F., Abbass, A., Hilsenroth, M. J., Luyten, P., Munder, T., Rabung, S., & Steinert, C. (2018). "Gold standards," plurality and monocultures: The need for diversity in psychotherapy. *Frontiers in Psychiatry, 9,* Article 159.

Lilienfeld, S. O. (2010). Can psychology become a science? *Personality and Individual Differences, 49,* 281–288.

Lilienfeld, S. O., Lynn, S. J., & Lohr, J. M. (2014). *Science and pseudoscience in clinical psychology.* Guilford.

Lilienfeld, S. O., Lynn, S. J., O'Donohue, W. T., & Latzman, R. D. (2017). Epistemic humility: An overarching educational philosophy for clinical psychology programs. *Clinical Psychologist, 70*, 6–14.

Lilienfeld, S. O., & Bowes, S. M. (2021). Intellectual humility: Ten key questions. In P. Graf & D. J. A. Dozois (Eds.), *Handbook on the state of the art in applied psychology* (pp. 449–467). Wiley.

Lilliengren, P., Johansson, R., Lindqvist, K., Mechler, J., & Andersson, G. (2016). Efficacy of experiential dynamic therapy for psychiatric conditions: A meta-analysis of randomized controlled trials. *Psychotherapy (Chicago, Ill.), 53*, 90–104.

Liu, C. Y., & Apuzzo, M. L. (2003). The genesis of neurosurgery and the evolution of the neurosurgical operative environment: Part I—Prehistory to 2003. *Neurosurgery, 52*, 3–19.

Meehl, P. E. (1956). Clinical versus actuarial prediction. In *Proceedings of the 1955 invitational conference on testing problems* (pp. 136–141). Princeton: Educational Testing Service.

Nickerson, R. S. (1998). Confirmation bias: A ubiquitous phenomenon in many guises. *Review of General Psychology, 2*, 175–220.

Norcross, J. C., VandenBos, G. R., & Freedheim, D. K. (2011). *History of psychotherapy: Continuity and change.* American Psychological Association.

Prochaska, J. O., & Norcross, J. C. (2018). *Systems of psychotherapy: A transtheoretical analysis* (8th ed.). Oxford University Press.

Pronin, E. (2007). Perception and misperception of bias in human judgment. *Trends in Cognitive Science, 11*, 37–43.

Pronin, E. (2008). How we see ourselves and how we see others. *Science 320*, 1177–1180.

Pronin E., Lin, D. Y., & Ross, L. (2002). The bias blind spot: Perceptions of bias in self versus others. *Personality and Social Psychology Bulletin, 28*, 369–381.

Pronin, E., Gilovich, T. D., & Ross, L. (2004). Objectivity in the eye of the beholder: Divergent perceptions of bias in self versus others. *Psychology Review, 111*, 781–799.

Rosenthal, R. (1979). The file drawer problem and tolerance for null results. *Psychological Bulletin, 86*, 638–641.

Scargle, J. D. (1999). Publication bias (the "file-drawer problem") in scientific inference. *Journal of Scientific Exploration, 14*(1), 91–106.

Shedler J. (2010). The efficacy of psychodynamic psychotherapy. *American Psychologist, 65*, 98–109.

Spring, B. (2007). Evidence-based practice in clinical psychology: What it is, why it matters; what you need to know. *Journal of Clinical Psychology, 63*, 611–631.

Steinert, C., Munder, T., Rabung, S., Hoyer, J., & Leichsenring, F. (2017). Psychodynamic therapy: As efficacious as other empirically supported treatments? A meta-analysis testing equivalence of outcomes. *American Journal of Psychiatry, 174*, 943–953.

Part II

Assessment

3 Dubious Diagnoses

Blake A. E. Boehme, Andres De Los Reyes, and Gordon J. G. Asmundson

There are many diagnoses that most practitioners in the health sciences do not recognize or do not have the technical means to identify. The symptoms of these diagnoses are often extremely troubling for the individual experiencing them, and many people who suffer from these symptoms do not find their interactions with health science practitioners fruitful. Often, these patients feel that these practitioners fail to identify or treat the root cause of their problem and do not allocate appropriate time and resources to evaluating the patient's concerns. There is, however, a group of practitioners who are knowledgeable about the condition that the patient has and can offer alternative treatments aimed at treating the root cause of their condition. Many diagnoses fit these criteria that these alternative practitioners can diagnose and treat, including chronic Lyme disease (cLd).

People diagnosed with cLd experience a chronic infection or the effects of a shorter-term infection of a bacterium that is carried by ticks. In this case, cLd can appear to be a valuable diagnosis as it allows for practitioners to identify the root cause of symptoms and provide alternative treatments that are typically not be prescribed by mainstream health science practitioners. The cLd diagnosis can also provide patients with a clearer understanding of why they have been experiencing their symptoms. Therefore, with the appropriate diagnosis, these patients can receive treatment, do their own research on their condition, and connect with others who have also received the same diagnosis.

Examining the Claims

As the level of understanding surrounding the influence that mental health has on both the psychological and physical well-being of humans has expanded, several professions with little or no mental health training have injected themselves into the mental health landscape. Many of these professions and individual clinicians have gone beyond incorporating expanding knowledge into their clinical practices.

DOI: 10.4324/9781003259510-5

Instead, many clinicians have begun incorporating mental health diagnoses or pseudo-diagnoses into their treatment planning – diagnoses provided with a questionable physical explanation for psychological distress that is not supported by science. Contemporary examples of these pseudo-diagnoses traverse physical and mental health areas, including cLd, a purported ongoing, often undetected illness due to untreated or poorly treated Lyme disease. Another contemporary example is called Morgellons and is typically a self-diagnosis in cases of delusional parasitosis, in which people believe they are infected with parasites. Some clinicians have continued to give this diagnosis despite no evidence of parasitic infection.

Exploitation versus Compassion

We wrote this chapter not to ridicule or criticize those who have been given a dubious diagnosis. Instead, we seek to articulate the motives and ways these diagnoses arise. There is no compelling evidence that most people who receive the questionable diagnoses discussed in this chapter are "faking it." People suffering from poorly understood or unexplained symptoms are often desperate for an explanation for their condition and effective treatment. Indeed, there is compelling evidence that people given dubious diagnoses experience a significant reduction in their quality of life (Johnson et al., 2014). The symptoms and distress they experience are real and should be treated with compassion; however, compassion and exploitation should not be mistaken for one another. Questionable diagnoses and treatment can delay or prevent the application of evidence-based practices, including receipt of an accurate diagnosis and case conceptualization and development of an effective treatment plan to address symptoms and impairments stemming from a patient's concerns (Johnson et al., 2018). These unfortunate outcomes are more likely to occur when individuals, organizations, and professions are less prone to relying on scientific evidence to inform the diagnostic process.

Evidence-Based Mental Health Diagnoses

The history of how mental health diagnoses moved from supernatural explanations of behavior to scientific endeavour is beyond the scope of this chapter (for a review, see Surís et al., 2016). However, the scientific principles that underlie the progression of diagnoses across time and how adherence to these principles creates a system in which diagnoses can be scrutinized and validated is crucial. Dubious diagnoses are either not supported by scientific evidence or are never exposed to the rigours of scientific review, often relying on small sample sizes, case studies, or strictly anecdotes (Savely & Stricker, 2007). Still, despite this limitation, the diagnoses are allowed to exist and thrive, primarily due to their often-non-specific and subjective symptoms and the cult-like atmosphere among proponents of the diagnoses (Nimnuan et al., 2001). For example, many or all dubious diagnoses are characterized by symptoms like fatigue, pain, "brain fog," depression, and anxiety. Although these symptoms can be helpful in the diagnostic process, they are subjective and do not provide evidence in and of themselves that a specific diagnosis should be made. Non-specific symptoms enable multiple invalid diagnoses; usually, the one(s) that the patient finds most compatible with their history and the beliefs their practitioner holds regarding the root of the patient's suffering, despite a lack of tangible evidence. By combining the patient's fears, non-specific symptoms, and hopes for diagnosis and relief, practitioners can *sell* a dubious diagnosis for significant monetary gain.

Expressions of Distress

An important factor when attempting to analyze how diagnoses without a sound evidence base are propagated is how culture and expressions of human distress influence the presentation of patients and their likelihood of receiving a dubious diagnosis. The body reliably produces symptoms like pain, fatigue, and fever in reaction to a stressor, mechanical forces like a broken bone, a foreign invader like a virus, or the strain of mental health conditions. These expressions of distress often co-occur. This co-occurrence allows for the detection of connected sets of relatively rare experiences and, in turn, facilitates the construction of syndromal patterns of symptoms that comprise core features of evidence-based, accurate clinical conditions (see also Achenbach, 2020). However, many dubious diagnoses are less than valid explanations of common, possibly culturally influenced expressions of distress that patients and practitioners latch onto due to multiple predictable factors, including cognitive biases. Still, there is significant evidence that as cultures move through time, the signs and symptoms that convey our anguish will likely change within the bounds of our physiology. These symptoms become common expressions of distress. For example, somatic complaints, specifically pain and fatigue, have become common expressions of distress, even though these symptoms often arise with no specific structural defect or insult (Rief & Broadbent, 2007). Diverse and interconnected factors in a culture, such as language, beliefs about health, social responses to symptoms of distress, beliefs about the diagnostic validity of specific symptoms, and the complex history of culture, all influence how distress is expressed (Nichter, 1981). There are two common misconceptions regarding culturally influenced expressions of distress relevant to dubious diagnoses: that the symptoms of distress within a culture are static and that Western cultures are insulated from these expressions of distress (Hughes, 1998).

Cognitive Biases in Diagnoses

Cognitive biases are errors in thinking that occur when people are processing information. All humans are prone to cognitive biases based on the shared structure and functioning of the brain and the shared environmental demands across our evolutionary past (Marshall et al., 2013). When these cognitive biases are active, we are more likely to come to conclusions about information that are less than objective. How cognitive biases play a role in diagnosis (Saposnik et al., 2016) and assessing treatment outcomes (Lilienfeld et al., 2014) has been a topic of significant interest in the health sciences. Although numerous cognitive biases can play a role in an inaccurate diagnosis, confirmation bias is the most impactful.

Confirmation bias is active when people seek information that supports a hypothesis while actively ignoring or suppressing information that questions their assumption (Nickerson, 1998). The confirmation bias punctuates the stories of those who seek and receive a questionable diagnosis and the behaviors of the practitioners who provide these diagnoses. When a person believes that they have a particular condition, even without a diagnosis, they are more likely to be on alert for symptoms that confirm their belief and seek out information that aligns with their preconceived notion. A typical example of looking for symptoms that fit a perceived pattern based on fear is headaches and the fear of brain tumors (Singh & Brown, 2016). Headaches, even frequent ones are a familiar and usually non-threatening human experience; however, upon experiencing a new headache, many people fear that the headache is a sign of a more severe problem like a brain tumor or aneurysm. The person may then search for symptoms associated with brain tumors and become hyperaware of their own experience, often becoming frightened that they are experiencing other "symptoms" despite no tumor existing. Because some practitioners may also believe that a condition exists despite a lack of scientific evidence or that they hold knowledge about a condition that others do not, they can become a source of information for the patient seeking guidance, diagnosis, and treatment, feeding the cycle of perceived patterns of symptoms. Despite scientific evidence to the contrary, many practitioners will claim that their diagnoses and treatment results "speak for themselves" and will often cite anecdotes to support their claims. The dubious information that practitioners promote can fuel individuals and groups by further confirming their bias and adding an air of legitimacy to the diagnosis and subsequent treatments, despite a lack of tangible evidence that they are accurate and effective.

The Signs of Dubious Diagnoses

Although cognitive biases play a role in dubious diagnoses, they do not provide a complete account of this phenomenon. In addition to cognitive biases, ulterior motives such as financial reward play a significant role, as well as inadequate training, standards, and regulation of many practitioners. The shared reasons and inadequacies are most commonly ignorance or false beliefs surrounding the practices necessary to provide an accurate diagnosis, a lack of training or education in mental health diagnosis, a lack of understanding of the fundamental principles and applications of the scientific method, and the desire to increase the practitioner's income. We also argue that all dubious diagnoses have standard features, which we identify as the signs of dubious mental health diagnoses. Many of these tell-tale features are also the hallmarks of mental health pseudoscience (Lilienfeld et al., 2015). These include:

1 *Rapid "explosion" of a diagnosis.* The diagnosis often arises and gains popularity at a meteoric rate, far exceeding what would be expected based on changes in human physiology, environment, culture, and behavior. Scientific breakthroughs, such as more accurate tests to detect the condition or increased scientific understanding of the condition, do not explain or warrant a subsequent increase in diagnostic rates. In most cases, the explosion of diagnoses surrounds common symptoms of distress, quite often symptoms that may have been attributed to another popular dubious diagnosis that has fallen out of favor. Still, despite a lack of objective evidence for a difference between conditions, it is labeled as a different condition across time. The new diagnosis becomes diagnosis de jour, often replacing or displacing the previous diagnosis, with information communications infrastructure (e.g., internet search engines) playing a crucial role in the rapidity of the spread.

2 *An extensive list of possible signs and symptoms.* In contrast to more evidence-based diagnoses, dubious diagnoses can be given, partly because proponents of the dubious diagnosis will provide long lists of possible symptoms. Because of a long list of non-specific symptoms, practitioners and patients can begin seeing a pattern emerging in their symptoms even though they may not be diagnostically specific. Identifying these symptoms as part of any diagnosis increases the likelihood of invoking the confirmation bias to find further patterns in symptoms that fit the concept of the dubious diagnosis held by either the patient or practitioner. This principle works hand in hand with the third standard feature.

3 *Many comorbid conditions or "comorbid infections."* These comorbid diagnoses can be used to not only "explain" to the patient why they are

experiencing what they are experiencing but also increase the likelihood of more extensive, prolonged, and costly treatments. To provide an all-encompassing explanation for the array of symptoms and complaints that a patient may have, practitioners who offer dubious diagnoses will often layer more diagnoses. Examples of common questionable comorbid diagnoses include "chronic" Epstein-Barr virus, adrenal fatigue, vertebral subluxation, mold toxicity/illness, "neuroinflammation," multiple chemical sensitivity, electromagnetic hypersensitivity, Morgellons disease, and chronic candidiasis. This list is incomplete; indeed, many comorbid conditions and co-infections are being thought up and sold to patients.

4 *No scientific peer review of the diagnosis.* Peer review provides another layer to the validity of a finding so that other scientists may use this work to refine their techniques, produce more compelling research, and inform the most appropriate practices, including diagnosis. Peer review involves expert appraisal of a scientist's claims that they have made in a study, including the statistical methods they have used and whether their conclusions are supported by their methods and results. Dubious diagnoses often evade rigorous scientific review, are not substantiated under peer review, or may be published in journals that do not follow sound peer review practices, including journals that specifically cater to fields based on pseudoscientific principles or those journals that publish papers for a fee.

5 *The practitioner claims to have hidden wisdom.* Practitioners who provide dubious diagnoses often claim to specialize in or understand the condition that the dubious diagnoses are based on better than other practitioners. Many such practitioners prey on the frustrations of their patients, often stemming from unfruitful experiences with other practitioners or the inability to find a reasonable or acceptable explanation for their symptoms. It is not uncommon that patients have seen multiple practitioners in the past who have repeatedly carried out significant investigations and testing. When the studies do not provide evidence that adequately explains to the patient why they are experiencing their symptoms, they can search out a practitioner who claims to treat any number of unfounded diagnoses – the practitioner's claims of expertise work hand in hand with the confirmation bias. Ultimately, the patient finally receives a diagnosis from an "expert" whose diagnosis and treatment fuel their belief that they have the diagnosed condition.

6 *Reliance on anecdotal evidence.* Practitioners who promote dubious diagnoses will often rely on testimonials or anecdotal evidence. A potent form of anecdote is now derived from celebrities or social media personalities. For example, celebrities such as Justin Bieber, Bella Hadid, Kelly Osbourne, Avril Lavigne, and Shania Twain have publicly

announced their Lyme disease diagnoses, with many describing other "co-infections" often diagnosed by practitioners who treat their conditions with dubious methods like "herbal remedies." This anecdotal evidence is spread quickly by modern social media networks and can be subject to a continuous process of manipulation and revision as it spreads from person to person. An individual's understanding of scientific principles can make them more or less likely to be manipulated by online pseudoscientific claims. As science literacy is often lacking in the digital space, these anecdotal claims can become the prevailing opinion of a large portion of the population.

7 *Significant monetary rewards for practitioners.* Practitioners who provide dubious diagnoses and treatment without an evidence base can reap substantial payments for their treatments. These practitioners often see patients in their clinic over the long term. Many practitioners also sell products (e.g., vitamins, supplements, equipment, cleanses) to their patients to further "treat" their condition. Promoting and often selling products in a clinical environment is especially common with chiropractors and naturopaths, who often encourage supplements and vitamins despite a lack of evidence that these supplements promote health in general or treat dubious conditions.

The Trouble with Language

Language is essential in promoting and propagating dubious diagnoses, specifically the misuse, misinterpretation, and misrepresentation of diagnostic vocabulary. Even many well-meaning practitioners need clarification on the language surrounding diagnosis and the correct contexts to use terminology. Defining the most confusing concepts and how they relate to diagnosis is essential. Examples of these types of concepts are disorder, illness, condition, disease, and syndrome.

Disorder in the context of mental health conditions describes the dysfunction related to a person's thoughts and behavior. An example of this type of dysfunction is generalized anxiety disorder. Most individuals will experience anxiety in their life as episodic, especially during challenging periods. However, suppose anxiety and the associated behaviors (i.e., avoiding anxiety-provoking situations) cause dysfunction in a person's life for a prolonged period. In that case, they may meet diagnostic criteria for a disorder.

Illness is an ambiguous term used to describe a disease or state of ill health. For example, a simple cold is often referred to as an illness. Still, mental health conditions associated with severe distress and dysfunction, such as schizophrenia, are also often referred to as an illness, and this adds confusion.

Condition is another ambiguous term in the mental health field. Still, it is generally used as a catch-all term for the vast array of mental health disorders, from those typically associated with less dysfunction to those with severe dysfunction.

Disease is the negative functioning of a part of or system in the body, which factors internal or external to the body can generate. For example, the disease of cancer is the uncontrolled growth of abnormal cells, which may be influenced by environmental factors like smoking tobacco or excessive drinking of alcohol, but also by genetic factors.

Finally, the term *syndrome* is the most confusing and misappropriated. Syndrome is also the term most likely to be used in the context of dubious diagnoses. A syndrome is a collection of statistically rare symptoms that, in combination, appear to characterize a specific disease or disorder. For example, mental impairment, stunted physical growth, and specific physical features (i.e., poor muscle tone, small chin, flattened nose) often co-occur after a child is born and begins to develop, indicating Down syndrome. Well-validated syndromes differ from those that practitioners who provide dubious diagnoses provide in their rarity. These practitioners take common and subjective symptoms, often arising from multiple systems in the body, and convey an illusory explanation for how these symptoms are related to the patient. Unlike validated syndromes, practitioners can choose any symptoms the patient reports to provide an already prevalent pseudoscientific syndrome or create a new pseudoscientific explanation. For example, some practitioners provide a long list of supposed cLd symptoms that are subjective, normally non-diagnostic without more sophisticated tests, and are used to describe "many patients who walk into our [chiropractor's] offices" (Langdon, 2019), the opposite of validated, rare, specific syndromes.

"Chronic" Lyme Disease

A prominent contemporary dubious diagnosis that can be used to highlight how questionable diagnoses are born and spread is the case of cLd. There is a significant difference between the proposed, unsubstantiated existence of a long-term condition called cLd and the long-standing and well-validated Lyme disease diagnosis. The latter is the most common tick-borne disease in North America. Lyme disease is caused by the bacterium *Borrelia burgdoreferi*, which can be transmitted to humans if infected black-legged ticks bite them. Lyme disease typically occurs in distinct areas of the United States and Canada. Lyme disease can be diagnosed based on the presentation of the patient's symptoms with or without the results of blood tests, as blood tests are often incapable of detecting Lyme (Kullberg et al., 2020). Early signs and symptoms of Lyme disease include a "bull's-eye" shaped rash, fever, chills, fatigue, muscle and joint aches, and headache. In contrast, later symptoms can more severely affect the neurological and cardiovascular systems and joints (i.e., arthritis).

Since 2006, the Lyme Disease Review Panel of the Infectious Diseases Society of America (IDSA) and other organizations have supported the evidence-based assessment for and treatment of Lyme disease (IDSA, 2006). The most extensively validated therapy for Lyme disease is a short course (10–28 days) of antibiotic treatment (Sanchez et al., 2016), with the use of long-term antibiotics discouraged by IDSA, the American Academy of Neurology (AAN), and the American College of Rheumatology (ACR; Lantos et al., 2021) and found to be of no benefit in extensive empirical studies (Berende et al., 2016). Despite these recommendations and the efficacy of short-term antibiotic treatment, many patients and practitioners endorse a cLd diagnosis despite a lack of scientific evidence that any such condition exists.

Many people who experience non-specific symptoms of fatigue, joint pain, anxiety, and depression either believe they have cLd or have been given a diagnosis despite a lack of evidence of current or previous infection (Hassett et al., 2009; Sigal, 1990). Those who receive such a diagnosis will often retrospectively endorse that a tick may have bitten them at some point. People who believe they have cLd will often report experiencing acute symptoms of Lyme, despite findings that up to 88% of these individuals show no evidence of ever having Lyme (Hassett et al., 2009; Sigal, 1990). Also, there is evidence that their clusters of symptoms would be atypical for classic Lyme disease (Lantos, 2015). Their symptoms are not the only problematic aspect of accurate diagnosis; in this case, for-profit laboratories offer dubious testing with extremely high false positive rates and findings that are not found by other, more reputable labs (Fallon et al., 2014). Some practitioners even refer to a "diagnosis of Lyme disease by exclusion" or that cLd is a "great imitator" and that some individuals who have been given diagnoses such as multiple sclerosis (MS) or amyotrophic lateral sclerosis (ALS) have cLd (Auwaerter et al., 2011). The combination of symptoms can appear as a part of hundreds of diagnoses and dubious testing results used as evidence for the dubious diagnosis of cLd. (For a critical appraisal of the cLd diagnosis, see; Feder et al., 2007.)

How, then, despite a lack of scientific evidence, does a diagnosis like cLd continue to gain popularity? Through the lens of the seven factors likely to predict a dubious diagnosis, we can see how a dubious diagnosis such as cLd can thrive.

Is There Evidence for a Rapid Increase in cLd Diagnosis?

Accurate assessment of an increase in the prevalence of cLd as a diagnosis in the scientific literature is challenged by the rise in Lyme disease and the ticks that carry the offending bacterium due in part to climate change (Mead, 2015). According to Google Trends, searches for "chronic Lyme disease" have increased exponentially since 2004, with massive increases in the search term coinciding with celebrities reporting they had received a Lyme disease or cLd diagnosis. As public awareness of Lyme disease has increased, along with pseudoscientific, ill-informed (Feder et al., 2007), and fear-mongering (Cohen, 2013) articles in the popular press surrounding the prevalence and prognosis of the condition, so have the number of people who believe they have cLd.

An Extensive List of Possible Symptoms?

A 2011 review found that popular Lyme disease websites promoted primarily subjective symptoms of cLd and Lyme disease (Auwaerter et al., 2011). Proponents of cLd as a legitimate entity provide exhausting lists of the symptoms that people with the condition may experience, with some providing lists in the hundreds (Sonnet, 2020). Examples of these subjective symptoms appearing on websites are chronic fatigue, headaches, pain, digestive issues, and depression (Olivieri Family Chiropractic, 2021), but this list is not exhaustive. Most of the symptoms endorsed by many patients and practitioners in cLd, such as pain and fatigue, even in their chronic forms, are widespread and often non-specific (Chen, 1986), challenging their diagnostic specificity. Alternative providers such as chiropractors and naturopaths will then claim to treat these symptoms and the underlying condition with their methods. Examples include the use of homeopathic "medicine" (Myerowitz Chiropractic, n.d.), acupuncture and herbs (Pulley, 2018), and "supplements" (Richmond Natural Medicine, 2019) for symptoms ranging from "liver detoxification issues" to lightheadedness.

Peer-Review Status?

Researchers have made significant efforts to provide studies and information to delineate the differences between cLd and the diagnostically valid condition of protracted ill health because of a diagnosed case of Lyme disease. Despite their efforts, researchers often use *chronic* Lyme disease when describing the latter. Despite many studies being published using this term, none offer evidence that the cLd diagnosis proposed by some patients and practitioners is valid or that there is any predictive value in the symptoms often reported by people who believe they have cLd. Therefore, scientific repositories are filled with studies with misleading titles and content that makes it difficult to establish which of these phenomena they are referring to.

Anecdotes? Social Media? Celebrities?

Chronic Lyme disease has become the dubious diagnosis of choice when providing desperate patients with an explanation for their symptoms and complaints, and its presence on the internet has grown exponentially. Practitioners who claim to diagnose and treat cLd use anecdotes and testimonials to promote the vast number of treatments and products they endorse (Lantos et al., 2015). Numerous celebrities have revealed that they had been experiencing common and non-specific symptoms of distress and, after previously fruitless experiences with practitioners, found one that diagnosed them with cLd. For example, one of *The Real Housewives of Beverly Hills* stars, Yolanda Hadid, claims she was diagnosed with cLd in 2012. Interestingly, she has also claimed that both of her children were diagnosed with cLd by the same practitioner. Other celebrities like musicians Avril Lavigne and Justin Bieber have joined Hadid in claiming that their long-standing non-specific symptoms were diagnosed as cLd. Bieber's treatment with questionable or unfounded methods, such as hyperbaric oxygen therapy, is the focus of a mini-documentary.

Promotion of Products?

The online world of cLd is rife with alternative, unfounded, and pseudo-scientific treatments promoted by "Lyme literate" physicians who primarily refuse to accept insurance and can charge exorbitant fees for their services (Lantos et al., 2015). A cursory review of websites promoting products to treat cLd provides many examples of how patients desperate for relief, combined with a dubious diagnosis, can be exploited monetarily. From physician and television celebrity Dr. Oz recommending supplements with no evidence-base (Oz, 2009) and chiropractors promoting "brain-based, robotic laser, cellular stimulation, and horizontal stimulation therapies" (Mounds View Chiropractic, n.d.), to naturopaths prescribing "hyperbaric oxygen, chelation, colonic, and IV therapies" (Nardella Clinic, n.d.) and Lyme literate physicians prescribing "UVB intravenous light therapy" (Kellman Wellness Center, n.d.). Based on these examples, it is easy to see how a person who believes they have cLd could spend a significant amount of money on products and treatments with no evidence base in a desperate attempt to seek relief for a dubious and amorphous diagnosis.

Summary and Conclusion

Although we have described the issue of dubious diagnosis using the example of cLd, this is just an example of the latest diagnosis given to people with non-specific symptoms seeking help. Previous diagnoses that cLd displaces include fibromyalgia and chronic fatigue, which many people with a cLd diagnosis have also been given (Hassett et al., 2009). There is evidence that people who receive dubious diagnoses have shared underlying psychological vulnerabilities such as focusing on their bodies more than others (Brown, 2004) and catastrophizing (convincing themselves that a severe condition causes the symptoms) when common experiences like pain and fatigue occur (Hassett et al., 2008). Some theories attempt to explain how psychological vulnerabilities may predispose a person to experience the symptoms at the core of dubious diagnoses; however, there is insufficient evidence to propose that mental health conditions are the origin of the symptoms that lead to receiving a dubious diagnosis. Still, the high rates of comorbidity are likely to influence diagnosis, treatment, and outcomes in this population. Indeed, many people experience "noisy bodies" (i.e., bodily sensations or changes, such as pain or rash) and assume disease-based explanations when, in many cases, the "noise" is the result of a mild illness, fatigue, or stress (Taylor & Asmundson, 2004). This is not to say that the experience is "all in the head" but that there are often non-disease-based explanations for the bodily sensation and changes that the patient is experiencing (Asmundson & Taylor, 2005). Unfortunately, disease conviction – the belief that any bodily sensation or changes are due to disease processes – is common (Fergus & Valentiner, 2010), making fertile the opportunities for those practitioners who benefit from dubious explanations of non-specific symptom presentations. The combination of psychological comorbidities or underlying psychological vulnerabilities means that mental health professionals often see these patients. These patients may be told directly, insinuated, or interpret that health science professionals believe their symptoms are "all in their head." This belief can lead to significant challenges in the practitioner–patient relationship. Therefore, increasing mental health students', professionals', and patients' knowledge of dubious diagnoses can raise awareness and inform better care for these patients.

Blake A. E. Boehme, BA, is a graduate student in the Department of Psychology at the University of Regina in Canada.

Andres De Los Reyes, PhD, is a professor of psychology at the University of Maryland. He also serves as editor for the *Journal of Clinical Child and Adolescent Psychology.*

Gordon J. G. Asmundson, PhD, is a professor of psychology at the University of Regina in Canada. He is also the Editor-in-Chief of *Clinical Psychology Review.*

References

Achenbach, T. M. (2020). Bottom-up and top-down paradigms for psycho-pathology: A half-century odyssey. *Annual Review of Clinical Psychology*, 16(1), 1–24. 10.1146/annurev-clinpsy-071119-115831

Asmundson, G. J., & Taylor, S. (2005). *It's not all in your head: How worrying about your health could be making you sick--and what you can do about it.* Guilford Press.

Auwaerter, P. G., Bakken, J. S., Dattwyler, R. J., Dumler, J. S., Halperin, J. J., McSweegan, E., Nadelman, R. B., O'Connell, S., Shapiro, E. D., Sood, S. K., Steere, A. C., Weinstein, A., & Wormser, G. P. (2011). Antiscience and ethical concerns associated with advocacy of Lyme disease. *The Lancet Infectious Diseases*, 11(9), 713–719. 10.1016/S1473-3099(11)70034-2

Berende, A., ter Hofstede, H. J. M., Vos, F. J., van Middendorp, H., Vogelaar, M. L., Tromp, M., van den Hoogen, F. H., Donders, A. R. T., Evers, A. W. M., & Kullberg, B. J. (2016). Randomized trial of longer-term therapy for symptoms attributed to Lyme disease. *New England Journal of Medicine*, 374(13), 1209–1220. 10.1056/NEJMoa1505425

Brown, R. J. (2004). Psychological mechanisms of medically unexplained symptoms: An integrative conceptual model. *Psychological Bulletin*, 130(5), 793–812. 10.1037/0033-2909.130.5.793

Chen, M. K. (1986). The epidemiology of self-perceived fatigue among adults. *Preventive Medicine*, 15(1), 74–81. 10.1016/0091-7435(86)90037-X

Cohen, S. (2013, August 28). *Feel Bad? It Could Be Lyme Unless Proven Otherwise.* Cohen. https://www.huffpost.com/entry/lyme-disease_b_3697817

Djukic, M., Schmidt-Samoa, C., Nau, R., von Steinbuchel, N., Eiffert, H., & Schmidt, H. (2011). The diagnostic spectrum in patients with suspected chronic Lyme neuroborreliosis – the experience from one year of a university hospitals Lyme neuroborreliosis outpatients clinic. *European Journal of Neurology*, 18, 547–555.

Fallon, B. A., Pavlicova, M., Coffino, S. W., & Brenner, C. (2014). A comparison of Lyme disease serologic test results from 4 laboratories in patients with persistent symptoms after antibiotic treatment. *Clinical Infectious Diseases*, 59(12), 1705–1710. 10.1093/cid/ciu703

Feder, H. M., Johnson, B. J. B., O'Connell, S., Shapiro, E. D., Steere, A. C., & Wormser, G. P. (2007). A critical appraisal of "chronic Lyme disease." *New England Journal of Medicine*, 357(14), 1422–1430. 10.1056/NEJMra072023

Fergus, T. A., & Valentiner, D. P. (2010). Disease phobia and disease conviction are separate dimensions underlying hypochondriasis. *Journal of Behavior Therapy and Experimental Psychiatry*, 41(4), 438–444. 10.1016/j.jbtep.2010.05.002

Hassett, A. L., Radvanski, D. C., Buyske, S., Savage, S. V., Gara, M., Escobar, J. I., & Sigal, L. H. (2008). Role of psychiatric comorbidity in chronic Lyme disease. *Arthritis Care & Research*, 59(12), 1742–1749. 10.1002/art.24314

Hassett, A. L., Radvanski, D. C., Buyske, S., Savage, S. V., & Sigal, L. H. (2009). Psychiatric comorbidity and other psychological factors in patients with "chronic Lyme disease." *The American Journal of Medicine*, 122(9), 843–850. 10.1016/j.amjmed.2009.02.022

Hughes, C. C. (1998). The glossary of 'Culture-Bound Syndromes' in DSM-IV: A critique. Transcultural *Psychiatry*, 35(3), 413–42110.1177/136346159803500307.

IDSA. (2006). *Final Report of the Lyme Disease Review Panel of the Infectious Diseases Society of America (IDSA)* (p. 65).

Johnson, L., Wilcox, S., Mankoff, J., & Stricker, R. B. (2014). Severity of chronic Lyme disease compared to other chronic conditions: A quality of life survey. *PeerJ*, 2, e322. 10.7717/peerj.322

Johnson, S. B., Park, H. S., Gross, C. P., & Yu, J. B. (2018). Use of alternative medicine for cancer and its impact on survival. *JNCI: Journal of the National Cancer Institute*, 110(1), 121–124. 10.1093/jnci/djx145

Kellman Wellness Center. (n.d.). *Lyme Disease Specialist NYC | Lyme Disease Doctor NYC*. Kellman Wellness Center. Retrieved September 7, 2022, from https://www.kellmancenter.com/lyme-disease.html

Kullberg, B. J., Vrijmoeth, H. D., van de Schoor, F., & Hovius, J. W. (2020). Lyme borreliosis: Diagnosis and management. *BMJ*, 369, m1041. 10.1136/bmj.m1041

Langdon, S. (2019, August 2). *Lyme crime: A chiropractor's perspective on Lyme disease*. https://www.cndoctor.ca/lyme-crime-5417/

Lantos, P. M. (2015). Chronic Lyme disease. *Infectious Disease Clinics of North America*, 29(2), 325–340. 10.1016/j.idc.2015.02.006

Lantos, P. M., Rumbaugh, J., Bockenstedt, L. K., Falck-Ytter, Y. T., Aguero-Rosenfeld, M. E., Auwaerter, P. G., Baldwin, K., Bannuru, R. R., Belani, K. K., Bowie, W. R., Branda, J. A., Clifford, D. B., DiMario, F. J., Halperin, J. J., Krause, P. J., Lavergne, V., Liang, M. H., Meissner, H. C., Nigrovic, L. E., …Zemel, L. S. (2021). Clinical practice guidelines by the infectious diseases Society of America (IDSA), American Academy of Neurology (AAN), and American College of Rheumatology (ACR): 2020 guidelines for the prevention, diagnosis and treatment of Lyme disease. *Clinical Infectious Diseases*, 72(1), e1–e48. 10.1093/cid/ciaa1215

Lantos, P. M., Shapiro, E. D., Auwaerter, P. G., Baker, P. J., Halperin, J. J., McSweegan, E., & Wormser, G. P. (2015). Unorthodox alternative therapies marketed to treat Lyme disease. *Clinical Infectious Diseases: An Official Publication of the Infectious Diseases Society of America*, 60(12), 1776–1782. 10.1093/cid/civ186

Lilienfeld, S. O., Lynn, S. J., & Lohr, J. M. (Eds.). (2015). *Science and pseudoscience in clinical psychology* (Second edition). The Guilford Press.

Lilienfeld, S. O., Ritschel, L. A., Lynn, S. J., Cautin, R. L., & Latzman, R. D. (2014). Why ineffective psychotherapies appear to work: A taxonomy of causes of spurious therapeutic effectiveness. *Perspectives on Psychological Science*, 9(4), 355–387. 10.1177/1745691614535216

Marshall, J. A. R., Trimmer, P. C., Houston, A. I., & McNamara, J. M. (2013). On evolutionary explanations of cognitive biases. *Trends in Ecology & Evolution*, 28(8), 469–473. 10.1016/j.tree.2013.05.013

Mead, P. S. (2015). Epidemiology of lyme disease. *Infectious Disease Clinics of North America*, 29(2), 187–21010.1016/j.idc.2015.02.010.

Mounds View Chiropractic. (n.d.). *Post Treatment Lyme Disease Syndrome (PTLDS)*. Mounds View Chiropractic. Retrieved September 1, 2022, from https://www.moundsviewchiro.com/post-treatment-lyme-disease-syndrome-ptlds

Myerowitz Chiropractic. (n.d.). Lyme Disease—Myerowitz Chiropractic—Bangor, Maine. *Myerowitz Chiropractic*. Retrieved September 1, 2022, from https://www.myerowitzchiroacu.com/lyme-disease/

Nardella Clinic. (n.d.). Lyme and Tick-borne Disease Naturopathic Treatment Calgary, Alberta. *Nardella Clinic*. Retrieved September 1, 2022, from https://nardellaclinic.com/naturopathic-therapies/lyme-and-tick-borne-disease-naturopathic-treatment/

Nickerson, R. S. (1998). Confirmation bias: A ubiquitous phenomenon in many guises. *Review of General Psychology, 2*(2), 175–220. 10.1037/1089-2680. 2.2.175

Nimnuan, C., Hotopf, M., & Wessely, S. (2001). Medically unexplained symptoms: An epidemiological study in seven specialities. *Journal of Psychosomatic Research, 51*(1), 361–367. 10.1016/S0022-3999(01)00223-9

Nichter, M. (1981). Idioms of distress: Alternatives in the expression of psychosocial distress: A case study from South India. *Culture, Medicine and Psychiatry, 5*(4), 379-408.

Olivieri Family Chiropractic. (2021). *Chiropractic and Lyme Disease*. Olivieri Family Chiropractic. https://www.olivierichiro.com/new-blog/chiropractic-and-lyme-disease

Oz, M. (2009). *Chronic Lyme Disease: Myth or Reality?* Oprah.Com. Retrieved September 1, 2022, from https://www.oprah.com/health/dr-oz-treating-lyme-disease

Porcino, A. J., Solomonian, L., Zylich, S., Doucet, C., Gluvic, B., & Vohra, S. (2019). Pediatric natural health products recommended by chiropractic and naturopathic doctors in Canada. *Complementary Therapies in Medicine, 43,* 196–200. 10.1016/j.ctim.2019.02.001

Pulley, J. (2018, December 11). Do You Have Lyme Disease? *Pulley Chiropratic & Acupuncture*. https://www.pulleychiropractic.com/do-you-have-lyme-disease/

Rief, W., & Broadbent, E. (2007). Explaining medically unexplained symptoms-models and mechanisms. *Clinical Psychology Review, 27*(7), 821–841. 10.101 6/j.cpr.2007.07.005.

Richmond Natural Medicine. (2019, August 22). A Naturopathic Perspective on Lyme Disease. *Richmond Natural Medicine*. https://richmondnaturalmed.com/a-naturopathic-perspective-on-lyme-disease/

Sanchez, E., Vannier, E., Wormser, G. P., & Hu, L. T. (2016). Diagnosis, treatment, and prevention of Lyme disease, human granulocytic anaplasmosis, and babesiosis: A review. *JAMA, 315*(16), 1767. 10.1001/jama.2016.2884

Saposnik, G., Redelmeier, D., Ruff, C.C., & Tobler, P. N. (2016). Cognitive biases associated with medical decisions: a systematic review.*BMC Medical Informatics and Decision Making, 16*(1), 138.

Savely, V. R., & Stricker, R. B. (2007). Morgellons disease: The mystery unfolds. *Expert Review of Dermatology, 2*(5), 585–591. 10.1586/17469872.2.5.585

Sigal, L. H. (1990). Summary of the first 100 patients seen at a Lyme disease referral center. *The American Journal of Medicine, 88*(6), 577–581. 10.1016/0002-9343(90)90520-N

Singh, K., & Brown, R. J. (2016). From headache to tumour: An examination of health anxiety, health-related Internet use and 'query escalation'. *Journal of Health Psychology*, 21(9), 2008–2020. 10.1177/1359105315569620

Sonnet, C. (2020). *What is Lyme Disease?* http://www.caravansonnet.com/2014/05/what-is-lyme-disease.html

Surís, A., Holliday, R., & North, C. S. (2016). The evolution of the classification of psychiatric disorders. *Behavioral Sciences*, 6(1), 5. 10.3390/bs6010005

Taylor, S., Asmundson, G. J., & Hyprochondria. (2004). *Treating health anxiety: A cognitive-behavioral approach* (Vol. 494, p. 495). New York: Guilford Press.

4 Rorschach Inkblots

James M. Wood, M. Teresa Nezworski, and Howard N. Garb

The Rorschach Inkblot Test was developed more than a century ago by Hermann Rorschach, a Swiss psychiatrist who worked with patients with severe mental illness in a hospital for the "insane" (Searls, 2017). Rorschach created a set of odd, intriguing inkblots, some pastel colored, others gray and white. He then showed the blots to his patients and asked them to describe what they saw in the quirky spatters and clouds of color. Rorschach came to believe that his patients' responses – that is, their descriptions of the blots – revealed their mental disorders and personalities. For instance, he had the impression that patients who reported many responses involving color were emotional and impulsive.

In 1921, Rorschach (1921/1964) published *Psychodiagnostics*, a book that included 10 of his inkblots and described how his patients responded to them. Shortly afterward he died unexpectedly of appendicitis at the age of 37. Although his book had attracted little attention while he was alive, in the following years Rorschach's reputation and test gradually spread across Europe and the United States. By 1950, the Rorschach Inkblot Test had become highly popular among American psychologists, who considered it a sort of mental X-ray that allowed them to peer deep into the minds and hearts of their patients.

To this day, some psychologists continue to claim that the Rorschach Inkblot Test provides a rich and complete picture of a patient's personality and psychological problems. Advocates of the Rorschach like to say that other assessment techniques, such as questionnaires and clinical interviews, reflect merely what patients are willing or able to tell about themselves, whereas the Rorschach reveals much more. It supposedly has the power to expose emotions, thoughts, and other psychological qualities that are hidden out of sight inside the patient, beyond the patient's conscious awareness. That is, the Rorschach is considered to be a type of *projective* test.

The Rorschach Test is claimed to be highly sensitive for identifying psychiatric symptoms and diagnosing mental disorders. Advocates claim

DOI: 10.4324/9781003259510-6

that it has a solid scientific basis and is widely accepted among clinical psychologists as useful in clinical and legal settings. In the past, claim advocates, the Rorschach was unfairly attacked by a small number of critics who misunderstood its unique potential for providing clinical insight. Advocates concede that a few of the criticisms leveled against the test were legitimate, but claim that the problems identified have been corrected in present-day versions of the Rorschach.

Examining the Claims

The Rorschach Test is administered one on one. The psychologist, sitting beside the patient, hands them 10 Rorschach cards, one at a time, and asks, "What might that be?" Each card is approximately the size of a *National Geographic* magazine cover and bears one of the intriguing inkblots that Hermann Rorschach created more than a century ago (Exner, 2003; Meyer et al., 2011). Image 4.1 is a replica example of what an inkblot looks like.

The inkblots are intentionally ambiguous. Patients see many things in them, such as bats, lobsters, flowers, monsters, and scenes of people fighting or dancing. Patients typically give about 2 responses per card, or about 20 responses total for the entire test. The psychologist attempts to write down each response in the patient's exact words. After the patient has responded to all the cards, the psychologist goes through them a second time, asking the patient to clarify exactly what images were seen in the blots and where they appeared.

After the testing session is over, the psychologist scores and interprets the patient's responses. Scoring the Rorschach is challenging and time-consuming because there are dozens of scores to be calculated. For instance, one important score indicates the number of responses given by the patient that involve the use of color. Another indicates the number of responses that describe people acting in cooperation with each other ("two women preparing a meal together"). There are also many Rorschach "composite" scores, which are calculated by adding or subtracting two scores from each other, or by dividing one score by another. For instance, one composite score is calculated by first adding up the number of responses that describe people moving, and then dividing this sum by the number of responses that involve the use of color.

After the Rorschach scores have been calculated, the psychologist interprets their meaning. In most cases, the scores have a straightforward interpretation. For example, as mentioned earlier, if a patient has given a high number of color responses, this will generally be interpreted to mean that the patient is impulsive or tends to act under the influence of strong emotions. As another example, if a patient has given several responses that describe people engaged in cooperative activity, the psychologist will

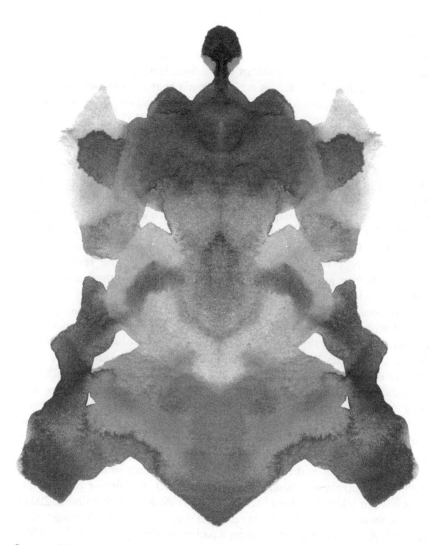

Image 4.1
Copyright © 2002 Patrice N. Griffitts. Used by permission.

probably conclude that the patient views interactions with other people as being positive and helpful rather than antagonistic.

The Rorschach interpretations made by psychologists are typically used in clinical settings to shed light on patients' behaviors, personality, and psychological problems and to help guide treatment decisions. The Rorschach is also used in legal settings, for instance, for child custody disputes, criminal trials, and parole hearings.

Is the Rorschach Good for Anything?

In light of the Rorschach's long history of scientific controversy, it is sensible to ask whether the test is good for anything. The answer is, "Yes, the Rorschach can do a few things well." Specifically, it has some validity for detecting disorders such as schizophrenia that involve perceptual distortion and disorganized thinking. In addition, some of its scores are related to IQ (Mihura et al., 2013; Wood et al., 2015).

When conducting his research with hospital patients, Hermann Rorschach scored each of their responses as having either "good" form quality or "poor" form quality. "Good" form quality indicated that the image reported by the patient fit the shape or "form" of the inkblot, whereas "poor" form quality indicated that the image didn't fit the blot's shape. For instance, the shape of one of Rorschach's inkblots very strongly resembled a bat. For this inkblot, if a patient reported seeing a "bat" or "butterfly," Rorschach scored the response as having good form quality. If the patient reported seeing a "cat" or "kangaroo," the response was scored as having poor form quality because the shape of these animals did not fit the blot's shape.

Hermann Rorschach's book reported that patients with schizophrenia tended to give an unusually high number of responses with poor form quality. Research in the 1950s confirmed Rorschach's observations, as have more recent studies (Chambers & Hamlin, 1957; Little & Shneidman, 1959; Mihura et al., 2013). Many people who take the Rorschach test, including individuals without any disorders, may give at least a few responses with poor form quality. However, patients with schizophrenia, a very severe mental disorder involving loss of contact with reality, tend to give substantially more such responses than other people. So do other patients with perceptual distortions, severe mental impairments, or psychoses.

In the late 1940s and early 1950s, researchers demonstrated that patients with schizophrenia also tend to show *disordered thinking* or *disorganized speech* when taking the Rorschach (Kleiger, 1999; Kleiger & Mihura, 2021). That is, these patients often display illogical reasoning or say odd things when responding to the blots. For instance, a patient might say, "This little red blot looks like a drop of blood. And it looks like an island in the ocean. It must be Haiti, because that's the island where there's been a lot of bloody fighting." Such odd, illogical responses are more frequent not only among patients with schizophrenia, but also among patients with borderline personality disorder and other mental disorders with disorganized thinking or speech (Mihura et al., 2013). Although the Rorschach is a valid measure of disordered thinking or disorganized speech, an interviewer can also detect these problems without the Rorschach, and so it is not clear how often the addition of a Rorschach to an interview will result in more accurate diagnoses.

Other Rorschach scores are related to intelligence and mental ability. For instance, studies have shown that individuals with higher IQ scores tend to give more responses on the Rorschach than other people, and those responses tend to be more complex, with several parts of the inkblot combined and integrated into a unifying image. In addition, research has shown that patients with higher IQs tend to use more sophisticated vocabulary when describing what they see in the blots (Davis, 1961; Mihura et al., 2013; Trier, 1958).

Rorschach scores often do not measure what they are supposed to measure. The test is generally, but not always, unrelated to other mental disorders, diagnoses, and symptoms (Meyer et al., 2017, p. 78; Wood et al., 2000). While a recent review of the published scientific literature identified several Rorschach scores as potentially useful for identifying the presence of distressing emotions, impulsivity, dependency, current level of coping ability, or other characteristics (Mihura et al., 2013), the validity and clinical utility of most of these scores has been questioned and remains controversial (Wood et al., 2015; see also Wood et al., 2003, p. 244; but see Mihura et al., 2015).

Rorschach Myths and Problems

As the preceding section has explained, the Rorschach can do a few things relatively well. The test has been controversial for more than half a century not because it is worthless, but because it has so often been promoted with misleading claims and used for purposes for which it has little or no scientific support. Furthermore, under some circumstances, use of the Rorschach can cause serious harm to patients. The present section identifies the myths that are most commonly held forth on behalf of the test and then discusses how the use of the Rorschach can cause harm.

Claim #1: The Rorschach Provides a "Rich" and "Complete" Understanding of Personality

In the 1940s and early 1950s, when the Rorschach was at its peak popularity, enthusiasts claimed that the test offered a rich source of clinical insight and a complete picture of a patient's personality and psychological problems. For instance, according to Bruno Klopfer, the most influential Rorschach expert of that era, a skilled interpreter could extract a total psychological understanding of a patient simply by examining the inkblot responses, without any other clinical information about the patient's history or test scores (Klopfer & Kelley, 1946, pp. 18, 21–22).

Klopfer's grandiose claims should have awakened serious doubts among the members of the psychological community, particularly because there was no research to support them. Imagine that a pharmaceutical company, without any good scientific evidence, were to announce that it had developed a blood test that could provide a "complete" medical understanding of every patient and thus eliminate any need to conduct additional physical examinations or diagnostic imaging. Such a claim would instantly be recognized as preposterous by the medical community. However, Klopfer's equally absurd claims were widely accepted by psychologists of the early 1950s. Only in the following years, as hundreds of studies, often by leading researchers, reported disappointing results did the dismal truth about the Rorschach become clear: Far from giving a "complete" picture of patients' personalities, it was worthless for most purposes. As summed up by Lee J. Cronbach of Stanford University, one of the most respected psychologists of the 20th century: "It is not demonstrated that the test is precise enough or invariant enough for clinical decisions. The test has repeatedly failed as a predictor of practical criteria... There is nothing in the literature to encourage reliance on Rorschach interpretations" (Cronbach, 1956, p. 184).

Despite the mainly negative research findings, enthusiasm for the Rorschach has remained inexplicably high among a minority of clinical psychologists who often show the same unrealistic zeal as in the 1940s. At present there are two leading approaches or "systems" that these psychologists use when administering, scoring, and interpreting the Rorschach. The first and more popular approach is John Exner's "Comprehensive System for the Rorschach" or "CS" (Exner, 2003). The second and newer approach is the "Rorschach Performance Assessment System" or "R-PAS," introduced in 2011 (Meyer et al., 2011).

Both of these systems have been promoted by their creators in extravagant terms. Exner, like Klopfer, has claimed that his Rorschach system, the Comprehensive System, provides a "complete understanding" of a patient (Exner, 2003). The R-PAS developers claim that its approach yields "rich, multi-faceted descriptions," contains "a wealth of idiographic information," and provides psychologists the means of "observing and measuring personality in action" (Meyer et al., 2011 pp. 1–2, 320).

Such expansive promises are misleading, however. Although both the Comprehensive System and R-PAS include dozens upon dozens of Rorschach scores, these scores do not reveal dozens upon dozens of aspects of personality. In fact, there is no well-accepted scientific basis for believing that these scores reveal much about personality, beyond their relation to perceptual distortion, thought disorder, or intelligence. It is true that research has shown that a handful of scores – perhaps eight or so – may have a weak relationship to other aspects of personality. For the practicing clinician, however, these Rorschach scores cannot be interpreted in any way that is both scientifically grounded and useful for guiding clinical work. Psychologists who use the Rorschach in hopes that its multitude of scores will provide a "rich" and "complete" understanding of their patients are misleading both themselves and the patients.

Claim #2: The Rorschach Is Like a Psychological X-Ray

Another famous claim made by Bruno Klopfer in the 1940s was that the Rorschach is like a psychological X-ray (Klopfer, 1940, p. 26). He promoted the idea that the test has the power to look inside a patient and detect hidden things – problems that psychiatrists and psychologists cannot hope to observe otherwise, or that the patient is unaware of and thus cannot describe. According to Klopfer, a psychologist using the Rorschach has privileged access to information about patients that is simply unavailable to other mental health professionals.

Research in the 1950s and afterward exploded Klopfer's claim that psychologists using the Rorschach have special access to insights that their colleagues lack. In fact, studies showed that psychologists who relied on the Rorschach were actually *less* accurate in their assessments of patients than were psychologists who simply read the patient's history or used the *Minnesota Multiphasic Personality Inventory* (MMPI), a psychological test filled out by patients to report their psychological symptoms and problems (Guilford, 1948; Kelly & Fiske, 1950; Holtzman & Sells, 1954; Little & Shneidman, 1959; Sines, 1959; Whitehead, 1985).

The seductive notion that the Rorschach provides a special window into patients' innermost unconscious feelings and thoughts is still alive today, however. For example, the creators of the R-PAS, the new Rorschach system, claim that the Rorschach reveals "implicit" aspects of personality, by which they mean "characteristics that may not be recognized by the respondent him or herself" (Meyer et al., 2011, p. 1). They also claim that "the Rorschach can provide psychological information that may reside outside of the client's immediate or conscious awareness..." (Meyer & Mihura, 2020, p. 283). For example, according to the creators of the R-PAS, several scores indicate "implicit" distress. Because these negative feelings are "implicit," claim the R-PAS authors, the patient may be unconscious of them and thus cannot be said to actually *feel* the distress (Meyer et al., 2017, pp. 76–77).

The R-PAS scores that supposedly indicate "implicit" distress are among the controversial scores we have already discussed. Furthermore, the notion proposed by the R-PAS authors that these scores indicate *unconscious* distress leads to strange and troubling paradoxes: If a person is psychologically distressed but does not know it, is that person really distressed at all? Isn't that like claiming that a person feels "unconscious pain," even though they say they aren't feeling any pain at all? And what if a patient reports that they feel fine, but their Rorschach indicates "implicit" distress? Should a psychologist using the Rorschach disregard what the patient says and conclude that the patient is psychologically in pain, suffering perhaps from "unconscious depression"?

Claim #3: Validation Studies Are Unnecessary because "Clinical Validation" Is Enough

Validity is a scientific term that can be used to describe how well a test measures what it is supposed to. To evaluate the validity of psychological and medical tests, researchers undertake what are called *validation studies*. For example, in 2002, researchers at Clemson University conducted a validation study of the *Beck Depression Inventory–II* (BDI-II), a questionnaire used to measure depressive symptoms (Sprinkle et al., 2002). They found that in a sample of therapy patients at a university counseling center, the correlation of BDI-II scores with the number of depressive symptoms reported by the patients during a diagnostic interview was 0.83. This correlation, called a *validity coefficient*, was very high and indicated that the BDI-II has strong validity. That is, the study showed that the BDI-II has a strong relationship with depression, the disorder it is supposed to measure.

In the 1930s and 1940s, Klopfer contended that such validity studies were unnecessary where the Rorschach was concerned. Instead, he and his followers proposed to substitute a procedure that they called "clinical validation" (Klopfer, 1939, p. 47). Specifically, they argued that the Rorschach's worth could be demonstrated by positive testimonials from the psychologists who used it clinically (Krugman, 1940).

Klopfer's dismissal of systematic validation studies, and his trust in the testimonials of clinicians, ignored the hard-earned experience of the American medical profession during the preceding half century. In the years leading up to the 1930s, bitter experience had shown that testimonials by physicians about the effectiveness of medical procedures could be misleading and downright dangerous (Haines, 2002; McCoy, 2000; Young, 1967). In several highly publicized scandals, prominent doctors enthusiastically promoted scientifically unsupported medical tests and medications that were later found to be harmful and even fatal to their patients.

At the time that most Rorschach users were uncritically accepting Klopfer's dubious ideas about clinical validation and the value of testimonials, at least a few perceptive psychologists resisted. For example, Donald Super of Columbia University warned his Rorschach-smitten colleagues: "Unorganized experience, unanalyzed data, and tradition are often misleading. Validation should be accomplished by evidence gathered in controlled investigations and analyzed objectively, not by the opinions of authorities and the impressions of observers" (Buros, 1949, p. 167).

The warnings by Super and other skeptics were eventually vindicated in the 1950s, as we have already described, when the results of systematic validity studies showed that the Rorschach was largely worthless and that clinicians' glowing testimonials on its behalf had been seriously in error. One might think that such a debacle would have convinced Rorschach users of the folly of clinical validation and the value of careful research. But instead, many Rorschach advocates simply brushed aside the research. For instance, Klopfer advised his followers to ignore the negative scientific findings regarding the test (Klopfer & Davidson, 1962, p. 24). Similarly, Samuel Beck, another prominent Rorschach leader, dismissed the findings as irrelevant: "Let it be said at once and unequivocally that validation such as is sought in a laboratory experiment is not at present to be expected for whole personality findings, whether by the Rorschach test or by any other" (Beck, 1959, p. 275).

The Rorschach tradition of using scores that lack support from systematic validation studies has never disappeared and continues to the present day. The Comprehensive System and the R-PAS both include a substantial number of Rorschach scores with little or no research support. Clinicians who use these scientifically untested scores are showing the same reckless naivete, and running the same risks with patients' well-being, that Klopfer and his followers did in the 1940s.

Claim #4: The Rorschach Is a Trustworthy Tool for Identifying Psychological Disturbances

The last and probably most serious problem with the Rorschach is the test's tendency to misidentify people as being psychologically disturbed when all other evidence indicates they are psychologically healthy. Researchers first exposed this flaw more than half a century ago. For instance, in one study in the 1950s, the Rorschach was administered to a group of men previously identified as well adjusted. The researchers were surprised to find that many of these men's Rorschach scores fell in the abnormal range and falsely indicated maladjustment (Brockway et al., 1954). In another study at the University of California at Berkeley, Rorschach experts evaluated adolescents from the community and identified two out of every three as "maladjusted" – an absurdly high number because, contrary to some stereotypes, most teenagers do not experience marked emotional disturbance (Grant et al., 1952; see also Chapter 11 of this book for more about the "storm and stress" of adolescence).

As these and other similar findings from the 1950s made clear, psychologists who used the Rorschach often found psychological disturbance and mental pathology where in fact there was none, a form of bias that is called *overpathologizing*. Nor has this problem disappeared with more recent approaches to the Rorschach. Research has shown that the most popular approach to the Rorschach today, Exner's Comprehensive System, often makes both adults and children appear psychologically disturbed even when no other evidence suggests that this is so (Viglione et al., 2022, p. 140). For instance, one study found that psychologists using the Comprehensive System misdiagnosed more than 75% of psychologically healthy individuals as disturbed (Mittman, 1983; see also Exner, 1991, pp. 432–433). Another study found that when psychologically school children were tested with the Comprehensive System, their Rorschach scores often wrongly indicated the presence of grave psychological problems, including distortion of reality, faulty reasoning, and difficulty maintaining interpersonal relationships (Hamel et al., 2000).

The consequences of overpathologizing can be devastating, particularly in high stakes settings that involve employment issues or legal decisions. For instance, in a legal case known to the authors of the present chapter (Wood et al., 2003, p. 301), an African American man sued his employer for racial discrimination. Although his mental health history was unremarkable, a psychologist testified in court that the man was seriously disturbed and that his Rorschach revealed paranoia and a tendency to distort reality when under stress. Because of the Rorschach's tendency to overpathologize, its use in legal cases or other high-stake settings has the potential to do serious harm.

Summary and Conclusion

Rorschach scores are related to perceptual distortions, disorganized thinking, and intelligence. However, there are much more valid, comprehensive, and efficient ways to assesses these traits. Further, the Rorschach's relationship to other diagnoses and personality characteristics is highly controversial and has been controversial for more than 50 years. Contrary to myths promoted by its proponents, the Rorschach does not provide a rich picture of patients' personalities or reveal hidden secrets about their emotions or thoughts. Worst of all, the Rorschach has a well-documented bias that causes it to misidentify psychologically healthy people as being psychologically disturbed. Use of the test in educational, employment, or legal settings is strongly discouraged. Readers who would like more information on the Rorschach and its many problems may wish to consult the authors' book, *What's Wrong With the Rorschach?* (Wood et al., 2003).

James M. Wood, PhD, is a clinical psychologist and professor emeritus at the University of Texas at El Paso. He is also author of the book *What's Wrong with the Rorschach? Science Confronts the Controversial Inkblot Test.*

M. Teresa Nezworski, PhD, is a clinical and developmental psychologist and a retired associate professor at the University of Texas at Dallas. She is also editor of the book *Clinical Implications of Attachment.*

Howard N. Garb, PhD, is a clinical psychologist, the author of *Judging the Clinician: Judgment Research and Psychological Assessment,* and a retired research psychologist with the United States Air Force.

References

Beck, S. J. (1959). Review of the Rorschach Inkblot Test. In O. K. Buros (Ed.), *The fifth mental measurements yearbook* (pp. 273–276). Gryphon.

Brockway, A. L., Gleser, G. C., & Ulett, G. A. (1954). Rorschach concepts of normality. *Journal of Consulting Psychology, 18,* 259–265. 10.1037/h0061109

Buros, O. K. (Ed.) (1949). *The third mental measurements yearbook.* Rutgers University Press.

Chambers, G. S., & Hamlin, R. M. (1957). The validity of judgments based on "blind" Rorschach records. *Journal of Consulting Psychology, 21,* 105–109. 10.1037/h0040368

Cronbach, L. J. (1956). Assessment of individual differences. *Annual Review of Psychology, 7,* 173–196. 10.1146/annurev.ps.07.020156.001133

Davis, H. S. (1961). Judgments of intellectual level from various features of the Rorschach including vocabulary. *Journal of Projective Techniques, 25,* 155–157. 10.1080/08853126.1961.10381018

Exner, J. E. (1991). *The Rorschach: A comprehensive system. volume 2: Interpretation* (2nd ed.). New York: Wiley.

Exner, J. E. (2003). *The Rorschach: A comprehensive system* (4th ed., Vol. 1). John Wiley & Sons, Inc.

Grant, M. Q., Ives, V., & Ranzoni, J. H. (1952). Reliability and validity of judges' ratings of adjustment on the Rorschach. *Psychological Monographs, 66*(2), Whole issue. 10.1037/h0093603

Guilford, J. P. (1948). Some lessons from aviation psychology. *American Psychologist, 3,* 3–11. 10.1037/h0056736

Haines, J. D. (2002). The king of quacks: Albert Abrams, M. D. *Skeptical Inquirer, 26*(3), 45–48.

Hamel, M., Shaffer, T. W., & Erdberg, P. (2000). A study of nonpatient pre-adolescent Rorschach protocols. *Journal of Personality Assessment, 75,* 280–294. 10.1207/S15327752JPA7502_8

Holtzman, W. H., & Sells, S. B. (1954). Prediction of flying success by clinical analysis of test protocols. *Journal of Abnormal and Social Psychology, 49,* 485–490. 10.1037/h0059895

Kelly, E. L., & Fiske, D. W. (1950). The prediction of success in the VA training program in clinical psychology. *American Psychologist, 5,* 395–406. 10.1037/h0062436

Kleiger, J. H. (1999). *Disordered thinking and the Rorschach.* The Analytic Press.

Kleiger, J. H., & Mihura, J. L. (2021). Developments in the Rorschach assessment of disordered thinking and communication. *Rorschachiana, 42,* 265–280. 10. 1027/1192-5604/a000132

Klopfer, B. (1939). Shall the Rorschach method be standardized?*Rorschach Research Exchange, 3,* 45–54. 10.1080/08934037.1939.10381511

Klopfer, B. (1940). Personality aspects revealed by the Rorschach method. *Rorschach Research Exchange, 4,* 26–29. 10.1080/08934037.1940.10381240

Klopfer, B., & Davidson, H. H. (1962). *The Rorschach technique: An introductory manual.* Harcourt Brace Jovanovich.

Klopfer, B., & Kelley, D. M. (1946). *The Rorschach technique.* World Book.

Krugman, M. (1940). Out of the ink well: The Rorschach method. *Rorschach Research Exchange, 4,* 91–101. 10.1111/j.1467-6494.1940.tb02200.x

Little, K. B., & Shneidman, E. S. (1959). Congruencies among interpretations of psychological test and anamnestic data. *Psychological Monographs, 73* (6, Whole No. 476). 10.1037/h0093742

McCoy, B. (2000). *Quack! Tales of medical fraud from the Museum of Questionable Medical Devices.* Santa Monica Press.

Meyer, G. J., Viglione, D. J., Mihura, J. L., Erard, R. E., & Erdberg, P. (2011). *Rorschach Performance Assessment System: Administration, coding, interpretation, and technical manual.* Rorschach Performance Assessment System LLC.

Meyer, G. J., Viglione, D. J., & Mihura, J. L. (2017). Psychometric foundations of the Rorschach Performance Assessment System (R-PAS). In R. E. Erard & F. Barton Evans (Eds.), *The Rorschach in multimethod forensic assessment: Conceptual foundations and practical applications* (pp. 23–91). Taylor & Francis Group.

Meyer, G. J., & Mihura, J. L. (2020). Performance-based techniques. In M. Sellbom & J. A. Suhr, *The Cambridge handbook of clinical assessment and diagnosis* (pp. 278–290). Cambridge University Press.

Mihura, J. L., Meyer, G. J., Bombel, G., & Dumitrascu, N. (2015). Standards, accuracy, and questions of bias in Rorschach meta-analyses: Reply to Wood, Garb, Nezworski, Lilienfeld, and Duke (2015). *Psychological Bulletin, 141,* 250–260. 10.1037/a0038445

Mihura, J. L., Meyer, G. J., Dumitrascu, N., & Bombel, G. (2013). The validity of individual Rorschach variables: Systematic reviews and meta-analyses of the comprehensive system. *Psychological Bulletin, 139,* 548–605. 10.1037/a0029406

Mittman, B. L. (1983). Judges' ability to diagnose schizophrenia on the Rorschach: The effect of malingering (Unpublished dissertation, Long Island University, The Brooklyn Center, 1983). *Dissertation Abstracts International, 44,* 1248B.

Rorschach, H. (1921/1964). *Psychodiagnostics.* New York: Grune & Stratton. (Original work published in German in 1921 and in English in 1942).

Searls, D. (2017). *The inkblots: Hermann Rorschach, his iconic test, and the power of seeing.* New York: Crown Publishers.

Sines, L. K. (1959). The relative contribution of four kinds of data to accuracy in personality assessment. *Journal of Consulting Psychology, 23,* 483–492. 10.103 7/h0046083

Sprinkle, S. D., Lurie, D., Insko, S. L., Atkinson, G., Jones, G. L., Logan, A. R., & Bissada, N. N. (2002). Criterion validity, severity cut scores, and test-retest reliability of the beck depression inventory-II in a university counseling center sample. *Journal of Counseling Psychology, 49*, 381–385. 10.1037/0022-0167. 49.3.381

Trier, T. R. (1958). Vocabulary as a basis for estimating intelligence from the Rorschach. *Journal of Consulting Psychology, 22*, 289–291. 10.1037/h0044585

Viglione, D. J., de Ruiter, C., King, C. M., Meyer, G. J.; Kivisto, A. J., Rubin, B. A., & Hunsley, J. (2022) Legal admissibility of the Rorschach and R-PAS: A review of research, practice, and case law. *Journal of Personality Assessment, 104*, 137–161. 10.1080/00223891.2022.2028795

Whitehead, W. C. (1985). *Clinical decision making on the basis of Rorschach, MMPI, and automated MMPI report data.* Unpublished doctoral dissertation, University of Texas Health Science Center at Dallas.

Wood, J. M., Garb, H. N., Nezworski, M. T., Lilienfeld, S. O., & Duke, M. C. (2015). A second look at the validity of widely used Rorschach indices: Comment on Mihura, Meyer, Dumitrascu, and Bombel (2013). *Psychological Bulletin, 141*, 236–249. 10.1037/a0036005

Wood, J. M., Lilienfeld, S. O., Garb, H. N., & Nezworski, M. T. (2000). The Rorschach test in clinical diagnosis: A critical review, with a backward look at Garfield (1947). *Journal of Clinical Psychology, 56*, 395–430. 10.1002/(SICI) 1097-4679(200003)56:3<395::AID-JCLP15>3.0.CO;2-O

Wood, J. M., Nezworski, M. T., Lilienfeld, S. O., & Garb, H. N. (2003). *What's wrong with the Rorschach? Science confronts the controversial inkblot test.* Jossey-Bass.

Young, J. H. (1967). *The medical messiahs: A social history of health quackery in twentieth-century America.* Princeton, New Jersey: Princeton University Press. (This book can be read without charge on the World Wide Web at http://www. quackwatch.com/. Accessed on February 24, 2023)

5   Personality Assessment

Gerald P. Koocher and Yilong Peng

Creating a valid and useful personality assessment tool presents a daunting problem. A key part of the challenge involves the matter of construct validity. Human personality is a hypothetical construct: a psychological tool or set of explanatory variables not directly observable or intrinsically measurable. We can easily and reliably measure a person's height and weight, the speed at which they complete a specific task, the pitch of their voice, their ability to reproduce a complex design from memory, and many other aspects of human behavior. In the case of any hypothetical variable, we must begin with a theory or defining framework and acknowledge that such definitions will restrict the acceptability of measurement strategies to those who share similar theoretical perspectives. This chapter discusses three assessment tools framed with superficial theoretical foundations and offering little to no predictive validity.

Examining the Claims

We have chosen three approaches to personality assessment that share highly questionable scientific foundations despite varying degrees of professional and public acceptance and illustrate how the key elements common to pseudoscience apply. These include the Szondi test, the Blacky Pictures, and Myers-Briggs Type Indicator (MBTI).

Assessing Fate and Hereditobiology: The Szondi Test

Léopold (Lipót) Szondi was born in Hungary in 1893 and died in Zurich in 1986. He earned a medical degree from the University of Budapest in 1919 and lived there until fleeing the Nazis in 1941 and settling in Zurich in 1944. He practiced psychoanalysis and focused his career on "schicksal (fate) psychology." Szondi's main work is a five-volume series published between 1944 and 1963 on fate analysis (sic: Schicksalsanalyse). An English language version of the first volume titled: *Experimental Diagnostics of*

DOI: 10.4324/9781003259510-7

Drives appeared in 1952. Szondi framed his drive theory based on eight deeply unconscious needs corresponding to "collective archetype of instinctive action."

As published in 1935, the test required no verbal responses. The examiner would display a series of facial photographs in six groups of eight. Copies of the photos can be readily found online. All 48 people depicted in the photographs were hospitalized mental patients. Sample instructions: "I shall lay before you 8 photographs. Observe all these photographs carefully and from the group give me the first picture toward which you are most sympathetic, then the one toward which you are secondly most sympathetic" (*Experimentelle Treibdiagnostik*, p. 26). In essence, each examinee chooses the two most appealing and then the two least appealing or most repulsive photos from each group. These choices supposedly reveal the patient's satisfied and unsatisfied instinctive drive needs, and dimensions of their personality.

Each group of eight included a photo of an individual whose personality Szondi classified as "hermaphrodite, sadist, epileptic, hysteric, katatonic, paranoid, depressive and maniac." For example, the h-drive need, named after hermaphroditism (i.e., homosexual leanings), represented the needs for personal or collective love, tenderness, motherliness, passivity, femininity, and bisexuality. The e-drive need, for epilepsy, represented coarse emotions such as anger, hatred, rage, envy, jealousy, and revenge. In such individuals these needs supposedly simmer until suddenly and explosively discharge as if in a seizure, much to the surprise and shock of others. From Szondi's perspective, each photo acts as a stimulus to detect the "pulsional drive tendencies" of the examinee, causing the main personality traits to surface. He reported some examinees with mental illness could experience a crisis and convulsions during the test in response to viewing the photo of a patient with the same pathology.

Szondi's inspiration for the concept occurred when, "He began treatment of a young woman accompanied by her husband and noted a striking resemblance to an old lady from the country whom he had treated several years before. The old lady turned out to be the mother of the young woman's husband. The incident made a significant impression on him and intensified his interest in genealogy and hereditobiology and hereditopathology and the familial unconscious" (Webb, page ix in preface to Szondi et al., 1959). Szondi believed that people feel inherently attracted to others based on appearance or mannerisms resulting from genotropism (i.e., specific genes regulating mate selection causing people with similar genetics to seek each other out). Thus, the man had married a woman who looked like his mother, clearly demonstrating the power of hereditobiology (at least in Szondi's reasoning).

Those seeking scientific data in support of the approach will encounter other dramatic undocumented claims such as:

"He has placed the hitherto occult concept of human destiny upon a medical and a psychoanalytic basis ... with a hitherto unknown degree of precision."

(Webb, page viii in preface to Szondi et al., 1959)

Some adherents disparaged or dismissed disbelievers. Anticipating scientific criticism in the United States, Szondi wrote in the introduction to an English language book on his technique:

"We Europeans still pursue an 'epic' form of psychology of a kind that we learned from Dostoevsky and Freud. This epic form of presentation is inadequate to the American tempo of thinking."

(Deri, 1949, pages vii–viii)

Susan Deri, a Hungarian Szondi contemporary who later published a book on the technique while living in the United States, also dismissed anticipated critics as "autistic" in the introduction to her book, claiming unique knowledge not shared with others:

" ... anybody who finds the Rorschach and psychoanalysis 'worthless and vague' also will be dissatisfied with the Szondi ... I am fully aware of the autistic nature of this reasoning since ... I am the only one who received the accumulative evidence of all these individual clinical validations."

(Deri, 1949, page xi)

Because of its weak psychometric properties and total lack of any concurrent or predictive validity, the instrument is not widely used, although a 1954 bibliography identified 330 references (David, 1954). Psychometrician, Paul Meehl, reviewed the technique for the *American Journal of Psychiatry* writing in part,

" ... even though it is unfair to criticize a book for not achieving aims ... it is perhaps fair to ask why no systematic validity data are presented?"

(Meehl, 1950)

Much of the more recent research using the instrument appears in *Szondiana,* an occasional publication of the Szondi Institut Foundation of Zurich, or other obscure publications. For example, a study published in *Pszichológia,* a now discontinued Hungarian journal, found that, "Tests of the reliability of 8 Szondi-factors along 10 consecutive administrations of the test ... show that three factors (e, hy, and k) have no better internal consistency than a randomly composed set of pictures no matter how many times the test was administered. The results also indicate a weak to moderate reliability level of the remaining factors since none of them had significant longitudinal consistency. This finding directly contradicts Szondi's theory" (Vargha, 1994). Nonetheless, after Szondi died in 1986, at the age of 93, his obituary published in the *American Psychologist* described his work as a "potent analytic modality." Unfortunately, that conclusion is likely biased by the fact that the author was the American psychologist who co-authored the English translation to his book (Webb, 1987).

The most recent iteration of Szondi testing exists in the form of a Russian-crafted smartphone app of unknown validity. It promises purchasers the opportunity to discover one's hidden self. The app allows people to take the test and receive an analysis of their personality, along with potential vocations options. The app claims to diagnose emotional states and personality traits, emotional stress level, prediction of different diseases, prediction of behavior in extreme situations, and prediction of professional and criminal preferences.

Assessing Psychoanalytic Development Stages: The Blacky Pictures

The Blacky Pictures, created by Gerald S. Blum (1949), were designed to assist child psychoanalysts understand the changes in children's personalities as they progressed through the Freudian stages of psychosexual development. Born in Newark, NJ, Blum earned a bachelor of science degree and Phi Beta Kappa key at Rutgers University in 1941, a master of arts degree at Clark University in 1942, served in the military from 1942 to 1946, and then completed a doctorate degree at Stanford University in 1948. Blum served on faculty at the University of Michigan and retired after many years at the University of California at Santa Barbara. Many of his published works focused on psychoanalytic theories of personality. Clearly the ascendant school of psychotherapeutic thought through the 1950s, psychoanalysis certainly held considerable sway in the Zeitgeist of American psychology during Blum's education and early career. Freud's only lectures in America took place at Clark University, albeit 30-odd years before Blum studied there, but an imposing "sit beside" statue of Freud rests in front of the psychology building. In addition, the University of Michigan strongly favored psychoanalytic perspectives during the two decades Blum spent on its faculty. This history tells part of the puzzling story of a highly trained, well-known, and respected psychologist's invention of a relatively useless and discredited test.

Blum commissioned a set of the 12 cartoons comprising the Blacky Pictures to align with psychoanalytic theory and the Disney cartoon genre. He sought to "get at the deeper recesses of personality ... geared directly to dynamic interpretation" (Blum & Hunt, 1952, p. 239). The stimulus cards portray the so-called adventures of a dog of unidentified age and ambiguous gender named, Blacky. Readers can easily view the cartoons via internet searching. The first cartoon introduces the cast of characters, including: Blacky, Mama (easily identified by a bow tied behind her head and lipstick), Papa, and Tippy (a sibling figure also of unspecified age/gender). Blacky's character is all black in coloration, Papa and Mama are white with black spots, and Tippy is all white. Each of the other cartoons depict either a stage of Freudian psychosexual development (e.g., oral, anal) or a type of object relationship (oedipal strivings and sibling rivalry) framed in psychoanalytic development terms. One rather compelling card intended to trigger feelings about castration anxiety depicts Blacky observing a blindfolded Tippy whose tail rests on a chopping block as a machete knife descends from above. Some of Blacky's other adventures include defecating between Mama's and Papa's respective doghouses and suffering guilt induction by Tippy's angelic haloed spirit a few cards after the castration anxiety scene. The test is administered by showing the cards to patients in sequence and asking them to tell a story about what is happening in the picture. Follow-up questions include probes about how the characters feel or what they may have on their minds. Blum explained that dog cartoon figures were used to facilitate personal responses, "In situations where human figures might provoke an unduly inhibitory resistance as a result of being 'too close to home'" (Blum & Hunt, 1952, p. 239).

The challenge faced when designing a test aligned with a narrow theoretical perspective becomes complicated because the validating criteria must also align with key hypothetical constructs. The intentional design of the test to fit a psychoanalytic approach to personality and other demand characteristics (blatant cues as to what the examiner expects) or manifest content of the pictures led to a plethora of poorly validated research using children and adults as examinees. Another challenge to validity in this context is that responses and evaluations can have alternative explanations not considered in the unitheoretical model. For instance, differences in responses between people may more logically align with traits such as introverted or extraverted personality, rather than with an oral or anal personality type.

In the monograph presenting the test to the professional community for the first time noted:

"First, there is the assumption that the Blacky Test is actually measuring the psychoanalytic dimension which it is intended to measure. Apart from the face validity of the test ... the only evidence currently available comes from informed clinical support ... therefore the validity of the test is still indeterminant."

(Blum, 1949, p. 28)

A few years later, openly acknowledging major validity problems with the test, Blum began a literature review of first 10 papers published based on the test by writing,

"Just as there is more than one way to skin a cat, there are many ways to try to validate behavior ascribed to a dog."

(Blum & Hunt, 1952, p. 238)

To his credit, Blum seemed to ultimately recognize that the tool had little utility and reframed it as "exploratory" writing:

"These methodological frailties frequently, often unavoidably, characterize exploratory research in this area... (and) ... current findings on the validity of the Blacky Pictures."

(Blum & Hunt, 1952, p. 249)

Other studies were compromised by small, biased samples, confounding variables, or overblown attempts at generalization. An embarrassing case study report describes a nine-year-old boy referred for stealing toys. Readers learn that "Case material revealed a history of spying on his mother and stepfather at night, masturbation, homosexual, and heterosexual episodes. Excerpts from the patient's Blacky stories dramatically confirm and elaborate the severe oedipal ambivalence expected on the basis of the history" (Michal-Smith et al., 1951). The report relies heavily on the stories told to the highly charged pictures through a psychoanalytic lens that blatantly ignores alternative interpretations and causative dynamics, while specifying an archaic treatment approach that would not likely pass muster as legitimate today.

Serious clinical and research interest in the instrument seldom reached beyond the psychoanalytic community and largely evaporated by the 1960s (Taulbee & Stenmark, 1968). Much of the published work involved psychoanalytic case studies in which the findings would have been self-evident from the start. As an example, in one study, 22 psychologists were asked to rate the test scores on an analytic patient, which yielded good inter-rater reliability (agreement on how the responses aligned with expected psychoanalytic concepts) but did not constitute a valid personality assessment (Ellis, 1953). In later years, Blum ultimately retreated even further from the instrument he created as a graduate student in the face of withering criticism by others (e.g., Eysenck, 1990). The Blacky Pictures Test's worth, as a source of useful personality data, became fully discredited.

Assessing Personality Types: Myers-Briggs Type Indicator (MBTI)

The MBTI is a self-report personality assessment created in the 1940s by a mother-daughter duo. Katharine Cook Briggs (1875–1968) attended college at the age of 14 and studied agriculture, graduating at the top of her class. Despite her early academic success and a short career as an educator, the norms of the times likely drove her towards domestic life. She married Lyman James Briggs and their daughter, Isabel, arrived in 1897 (Block, 2018).

Isabel Briggs Myers (1897–1980), raised in Washington, DC, was homeschooled prior to attending Swarthmore College (major: study political science) and married a budding lawyer, Clarence "Chief" Myers. Mother and daughter purportedly shared an interest in using personality analysis to "enhance harmony and productivity in diverse groups" (Myers Briggs Foundation, 2022). Briggs, an avid reader of European psychology books, became enamored of Carl Jung's work on introversion and extroversion, sharing these with Isabel (Cunningham, 2013). Most notably, she shared Jung's *Psychological Types* (published in German in 1921 and English in 1923 as volume 6 of his collected works), which became the foundation of their theories on personality. While official sources skim over the next 30 years of refinement, psychological historians posit several notable factors leading to the MBTI's prominence. The test first found acceptance during World War II, where the military used it to match personnel to jobs. The broader social movement of women into the workplace during this era likely also contributed to Katharine and Isabel's efforts.

Students at George Washington University Medical School became the first participants in a longitudinal study of more than 5,000 students, one of the largest at its time and whose results provided a large body of data on which further analyses were based. Briggs leveraged that work to collect data on more than 10,000 nursing students (CAPT, 2022; Cunningham, 2013). With large, reported sample sizes, the assessment became widely disseminated through academic and corporate America, peaking after Isabel's death in 1980. To this day, the tool remains owned by the Myers-Briggs Company, which offers the basic instrument, more specific versions for corporate use, and consultants for interpreting the results.

Rooted in Jungian archetypes, the MBTI categorizes four key psychological concepts: sensation, intuition, feeling, and thinking (CAPT, 2022). Currently, the main iteration of the MBTI, known as Form M, uses 93 self-scorable items to draw a score between binary classifications in four categories: introversion/extraversion (I/E), sensing/intuition (S/I), thinking/

feeling (T/F), and judging/perceiving (J/P). Each item contains a statement designed to prompt self-reflection and asks test takers to score how closely they feel the statement aligns to their own personality, from "Strongly Disagree" to "Strongly Agree" using a Likert scale. This leads to production of 16 unique personality types. Next, four-letter buckets classify the taker, and allow them to compare their classification to prominent individuals in history, serving as a launching point for personal reflection, career advising, workplace dynamics, and possibly an enhanced fantasy life.

Unfortunately, the MBTI's greatest layperson appeal – of self-selected binary determinism along four wide spectra – also frames its primary weakness. Simply put, because the tool relies on self-reported personality traits and preferences along a set of forced questions (one cannot "skip" a non-applicable question), people have a greater likelihood of accepting and believing those outcomes. Engagement in the assessment and the apparent face validity of the content lead to belief in the findings, even when analyses of the data over a large group of people shows poor sta-tistical validity. This tendency to accept such generalized characteriza-tions, known as the Barnum effect, was first characterized by psychologist Bertram Forer in 1949 and elaborated on with a focus on the gullibility of personnel managers by Ross Stagner in 1958. Stagner administered a personality assessment to groups of personnel managers and psychology students giving them all generalized feedback instead of actual personal-ized information. For example:

- You have a great need for other people to like and admire you.
- You have a great deal of unused capacity, which you have not turned to your advantage.
- Disciplined and self-controlled outside, you tend to be worrisome and insecure inside.
- Security is one of your major goals in life.
- You pride yourself as an independent thinker and do not accept others' statements without satisfactory proof.
- Your sexual adjustment has presented problems for you.
- You tend to be critical of yourself.
- At times you have serious doubts as to whether you have made the right decision or done the right thing.
- At times you are extroverted, sociable, while at other times you are introverted, wary, reserved.

Despite the superficiality of such statements, a significant proportion of participants report that they feel accurately represented by their test "outcomes." What drives this phenomenon? Further analysis of the Barnum effect links it to the Pollyanna principle or positivity bias – a type of linguistic optimism stating that individuals will more likely use and accept positive words of feedback rather than negative (Boucher & Osgood, 1969). It should come as no surprise that most of the descriptors for the MBTI results use positive, horoscopic language for each possible personality outcome, likely to improve test takers' perception of themselves and, subsequently, the results.

So, we know that test-takers have an understandable tendency to accept the feedback they receive. Unfortunately, the internal and external validity of the MBTI itself remain in heavy contention compared to the claims of its proponents. Firstly, the self-administration process combined with the vagueness of the results inherently creates a spectrum of personality stereotypes rather than truly individualized profiles. The failure of the MBTI to account for the degree to which an individual leans in any of the dichotomies further complicates matters. For instance, someone who scores 55/45 on I/E receives the same tag of introversion as someone who scores 90/10. Detailed quantitative breakdowns are available if requested but not heavily featured in how individuals use and apply their results. The sub-interactions between each duo and trio of each proposed dichotomy remain underexplored in favor of a composite bucket of the four scales together. The MBTI reduces the vast spectrum of personality – one of the most complex and least understood constructs in psychology – down to digestible biopsies sacrificing accuracy for acceptability.

The nature of the dichotomy approach also generates a statistical problem. Most psychological data gathered with adequate sampling shows a unimodal, normal distribution – the classic bell-curve shape, with a central mean and dwindling deviations to either side. If we consider the direction of the dichotomy (I versus E) as ultimately more important than the degree (55/45 versus 90/10), then we would expect the MBTI scores to show a bimodal distribution – we would expect to see two bell-curve shapes at each extreme, with a lower number of test takers in the middle, indicating very few people who are 55/45 (people are either 90/10 or 10/90). Instead, statistical sampling of many MBTI results indicates that its scales follow a unimodal, normal distribution; more people score closer to 55/45 or 45/55 than on either extreme end of any of the four scales (Bess & Harvey, 2002). This gives further weight to the argument that the degree of the trait itself matters more than the binary classification of type – a "55/45" Introvert will likely differ significantly from a "90/10" Introvert, based simply on frequency found within the general population; a nuance that the MBTI fails to acknowledge.

Other sources have offered similar criticisms of the MBTI's statistical approach. Reviews in the *Mental Measurement Yearbook* (Cohen & Swerdlik, 2005; Harris, 2013) point out that while the MBTI did have a large cohort analysis – close to 300,000 participants – during its development, little if any publicly available and verifiable information pertaining to these records used to develop the test exists. "The administrator's manual gives little meaningful information regarding the reliability of the instrument," the *Yearbook* reports, also note a failure to give actual numbers regarding the internal consistency of the scales. The MBTI manual drastically underutilizes historical sample size in determining test-retest reliability and validity, with $n = 39$ and $n = 17$, respectively. For validity, the 17 subjects sampled reported a median of 86% satisfaction with their results – a meaningless measure for establishing construct validity of a personality assessment tool. The *Yearbook* ultimately concludes that MBTI scores represent poorly defined constructs. Reliability and any form of validity are consistently weak and later versions of the MBTI (Step III, in this case) have become bloated with an excessive number of unvalidated scales making it difficult for an individual to interpret their results.

A review by Hess sought to establish concurrent validity of the MBTI with other established personality tests (Hess & Lanning, 2003). On these other assessments – including the *California Psychological Inventory* (CPI), *Fundamental Interpersonal Relationships Orientation-Behavior* (FIRO-B), *Eysenck Personality Questionnaire* (EPQ), and the *Rotter Locus of Control Scale* – Hess and Lanning reported "most of the correlations are in the expected direction, providing some evidence of concurrent validity," but qualifies this by noting, "One problem with this kind of data is that results in the other direction often can be explained away too facilely" (p. 611). Hess notes this research is officially unpublished or otherwise not peer reviewed. Hess and Lanning conclude that the test might serve as a valid "stimulus for dialog in counseling and employment," but caution against its use in "clinical, employment, or forensic decisions without further validational research" (p. 612).

One of the more widespread and persistent uses of the MBTI occurs in educational and career development. To their credit, the Myers-Briggs Company (2022) takes care not to endorse the use of the MBTI as a tool for the selection of job candidates or internal team/task placement. The same site highlights some of the MBTI's drawbacks that prevent it from demonstrating strong external validity in the most superficial way by describing all its questions as "clear-purpose" (not disguised), does not incorporate a social desirability or "lie scale" to explore responder honesty, and does acknowledge any delineation between personality and behavioral competency. Despite these cautions, many educational ventures have used the MBTI as a predictive assessment tool for career compatibility.

A study conducted in the United Kingdom during the 1980s surveyed physicians ($n = 464$) from a medical school in London seeking to identify broad personality trends and draw linkages to standards of clinical competence, particularly with respect to provider-patient communication (Clack et al., 2004). The study emphasized differences in the UK physician population mainstream – more Introverts (I), Intuitives (N), Thinking-deciders (T), and Judgers (J) – and concluded that disconnects would inevitably occur between physicians and their patients. This reasoning reveals the problematic extent of the MBTI's binary dichotomies in the investigators' statistical analysis: "For example, a patient with preferences for Sensing with Feeling (40.1% of the UK population) will have only a 1 in 6 chance of seeing a doctor with the same preferences. Similarly, a doctor with preferences for Intuition and Thinking (31.3% of this sample) will have only a 1 in 11 chance that the patient will be the same as them" (p. 182). As we described previously, because MBTI outcomes follow a unimodal rather than bimodal distribution, this extent of personality differences is far smaller than perceived. Broadcasting this classification of physicians as statistically inherently different from their patients qualifies as grossly inaccurate and could erode trust or cause anticipatory bias among patients. Furthermore, the paper frankly strains to attribute personality difference to these communication issues rather than any number of other considerations that might easily qualify as more actionable for application in physician education.

Other research has sought to link the choice of medical specialty among physicians-in-training using MBTI personality types. These studies (Stillwell et al., 2000; Yang et al., 2016) also demonstrate a poor understanding of the MBTI's validity and go one step deeper into bad science by not even attempting to explore the quantitative scales of the MBTI, instead opting to base their analysis on the one-letter classifications. The major danger of such publications could involve applying post-choice analysis to pre-choice decision making. One can imagine a medical school offering an MBTI at the beginning of students' training and then providing career "guidance" based on misguided data with potential to skew decision-making.

The Conceptual Challenge

Do we agree on a definition of personality that involves a systematic immutable developmental pattern, focuses on traits, heavily weighs contextual or mental state, represents intersecting continua with polar ends, requires interaction with others, flows directly from our genetic heritage, or some combination of these and other factors?

Once the question of theoretical framework is resolved, we must consider predictive validity. Does our system for measuring our hypothetical construct predict some future behavior? If so, how reliable (repeatable) are the resulting measurements and how accurately do these results predict behavior? If our personality test does indeed reliably and accurately predict future behavior, the framework or construct takes on greater construct validity unless alternative interpretations are equally or more plausible. Because of these complexities and the need to make foundational assumptions early in the process of designing a personality test, many heuristic biases on the part of would-be test developers – most notably representativeness, availability, anchoring, and confirmatory biases come into play (Kahneman et al., 1982; Norcross et al., 2017).

Representativeness bias occurs when people categorize things or events by using a prototype to represent a category, while ignoring base rates (e.g., assuming that a person is a criminal or has committed a criminal act because they have similarities to others in that category). *Anchoring* reflects a failure to adjust sufficiently from initial anchor points, even when those points are arbitrary (e.g., "If our existing categories work, why change?"). *Availability* refers to the ease with which a particular idea comes to mind (e.g., "I've seen certain people with particular personality characteristics, so I use those concepts"). Finally, *confirmation bias* occurs when people seek out opinions and facts supporting their beliefs and hypotheses (e.g., "I'm sure I'm right, I just need to find the proof").

Common Elements to the Popularity of Pseudoscientific Techniques

Four common elements typically align to enhance the popularity or acceptance of pseudoscientific assessment techniques and psychotherapeutic treatments. First, the approach addresses a difficult, complex, or refractory problem often based on a representativeness bias. Second, the approach poses a relatively simple solution with apparent face validity supported by availability and anchoring biases. Despite the complex scoring or interpretive systems associated with some such techniques, the underlying theory appears accurate or effective simply because of its stated aims and details. Third, the underlying reasoning or approach is "in sync" with the Zeitgeist or popular social movements and philosophies of the times in line with availability biases. Finally, the approach is promoted by a charismatic "expert" who typically presents an array of uniformly supportive "facts" while dismissing critics with a well-anchored confirmatory bias.

Summary and Conclusion

Attempts to measure the hypothetical construct of personality inevitably originate in the theoretical eyes of the beholder. Narrow models promoted by charismatic enthusiasts have at times found acceptance based more on intuition than scientific principles. As we seek to validate personality assessment tools, we should continue to exercise vigilance and caution against tests or batteries that claim to "explain it all" without a clear evidentiary basis. Historical reexamination and application of data science have discredited the purported validity of many of assessments. Some, like the Szondi and the Blacky Pictures, have faded from use. Others – most notably the MBTI – still attract professional and personal use despite well-described defects that demonstrate a lack of predictive validity and numerous statistical defects. As we advance our understanding of personality assessment, we must remain intellectually curious and rigorously critical of the tools we use in an attempt to do so.

Gerald P. Koocher, PhD, ABPP, is faculty at Harvard Medical School Bioethics Center, senior attending psychologist at Boston Children's Hospital, and the program director in Clinical and School Psychology at Capella University.

Yilong Peng, BS, is a medical student at Harvard Medical School.

References

Bess, T. L. & Harvey, R.J. (2002). Bimodal score distributions and the Myers-Briggs Type Indicator: fact or artifact? *Journal of Personality Assessment, 78* (1), 176–186. doi: 10.1207/S15327752JPA7801_11. PMID: 11936208.

Block, M. (2018). How The Myers-Briggs Personality Test Began in a Mother's Living Room. *NPR All Things Considered*, September 22, 2018. Downloaded f/ 21/2022 from: https://www.npr.org/2018/09/22/650019038/how-the-myers-briggs-personality-test-began-in-a-mothers-living-room-lab

Blum, G. S. (1949). A study of the psychoanalytic theory of psychosexual development. *Genetic Psychology Monographs, 55,* 141–172.

Blum, G. S., & Hunt, H. F. (1952). The validity of the Blacky Pictures. *Psychological Bulletin, 49*(3), 238–250. doi: 10.1037/h0057240.

Boucher, J. & Osgood, C.E. (1969). The Pollyanna hypothesis. *Journal of Verbal Learning and Verbal Behavior,* 8(1), 1–8. doi: 10.1016/S0022-5371(69) 80002-2.

CAPT – Center for Applications of Psychological Type (2022). The Story of Isabel Briggs Myers. Downloaded on 8/22/2022 from https://www.capt.org/mbti-assessment/isabel-myers.htm

Clack, G. B., Allen, J., Cooper, D. & Head, J. O. (2004). Personality differences between doctors and their patients: implications for the teaching of communication skills. *Medical Education, 38*(2), 177–186. doi: 10.1111/j.1365-2923 .2004.01752.x.

Cohen, R. J., & Swerdlik, M. E. (2005). *Psychological testing and assessment: Introduction to tests and measurement* (6th ed.). New York, NY: McGraw-Hill.

Cunningham, L. (2013). Myers-Briggs personality test embraced by employers, not all psychologists. *Seattle Times*, April 12, 2013. Downloaded on 8/22/2022 from: https://www.seattletimes.com/business/myers-briggs-personality-test-embraced-by-employers-not-all-psychologists/

David, H. P. (1954) A Szondi Test Bibliography, 1939–1953. *Journal of Projective Techniques*, 18(1), 17–32. doi: 10.1080/08853126.1954.10380530.

Deri, S. (1949) *Introduction to the Szondi test*. New York: Grune.

Earl S. Taulbee & David E. Stenmark (1968) The Blacky Pictures Test: A comprehensive annotated and indexed bibliography (1949–1967). *Journal of Projective Techniques and Personality Assessment*, 32(2), 105–137, doi: 10.1080/0091651X.1968.10120461.

Ellis, A. (1953). The Blacky Test used with a psychoanalytic patient. *Journal of Clinical Psychology*, 9, 167–172. 10.1002/1097-4679(195304)9:2<167::AID-JCLP2270090218>3.0.CO;2-A

Eysenck, H. (1990). *Decline and fall of the Freudian empire*. Washington, D.C.: Scott-Townsend Publishers.

Forer, B. R. (1949). The fallacy of personal validation: A classroom demonstration of gullibility. *Journal of Abnormal and Social Psychology*, 44, 118–123.

Harris, S. M. (2013). Development of the perceptions of mentoring relationships survey: A mixed methods approach. *International Journal of Multiple Research Approaches*, 7, 83–95. doi: 10.5172/mra.2013.2405.

Hess, A. K., & Lanning, K. (2003). Review of the Myers-Briggs Type Indicator Step II (Form Q). In B. S. Plake, J. C. Impara, & R. A. Spies, (Eds.), *The Fifteenth Mental Measurements Yearbook*. Lincoln, NE: Buros Institute of Mental Measurements.

Jung, C. G. (1921). *Psychologische Typen*. Zurich: Rascher & Cie.

Kahneman, D., Slovic, P. & Tversky, A. (1982). *Judgment under uncertainty: Heuristics and biases*. Cambridge, UK: Cambridge University Press.

Koocher, G. P., Norcross, J. C., McMann, M., & Stout, A. (2015). Consensus on Discredited Assessment and Treatment Techniques used with Children and Adolescents. *Journal of Clinical Child and Adolescent Psychology*, 44, 722–729. doi: 10.1080/15374416.2014.895941.

Lindner, H. (1953). The Blacky Pictures Test: A Study of Sexual and Non-Sexual Offenders, *Journal of Projective Techniques*, 17(1), 79–84, doi: 10.1080/08853126.1953.10380465.

Meehl, P. E. (1950). Introduction to the Szondi Test. *American Journal of Psychiatry*, 107(3), 237. doi: 10.1176/ajp.107.3.237.

Michal-Smith, H., Hammer, E. & Spitz, H. (1951). Use of the Blacky Pictures with a child whose oedipal desires are close to consciousness. *Journal of Clinical Psychology*, 7, 280–282.

Myers-Briggs Company (2022). *Answering your questions about the Myers-Briggs Type Indicator*. Retrieved on August 22, 2022 from https://www.themyersbriggs.com/en-US/Support/MBTI-Facts

Myers Briggs Foundation (2022). *Isabel Briggs Myers*. Downloaded on 8/22/2022 from: https://www.myersbriggs.org/my-mbti-personality-type/mbti-basics/isabel-briggs-myers.htm

Norcross, J. C., Hogan, T., Koocher, G. P. & Maggio, L. A. (2017). *Clinician's guide to evidence-based practices: Mental health and the addictions, 2nd Edition*. New York: Oxford University Press.

Norcross, J. C., Koocher, G. P., & Garofalo, G. P. (2006) Discredited Psychological Treatments and Tests: A Delphi Poll. *Professional Psychology: Research and Practice*, 37, 515–522. doi: 10.1037/0735-7028.37.5.515.

Stagner, R. (1958). The gullibility of personnel managers. *Personnel Psychology*, 11, 347–352.

Stilwell, N. A., Wallick, M.M., Thal, S. E., & Burleson, J.A. (2000). Myers-Briggs type and medical specialty choice: a new look at an old question. *Teaching and Learning in Medicine*, 12(1), 14–20. doi: 10.1207/S15328015TLM1201_3. PMID: 11228862.

Stricker, G. (1967). Stimulus Properties of the Blacky to a Sample of Pedophiles. *Journal of General Psychology*, 77, 35–39.

Szondi, L. & Aull, G. [translator] (1952) *Experimental diagnostics of drives*. New York: Grune and Stratton.

Szondi, L., Moser, U., & Webb, M. W. (1959). *The Szondi Test in diagnosis, prognosis, and treatment*. Philadelphia: Lippincott.

Vargha, A. (1994). A Szondi-teszt pszichometriája. (Psychometry of the Probe Test) *Pszichológia Pszichológiai Intézetenek folyóirata. (Journal of the Institute of Psychology)*, 14(2), 199–268.

Webb, M. W. (1987). Lipon Szondi (1893–1986). *American Psychologist*, 42(6), 600. doi: 10.1037/h0092050.

Yang, C., Richard, G., & Durkin, M. (2016). The association between Myers-Briggs Type Indicator and Psychiatry as the specialty choice. *International Journal of Medical Education*, 7, 48–51. doi: 10.5116/ijme.5698.e2cd. PMID: 26851600; PMCID: PMC4746054.

Part III
Intervention

6 Hypnosis and Hypnotherapy

Miranda A. L. van Tilburg

A common first image that enters one's mind when hearing "hypnosis" is people humiliating themselves on stage under the spell of a hypnotist. Yet hypnosis is so much more than what we see on television or in a Las Vegas show. Hypnosis has been a widely used technique in many areas, including business, sports, religion, medicine, and psychology. When hypnosis is used for treatment of health, including mental health, we call it hypnotherapy. Hypnotherapy has been used in medicine and psychological therapy for over 100 years. Yet the acceptance of and popularity of hypnotherapy has waxed and waned over the years. Currently, hypnosis is not considered a legitimate evidence-based treatment by many in the medical and psychological establishment. This is due to several reasons, such as the development of other evidence-based treatments, and the use of hypnosis in some dubious practices. The consequence is that few psychologists learn hypnotherapy in their training, and do not offer it in their practice. No licensure is needed to practice hypnotherapy and it has quickly become relegated to non-clinically trained "alternative medicine" providers, who also provide other unsupported treatments. Yet some evidence may suggest a legitimate use for hypnotherapy in some situations. Given its colorful history, and its time spent in the shadows of medicine and psychology, hypnosis has become surrounded by myths, pseudo-science, and false promises. This chapter will evaluate some of the most common claims about hypnosis.

Examining the Claims

There are a multitude of claims about hypnosis that often share a common origin. I have divided the claims in two sets. One set deals with the nature of hypnosis. Is hypnosis something special or something shared with other psychological processes? In this set of claims, I will explore what hypnosis means and focus on the pseudoscience of hypnosis, including whether it can help us access unconscious memories. The next set of claims is less

DOI: 10.4324/9781003259510-9

concerned with what hypnosis means and instead accepts it as one of the tools we can use in medicine or psychology. In other words, it is concerned with the evidence that hypnotherapy can treat certain health conditions. This section will examine the evidence base with a critical lens.

Is Hypnosis a Special State?

Consider the following claims:

- Hypnosis trance is a special state like no other.
- Hypnosis is like sleeping or sleep walking.
- Hypnosis accesses the unconscious.
- Hypnosis can access uncontrollable physiological processes in the body.
- Hypnosis can access previous life experiences.
- Hypnosis can access repressed memories.
- Hypnosis induces amnesia.
- The hypnotist controls you.
- You can be manipulated to commit crimes while under hypnosis.
- You can be manipulated to embarrass yourself on stage while under hypnosis.
- You can do amazing feats, such as defying physics, while under hypnosis.
- Hypnosis can alter your personality.
- Hypnosis can make you have exceptional new skills (e.g., an excellent singing voice).

The acceptance or rejection of the claims above is driven by how we conceptualize hypnosis. Culturally in many countries, hypnosis is portrayed as a special state unlike any other experience, in which we are open to suggestions that we otherwise would not accept. In this view, hypnosis is passive: Something that is done to you by the hypnotist, and potentially dangerous, which is under complete control of the hypnotist. These views are well documented in films, books, and other works of art. It is easy to see that popular media often portrays the use of hypnosis to covertly persuade people to commit a crime, murder, possess them, or alter their personalities. What is the root of these beliefs about hypnosis? For that we need to delve into the colorful history of hypnosis.

A Brief History of Hypnosis

Hypnotic techniques have been used from ancient times by healers and religious leaders including in India, Egypt, China, Africa, and pre-Columbian America. It was brought to Europe in the late 1400s, but it would take another 300 years before hypnosis became popular. Controversial Austrian physician Dr. Franz Anton Mesmer used hypnotic techniques for healing (Hammond, 2013), called "mesmerism." Mesmer believed in animal magnetism, which is the idea that all living beings possess an invisible natural force. Disturbance of this force can create disease, and mesmerism was offered to heal the invisible force. Mesmer created waves in the medical establishment with his very public, theatrical, and sometimes erotic sessions where he healed various kinds of afflictions mostly among women of society. After an investigation, mesmerism was discredited as "imagination" instead of an invisible force. Mesmer was ostracized from the medical community. Hypnosis became part of mystical and paranormal movements, not medicine.

In the early to mid-1800s, James Braid, a trained surgeon, was the first to collect evidence evaluating whether hypnotherapy works (Hammond, 2013). Wanting to distance himself from the Mesmer, Braid was the first to coin the term "hypnosis." He described hypnosis as the use of imagination and suggestions – psychological phenomena – to change physiological processes.

It wasn't until years later, in the early 19th century, that a new theory of hypnosis was coined, which remains the root of our current *cultural* understanding of hypnosis. Pierre Janet and Sigmund Freud described the existence of an unconscious mind, not known to us, but still affecting us. A famous example is the "Freudian slip": an unintentional error revealing unconscious feelings. For example, the quote: "The breast and the brightest" has been famously attributed to Edward Kennedy. Both Janet and Freud used hypnosis to access the unconscious mind, though Freud later replaced it for his "free association" technique (Hammond, 2013). As the idea of a Freudian unconscious mind fell out of scientific favor, so too did hypnosis. Yet by then, hypnosis was already solidly linked to the unconscious in our collective minds and remains so today.

Does Hypnosis Access the Unconscious?

The idea that hypnosis induces an altered state in which we can access our unconscious is what underlies many of the current claims about hypnosis. It drives the idea that hypnosis is a special state that can unlock unknown thoughts, feelings, and even talents (behaviors). To access the unconscious, we have been told to "dissociate" from our consciousness – almost as if one is sleeping or sleepwalking. This means you are not your normal self, and you are giving up control over what you say and do. The latter can have dire imaginative consequences, such as being manipulated to commit murder or displaying a yet-unknown talent. Thus, the idea that hypnosis can access the unconscious drives many of the claims stated above. Yet what is the evidence that hypnosis accesses the unconscious?

Some have argued that evidence for the unconscious comes from the fact that under hypnosis we are able to alter physiological processes that are usually not under our control. For example, under hypnosis we can change our gastric acid secretion (Klein & Spiegel, 1989). That seems very extreme indeed and will convince many that an unconscious part of brain must exist. But it's a ruse. What we're really meaning when we say "unconscious" is that these processes are automatic. Automatic bodily processes are under the influence of the autonomic nervous system, which is *partially* under our control. For example, we can manipulate our breathing, but it occurs automatically as well. Through deliberate practice we can make processes automatic by practicing them. That is how we all learned to walk and read. Thus, there is nothing special about automatic behaviors and we usually do not attribute them to an unconscious mind. The fact that hypnosis can influence automatic bodily processes, is not evidence for the existence of an unconscious. Furthermore, some automatic processes that are difficult to control, such as our blood pressure, can be influenced not just by hypnosis but by other techniques, such as meditation (Park & Han, 2017), biofeedback (Wang et al., 2010), or high resistance breathing (Craighead et al., 2022), actions with which we do not attribute to an unconscious mind. Given that we cannot disprove the existence of a "special state of consciousness," some might consider the study of the nature of hypnosis to fall outside of the realm of science and into pseudoscientific territory.

If hypnosis does not access the unconscious, then what is it and why does some evidence demonstrate that it may work in some scenarios? In the mid- and late 1900s, multiple other theories of hypnosis were proposed (see Kirsch & Lynn, 1995) for an in-depth discussion. Many of the newer theories claim hypnosis is a normal state many of us can experience and that it share commonalities with other socio-cognitive processes (Kirsch & Lynn, 1995). Indeed, there is evidence for this idea. For example, Spanos and colleagues (1989) showed simple suggestions to reduce pain worked just as well as suggestions during hypnosis. Thus, similar to the ideas of Braid, hypnosis can be understood as a common state of hyper-focused attention that uses imagery and suggestion to elicit psychological and physiological changes.

Can Hypnosis Retrieve Repressed Memories?

In the mid-20th century, the idea was popularized that the mind may protect oneself after a traumatic experience by banning the memory to the unconscious. These repressed memories could be accessed through hypnosis. Celebrities jumped into the discussion. For example, actress Roseanne Barr (Barr, 1991) claimed to remember that her mother abused her in infancy.

Repressed memories made their ways into court and people were convicted based on discovery of repressed memories. For example, George Franklin was convicted for a murder of an eight-year-old girl, after his daughter, Eileen, recovered the memory during hypnosis 20 years after the event. Hundreds of such cases were running through the courts at that time worldwide.

Were the rediscovered memories real or false? The memories seemed distinct: more vivid and containing details that typical memories don't include. Sometimes they even contained details that were not known to the public. In other words, they seemed real. Yet, many of them also contained elements that were unlikely (e.g., sadistic cults), impossible (e.g., time travel), or factually untrue (e.g., DNA evidence exonerated the accused). In a famous experiment, Loftus and Pickrell (1995) showed that planting of false memories is fairly easy. They asked participants to remember details of several events from their childhood, chosen by an older relative. Unknown to the participants, one scenario was untrue: being lost in a mall. One out of three participants remembered the false event. This shows that by suggesting the event happened, we can create a false memory. Much research followed and we now understand that false memories can be (un)intentionally planted (Davis & Loftus, 2006; Perry & Gold, 1995). Memories are not "pictures" of what we observed. They are changed through interpretation, suggestions, and repetition. Suggestions given under hypnosis may therefore alter memory, increasing the chances of planting false memories.

This practice of uncovering "repressed traumatic memories" caused havoc on people who were unfairly accused. George Franklin was eventually exonerated for his crime six years later when facts came to light that his daughter's testimony was unreliable. One can only try to imagine the amount of distress and disruption to his life. Yet "repressed traumatic memories" also cause distress to the victims themselves. To discover a traumatic memory and then to be told later it is not true, can have far reaching consequences. First, it can be harmful to (re)traumatize a person for abuse they may have forgotten or never experienced. Second, who are we when we cannot trust our own memories? I urge the reader to familiarize themselves with the story of Nicole Klemper (Watt, 2017). At age 6, Nicole described sexual abuse by her mother, who lost her battle for custody in court based on this description. Nicole did not remember the event at age 17, but this "repressed memory" came back after watching a videotape of her younger self. At age 39, Nicole still wonders what is true and how to reconcile what happened to her and her family.

Although largely found to be untrue, the practice of recovering repressed memories has not disappeared as a method of treatment. In a 2019 nationally representative sample of adults in the United States, 9%

reported seeing a therapist who discussed the possibility of repressed abuse, and 5% reported recovering memories of abuse in therapy of which they had no previous memory (Patihis & Pendergrast, 2019). More than 40% of people who recovered such memories cut off contact with families due to new memories and about 93% believed their memories were true. Clearly, discovering "repressed traumatic memories" can be harmful.

Recognizing the issues with false memories obtained during hypnosis, the U.S. federal court has deemed repressed memories accessed before the trial as inadmissible evidence in court. However, they do allow for forensic hypnosis to be used in the investigative process. Memories retrieved during hypnosis need to be corroborated with other evidence and hypnosis cannot be the first aid to memory retrieval (Criminal Resource Manual 288).

Can Hypnosis Help with Past Life Regression Therapy?

The premise that one may access previous life experiences assumes that reincarnation is possible. The idea that we have a life after death is common in many religions. One-third of Americans believe in reincarnation (Center, 2021). Yet the fact that there is life after death or a continuation of a past life is scientifically untestable. It is belief, not science. Andrade (2017) cites three major reasons why the belief in reincarnation is problematic. First, reincarnation proposes a soul after death will seek a new body. Then how can we account for population growth? Where do these new souls come from? Second, how do those souls, that are a nonmaterial substance, enter the physical world and become the main driver of the body? There is no plausible theory of this mechanism. Lastly, reincarnation assumes psychological continuity. You would be the same person in a previous life and now. As famously argued by philosopher John Locke: Would then a prince who died and become a cobbler not still be the prince? Furthermore, if most of us do not remember past lives, how can we ascertain psychological continuity of who we were or are?

Proponents of reincarnation argue there is evidence for its existence. They base this on multiple anecdotal accounts of mostly young children (ages 2–6) who remember a past life (Andrade, 2017). These children may claim to be a person whom the child never knew personally. They may have birthmarks at places where their previous selves had been mortally wounded. The University of Virginia has a collection of 2,500 such stories (Bonilla, 2015). These anecdotes can be very convincing, yet they cannot be considered high-quality scientific evidence by any stretch, especially in the context of the broader scientific literature. In science, case studies are used to generate hypotheses. These hypotheses are tested in more rigorous studies. For example, in the case of reincarnation memories by children, we would examine a large group of children with birthmarks and question them about their traumatic deaths in previous lives. Such studies have never been done. This would be highly unethical. But the main reason more thorough studies are not done is because in pseudoscience, anecdotes are often considered to be the highest level of evidence. Anecdotes tug at our heartstrings and make us believe something is true because we feel and see it. Yet, there may be alternative explanations for the findings. For example, many of the children claimed to remember past lives of dead family members. This opens the possibility that adults in their lives may have unknowingly informed children of facts "they cannot know." The co-creation of a memory between two people is a common psychological phenomenon (Jakubik, 2008) and not unique to past life experiences.

If one believes reincarnation is possible, it might be logical to assume that trauma from a previous life can cause problems in the current one. When a client has significant anxiety, for example, they may attribute their anxiety to a trauma in a past life and they may believe that treating it can be helpful via a therapy known as past life regression therapy. As it is impossible for most adults to remember their past lives, hypnosis is a tool used in past life regression therapy to access their past lives. Given the previous discussion on how easy it is to plant false memories during hypnosis, the same may be true here: false memories of past lives can easily be planted. This is a far more likely mechanism than reincarnation. This means that at best, past life regression therapy is a way to work with the mental mindset of a client who believes a trauma from a previous life is psychologically affecting them. Yet it is most likely that the therapist also believes in reincarnation, and in past life regression therapy. At worst, these shared beliefs can do great harm by implanting false memories of past trauma that the client now experiences as real. Given almost no adults will remember past lives, and there are evidence-based treatments for anxiety and other psychological issues that do not rely on discovering past trauma, the potential harms of past life regression therapy do not outweigh their benefits (if any). These treatments are unethical.

Does Stage Hypnosis Work?

Stage hypnosis is not used as treatment, yet it is the most common way people have observed "the power of hypnosis." It creates strong associations of hypnosis with mind control: floating bodies, loss of self-control, etc. Our eyes did not deceive us, or did they? Like magic, stage hypnosis employs several tricks to give us a memorable night. These include volunteer selection, social pressure, and deception (Meeker & Barber, 1971).

82 *Miranda A. L. van Tilburg*

Volunteer Selection

Most stage hypnotists start the show with a group induction to see who is most hypnotizable and who is most extraverted, which are used as indicators for people most likely to do comply on stage. Thus, these volunteers are unique insofar as the hypnotist would be unable to convince most of the audience to cluck like a chicken on stage, and it is valuable to know who is the most convincing at playing along.

Social Pressure

There is an explicit way we expect the volunteers to act. Once on stage, a person may feel pressure to do exactly what they are told by the hypnotists to meet this social obligation. The laughs and encouragement of the audience may further reinforce compliance. Hypnosis may have little to do with this, rather it is a previously agreed upon script that all of us carry in our minds: "When hypnotized, do all that the hypnotist asks from you." Some people may not be pressured easily, and stage hypnotists may ask people to leave the stage if they do not play along. Some scientists have gone so far to suggest that all hypnosis relies on participants feeling pressured to do what the hypnotist tells them (Kirsch & Lynn, 1995). No doubt this happens on stage.

Deception

Some of the tricks during stage hypnosis are borrowed from illusionists and have nothing to do with hypnosis. For example, hypnosis is often assumed to make people cataleptic: severe muscle rigidity together with suspension of all sensation. Many of us have seen this in action by observing the human plank: where a rigid hypnotized participant is supported only at the head and feet but will not bend even when the hypnotist stands on them. Superhuman powers! How is this even possible? Alas, this has nothing to do with hypnosis and plays on our imaginations as well as expectations. It is a simple magic trick.

Other types of deceptions may be used. Some have claimed hypnotists may whisper directions in participants ear to "fool" the audience, or employ stooges who are paid actors who appear to be just one of the audience members (Meeker & Barber, 1971).

No matter the mechanism of stage hypnosis, it has an effect on the participants. In a 1987 study, 1 in 5 participants reported negative effects during the performance or even afterwards (Echterling & Emmerling, 1987). Many reported feeling embarrassed, but pressured to comply. In several countries (i.e., United Kingdom, Denmark, Israel, Belgium) stage hypnosis is banned or heavily regulated, but these laws are not commonly enforced. Ponder the potential of harm to you or stage volunteers before you attend such a performance. A magic show may be more up your alley. In the words of the former magician and renowned pseudoscience critic, James Randi: "Magicians are the most honest people in the world; they tell you they're gonna fool you, and then they do it."

Is Hypnosis Good for Anything at All?

The evidence shows that hypnosis is not a special state and does not access your "subconscious" mind. However, hypnosis may have positive effects which will be discussed in the next section. Hypnosis can induce changes in the brain associated with shifts in attention or valence for certain stimuli. For example, in some cases a painful stimulus can still be sensed (i.e., in somatosensory brain regions), but not valued as quite as painful (i.e., as represented by changes in emotional brain regions such as the anterior cingulate cortex) (Bicego et al., 2022; Wolf et al., 2022). These types of brain changes have also been found with other psychological treatments such as cognitive-behavioral therapy, and are likely not unique to hypnosis. In fact, hypnosis relies on cognitive-emotive processes such as relaxation, imagery, and suggestion. These are also used in many other psychological treatments such as guided imagery, progressive muscle relaxation, and meditation. In fact, the difference between some of these techniques and hypnosis can be minimal. For example, guided imagery is often used in hypnosis and is then followed by giving suggestions for improvement. Yet, guided imagery is also often followed by suggestions for increased well-being and comfort. Both rely on similar cognitive-emotive processes and sometimes are hard to distinguish one from the other. Yet some people assign mythical status to hypnosis but not guided imagery.

Is Hypnotherapy Helpful for Treating Medical and Psychological Conditions?

Is hypnosis used during therapy an evidence-based treatment or is it an example of pseudoscience? There are fervent defenders on each side, but the truth likely lays somewhere in the middle. After hundreds of years of a tumultuous history, with many mishaps and shady applications, hypnosis is currently experiencing somewhat of a scientific and clinical revival. Increasingly, it is (re)discovered that the power of imagination and suggestion can indeed be helpful. With newer and less biased methods, we are now in a place where we can empirically study the effects of hypnosis as well as its mechanism.

Consider the following claims:

- Hypnotherapy can treat irritable bowel syndrome.
- Hypnotherapy can treat pain.
- Hypnotherapy can treat nausea.
- Hypnotherapy can treat sleep problems.
- Hypnotherapy can help cure cancer.
- Hypnotherapy can help cure HIV.

Hypnosis is not and cannot be a panacea. One hypnosis website claims 145 conditions can be helped with hypnosis from bedwetting to surgical recovery. Such widespread statements are unfortunate as they delegitimize hypnotherapy by making it a "magical" cure. Yet a wide body of evidence exists that hypnotherapy can be helpful in certain situations.

One of the most active areas of study is in irritable bowel syndrome (IBS). IBS is a condition characterized by abdominal pain in combination with changes in stool frequency or consistency (e.g., diarrhea or constipation). There are more than 12 randomized controlled trials studying the efficacy of hypnotherapy in IBS, and recent meta-analyses have indicated it helps 70% of patients. It is an efficacious psychological treatment of IBS, and long-term effects (5+ years) have been reported indicating people learn skills that are helpful long after treatment has stopped (Black et al., 2020). Hypnosis is now a recommended therapy for IBS by all major medical gut societies ("Irritable Bowel Syndrome in Adults (IBS-D): Clinical Decision Support Tool," 2019; Lacy et al., 2021). (Note: Cognitive-behavioral therapy is another efficacious psychological treatment for IBS; see Chapter 15 for more.)

Besides IBS, there is some evidence that hypnosis can affect other chronic and acute pain such as labor pain (Gueguen et al., 2021), post-surgical pain (Holler et al., 2021), or painful medical and dental procedures (Moss & Willmarth, 2019; Venkiteswaran & Tandon, 2021), as well as nausea (Browne et al., 2022; McCormack, 2010), and sleep (Mamoune et al., 2022). Two meta-analyses found moderate to large effect sizes for hypnotherapy for the treatment of anxiety (general and specific) (Valentine et al., 2019) as well as depression (Milling et al., 2019). However, most of these trials have major methodological flaws including low number of participants and failure to control for expectancy (part of the placebo effect). Conducting a well-designed trial is expensive, and companies as well as governments are unlikely to fund studies testing hypnosis. When funding is received, adequate methodologies are applied. For example, see the studies by Benninga and Vlieger for children with IBS (Vlieger et al., 2007; Vlieger et al., 2012). Note that this well-funded, well controlled, adequately powered trial found positive results for hypnosis. Second, one cannot blind a person to being hypnotized and this creates problems with controlling for the placebo effect. Placebos are used to control for the expectancy a treatment will work. We can control for expectancy by offering a control treatment that is expected to have an equal effect but in reality, is of less value. For example, in the trial by Vlieger and colleagues, children with IBS received equal number of sessions with a pediatrician to address their symptoms. This is highly credible. However, few trials have gone through such efforts and the literature on hypnosis is still suggestive but not definitive. Much more studies are needed.

If the change mechanisms of hypnosis operate through altering brain processes, the conditions it should affect would be those stemming from involvement of our central nervous system, such as pain, sleep, and well-being. We would not propose that hypnotherapy can be helpful in curing cancer or HIV, for example, though there is evidence it can help with pain control and nausea in these conditions (Carlson et al., 2018).

Summary and Conclusion

Is hypnosis science or pseudoscience? It is a little of both. There is evidence that hypnotherapy can be a helpful technique to reduce pain and nausea, help with sleep, and increase well-being. It has very few side effects and generally participants enjoy the sessions. Keep in mind that hypnotherapy is just one tool in the toolbox of a therapist to address these symptoms. Other evidence-based treatments are available. Yet there is increased recognition that the benefits outweigh the harms and that hypnotherapy is a legitimate way to treat these conditions. On the other hand, hypnosis has been used in many non-supported and often harmful ways, including stage hypnosis, discovering repressed memories, and past life regression therapy. For these uses, the harms always outweigh any suggested benefits and the use of hypnosis is highly unethical.

Many myths and superstitions continue to exist around hypnosis. It is not a special trance state, it does not access the unconscious, it is not related to sleepiness (quite the opposite: people are hyperattentive), it cannot access past lives, it is problematic in planting false memories, and it is not a magical cure-all. Many of the outrageous claims and problems with hypnosis have played out publicly in the media, creating a public distrust of the use of hypnotherapy. And with good reason. For those seeking hypnotherapy care, find a hypnotherapist who is a licensed health professional (e.g., psychologist, nurse), who does not promise a miracle cure or help with repressed memories, and who adheres to an evidence-based care philosophy.

Miranda A.L. van Tilburg, PhD, is the research director at Cape Fear Valley Medical Center, professor of medicine at Marshall University, adjunct professor of medicine at the University of North Carolina, and an affiliate professor of social work at the University of Washington.

References

Andrade, G. (2017). Is past life regression therapy ethical? *Journal of Medical Ethics and History of Medicine, 10*, 1–11.

Barr, R. (1991, October 7 1991). A star cries incest. *People Magazine*.

Bicego, A., Rousseaux, F., Faymonville, M. E., Nyssen, A. S., & Vanhaudenhuyse, A. (2022). Neurophysiology of hypnosis in chronic pain: A review of recent literature. *American Journal of Clinical Hypnosis, 64*(1), 62–80. 10.1080/00029157.2020. 1869517

Black, C. J., Thakur, E. R., Houghton, L. A., Quigley, E. M. M., Moayyedi, P., & Ford, A. C. (2020). Efficacy of psychological therapies for irritable bowel syndrome: Systematic review and network meta-analysis. *Gut, 69*(8), 1441–1451. 10.1136/gutjnl-2020-321191

Bonilla, E. (2015). [Evidence that suggest the reality of reincarnation]. *Invest Clin, 56*(2), 215–240. (Evidencias que sugieren la realidad de la reencarnación.)

Browne, P. D., de Bruijn, C. M. A., Speksnijder, E. M., Hollander, B. D., van Wering, H. M., Wessels, M. M. S., Groeneweg, M., Goede, J., Frankenhuis, C., Tromp, E., Benninga, M. A., & Vlieger, A. M. (2022). Skills or pills: Randomized trial comparing hypnotherapy to medical treatment in children with functional nausea. *Clinical Gastroenterology and Hepatology, 20*(8), 1847–1856.e1846. 10.1016/j.cgh.2021.10.029

Carlson, L. E., Toivonen, K., Flynn, M., Deleemans, J., Piedalue, K. A., Tolsdorf, E., & Subnis, U. (2018). The role of hypnosis in cancer care. *Current Oncology Reports, 20*(12), 93. 10.1007/s11912-018-0739-1

Center, P. R. (2021). *Few Americans blame God or say faith has been shaken amid pandemic, other tragedies: 2. Views on the afterlife*. Retrieved October from https://www.pewresearch.org/religion/?p=36467

Craighead, D. H., Tavoian, D., Freeberg, K. A., Mazzone, J. L., Vranish, J. R., DeLucia, C. M., Seals, D. R., & Bailey, E. F. (2022). A multi-trial, retrospective analysis of the antihypertensive effects of high-resistance, low-volume inspiratory muscle strength training.*Journal of Applied Physiology (1985), 133*(4), 1001–1010. 10.1152/japplphysiol.00425.2022

Davis, D., & Loftus, E. F. (2006). Recovered memories. *Annual Review of Clinical Psychology, 2*, 469–498. 10.1146/annurev.clinpsy.2.022305.095315

Echterling, L. G., & Emmerling, D. A. (1987). Impact of stage hypnosis. *American Journal of Clinical Hypnosis, 29*(3), 149–154. 10.1080/00029157.1987. 10734344

Gueguen, J., Huas, C., Orri, M., & Falissard, B. (2021). Hypnosis for labour and childbirth: A meta-integration of qualitative and quantitative studies. *Complementary Therapies in Clinical Practice, 43*, 101380. 10.1016/j.ctcp. 2021.101380

Hammond, D. C. (2013). A review of the history of hypnosis through the late 19th century. *American Journal of Clinical Hypnosis, 56*, 174–191.

Holler, M., Koranyi, S., Strauss, B., & Rosendahl, J. (2021). Efficacy of hypnosis in adults undergoing surgical procedures: A meta-analytic update. *Clinical Psychology Review*, *85*, 102001. 10.1016/j.cpr.2021.102001

Irritable Bowel Syndrome in Adults (IBS-D): Clinical Decision Support Tool. (2019). *Gastroenterology*, *157*(3), 855. 10.1053/j.gastro.2019.07.008

Jakubik, M. (2008). Experiencing collaborative knowledge creation processes. *Learning Organization*, *15*(1), 5–25.

Kirsch, I., & Lynn, S. J. (1995). The altered state of hypnosis: Changes in the theoretical landscape. *American Psychologist*, *50*(10), 846–858.

Klein, K. B., & Spiegel, D. (1989). Modulation of gastric acid secretion by hypnosis. *Gastroenterology*, *96*(6), 1383–1387. PM:2714570 (NOT IN FILE)

Lacy, B. E., Pimentel, M., Brenner, D. M., Chey, W. D., Keefer, L. A., Long, M. D., & Moshiree, B. (2021). ACG clinical guideline: Management of irritable bowel syndrome. *The American Journal of Gastroenterology*, *116*(1), 17–44. 10.14309/ajg.0000000000001036

Loftus, E. F., & Pickrell, J. E. (1995). The formation of false memories. *Psychiatric Annals*, *25*(12), 1201–1207. 10.3928/0048-5713-1995

Mamoune, S., Mener, E., Chapron, A., & Poimboeuf, J. (2022). Hypnotherapy and insomnia: A narrative review of the literature. *Complementary Therapies in Medicine*, *65*, 102805. 10.1016/j.ctim.2022.102805

McCormack, D. (2010). Hypnosis for hyperemesis gravidarum. *Journal of Obstetrics and Gynaecology*, *30*(7), 647–653. 10.3109/01443615.2010.509825

Meeker, W. B., & Barber, T. X. (1971). Toward an explanation of stage hypnosis. *Journal of Abnormal Psychology*, *77*(1), 61–70. 10.1037/h0030419

Milling, L. S., Valentine, K. E., McCarley, H. S., & LoStimolo, L. M. (2019). A meta-analysis of hypnotic interventions for depression symptoms: High hopes for hypnosis? *American Journal of Clinical Hypnosis*, *61*(3), 227–243. 10.1080/00029157.2018.1489777

Moss, D., & Willmarth, E. (2019). Hypnosis, anesthesia, pain management, and preparation for medical procedures.*Annals of Palliative Medicine*, *8*(4), 498–503. 10.21037/apm.2019.07.01

Park, S. H., & Han, K. S. (2017). Blood pressure response to meditation and yoga: A systematic review and meta-analysis. *Journal of Alternative and Complementary Medicine*, *23*(9), 685–695. 10.1089/acm.2016.0234

Patihis, L., & Pendergrast, M. H. (2019). Reports of recovered memories of abuse in therapy in a large age representative national sample: Therapy type and decade comparisons. *Clinical Psychological Science*, *7*(1), 3–21.

Perry, C., & Gold, A. D. (1995). Hypnosis and the elicitation of true and false mmeories of childhood sexual abuse. *Psychiatry, Psychology, and Law*, *2*(2), 127–138.

Spanos, N. P., Perlini, A. H., & Robertson, L. A. (1989). Hypnosis, suggestion, and placebo in the reduction of experimental pain. *Journal of Abnormal Psychology*, *98*(3), 285–293. 10.1037/0021-843X.98.3.285

Valentine, K. E., Milling, L. S., Clark, L. J., & Moriarty, C. L. (2019). The efficacy of hypnosis as a treatment for anxiety: A meta-analysis. *International Journal of Clinical and Experimental Hypnosis*, *67*(3), 336–363. 10.1080/00207144.2019.1613863

Venkiteswaran, A., & Tandon, S. (2021). Role of hypnosis in dental treatment: A narrative review. *Journal of International Society of Preventive & Community Dentistry, 11*(2), 115–124. 10.4103/jispcd.JISPCD_320_20

Vlieger, A. M., Menko-Frankenhuis, C., Wolfkamp, S. C., Tromp, E., & Benninga, M. A. (2007). Hypnotherapy for children with functional abdominal pain or irritable bowel syndrome: A randomized controlled trial. *Gastroenterology, 133*(5), 1430–1436. 10.1053/j.gastro.2007.08.072

Vlieger, A. M., Rutten, J. M., Govers, A. M., Frankenhuis, C., & Benninga, M. A. (2012). Long-term follow-up of gut-directed hypnotherapy vs. standard care in children with functional abdominal pain or irritable bowel syndrome. *The American Journal of Gastroenterology, 107*(4), 627–631. 10.1038/ajg.2011.487

Wang, S. Z., Li, S., Xu, X. Y., Lin, G. P., Shao, L., Zhao, Y., & Wang, T. H. (2010). Effect of slow abdominal breathing combined with biofeedback on blood pressure and heart rate variability in prehypertension. *Journal of Alternative and Complementary Medicine, 16*(10), 1039–1045. 10.1089/acm. 2009.0577

Watt, H. (2017, September 23 2017). Some days I think I was molested, others I'm not sure. *The Guardian.*

Wolf, T. G., Faerber, K. A., Rummel, C., Halsband, U., & Campus, G. (2022). Functional changes in brain activity using hypnosis: A systematic review. *Brain Sciences, 12*(1). 10.3390/brainsci12010108

7 Harmful Mental Health Interventions

Yevgeny Botanov, Alexander J. Williams,
John Sakaluk, and Robyn Kilshaw

Many positive trends indicate that mental health is becoming less stigmatized, seeking professional help for mental health problems is viewed in high esteem, and the public readily recommends mental health interventions (Angermeyer et al., 2017); and as psychologists we applaud these trends. Consequently, many individuals may generally believe that psychotherapy is almost always helpful, and if nothing else many people may assume that there is little risk of direct harm even when psychotherapy is ineffective. In this chapter, we will examine the core claim that psychosocial treatments rarely cause direct harms. Along the way, we'll examine several specific claims related to specific treatments such as recovered-memory techniques, facilitated communication, attachment therapies, critical incident stress debriefing, Scared Straight programs, and a few even older treatments.

Examining the Claims

Listening to a podcast or watching a YouTube video is seemingly impossible nowadays without being bombarded with advertisements for easy-to-access psychotherapy or a phone app that helps with mood or anxiety. Similarly, a quick YouTube search will return videos that provide explanations, advice, and instructions on almost every form of psychotherapy that ever existed while "Go to Therapy" memes spread easily through social media. Not long ago, most mental health clinicians and researchers could not have imagined watching Oprah Winfrey interview Prince Harry about his mental health treatment. When the cultural prominence of mental health treatment is incomparable to previous generations, it is no wonder that the mobile app Headspace has a $3 billion valuation. Likely, access to and information about mental health therapies is at an all-time high and, in part, due to the unprecedented access many people erroneously believe that mental health interventions, in any manner, are always helpful. However, despite the advertisements, YouTube videos, morning show segments, and memes,

DOI: 10.4324/9781003259510-10

many ineffective and even harmful therapies currently permeate the mental health landscape.

It can be confusing for the lay public and clinicians to identify bona fide mental health interventions even when the interventions are often advertised, commonly discussed, easily accessible, or appear to be supported by government policies or agencies. For researchers and clinicians, the goal of developing, evaluating, disseminating, and implementing a mental health intervention is often driven by the desire to *do good* or *beneficence*. Therefore, the lack of efficacious treatments for many mental health disorders often leads to new treatments, including some that may take an outside-the-box approach. However, individuals with a genuine desire to help can often overlook the converse to beneficence: the ethical obligation to also *do no harm* or *nonmaleficence*. Although it may seem that adherence to these two ethical principles is simple, oftentimes therapies can be both helpful *and* harmful. As this chapter will highlight, these intentionally distinct ethical pursuits are a consequence of a historical record rife with good intentions leading to unintentional harms. Nonmaleficence is an important ethical obligation that expressly applies a harm mitigation mechanism to counterbalance the oftentimes tunnel-visioned pursuit to do good.

Harmful Treatments from the Beginning

Trepanning – the drilling of holes in the human skull – is the oldest known health intervention, dating back to around 6000 B.C. For mental health, drilling holes in the skull treated the supernatural explanations (e.g., evil spirits in the head) that cultures had for conditions that we now identify as psychosis or severe depression. Despite its commonplace historical use, the survival rate for the treatment was as low as 40% (Kushner et al., 2018). Even in the earliest historical examples of health treatment, it is evident that humans were somewhat blinded to nonmaleficence in their pursuits of beneficence.

Bloodletting, popularized after Hippocrates' – the historical figure known for the Hippocratic Oath – humoral theory of health, was another commonplace health intervention with questionable benefit despite potential for harm. Although it represented an important leap in understanding health by examining biology as a cause of mental illness, rather than the supernatural explanations that led to trepanning, the inchoate perspective posited that a lack, or too much, of certain bodily liquids caused illness. When applied to mental disorders, for instance, mania was hypothesized to be caused by an excess of blood in the body, and letting out the blood was the necessary treatment (Farreras, 2019). With the historical record indicating bloodletting originated around 3,000 years ago in Ancient Egypt, it was not until the 17th century – more than 2,500 years later – that Jan

Baptist van Helmont proposed history's first *randomized* controlled clinical trial to assess bloodletting's purported efficacy and potential harm (Donaldson, 2016). Despite van Helmont's concerns, bloodletting continued as a commonplace practice for centuries. Indeed, leeching – an extension of traditional bloodletting but using leeches to extract blood from the body – became so popular in the 1830s for a host of problems, including mental health, that France's leech farms were unable to keep up with the demand and imported over 40 million leeches (Hyson, 2005). While less likely to be used for mental health, treatments based on the ideas of bloodletting still endure to this day.

Trepanning has similarly not escaped the grip of contemporary human interest (for review, see Gump, 2010). In the 1960s a small group of individuals began to practice trepanation as a method to enhance consciousness. The movement grew into an advocacy group in the 1970s and a two-time trepanner even ran for British Parliament in the late 1970s under the banner, *Trepanation for the National Health*. Cases of trepanning continued to crop up, including a publicized case in 2000 of two men attempting to treat a woman's chronic fatigue syndrome and depression with trepanning as a television crew recorded. Fortunately, the woman survived, and the men were prosecuted. The pattern of using treatments that harm in the pursuit to help continues to the present day and, unfortunately, harmful treatments have a knack for sticking around.

As a founding father of the United States, politician, social reformer, abolitionist, and educator, Benjamin Rush was a Renaissance man. As a physician, Rush turned his interests toward mental health. He was a key figure in the importation of moral treatment (or moral therapy) from Europe to the United States. Prior to this monumental shift, individuals with mental health problems were typically separated from society and housed in asylums, with often disastrous results for their quality of life. Moral therapy promised ethical improvements in mental health care. Unfortunately, while it increased mental health care outside of asylums, it still delivered harm. Rush and his contemporaries relied on popular interventions of the time, like bloodletting and mercury treatment. Mental health–specific "remedies," such as strapping patients to spinning boards and the use of so-called *tranquilizer* chairs, would be considered abuse nowadays (Fried, 2019).

The moral therapy movement transitioned to the institutional model by the start of the 20th century when a slew of new, and harmful, treatments were developed. For example, by deliberately lowering blood sugar levels until patients were in a short coma, insulin coma therapy, introduced in the 1920s, was purported to treat mental disorders by affecting brain pathways. However, prolonged coma or death could occur if patients did not respond to glucose afterward. Following a similar theory of treatment,

Metrazol therapy used stimulant medication to induce seizures, which could lead to fractured bones and torn muscles. Lobotomies or surgery on the prefrontal lobe of the brain – generally considered one of the most harmful and barbaric mental health interventions of the modern age – attempted to alter brain activity more directly and were so popular that nearly 60,000 lobotomies were performed in the United States between 1936 and 1956 (Robison, 2012).

Contemporary Harmful and Potentially Harmful Therapies

Unfortunately, harmful mental health treatments are not just a relic of the past but persist today, even in the form of psychotherapy. Josef Breuer and Sigmund Freud developed modern psychotherapy when they joined forces to examine a novel treatment idea, Breuer's *talking cure* for nervous disorders. Discussed in history books and introductory psychology textbooks, Anna O. was one of the foundational cases of this approach, but hers was likely a clearer example of psychotherapy leading to harm rather than a novel helpful treatment. Anna O. deteriorated (e.g., numerous hospitalizations, catatonia, commonplace use of potentially addictive hypnotics) throughout Breuer's treatment and only improved when she broke away from him (Crews, 2017). Breuer and Freud, seemingly blind to the harm they were causing, formulated the cathartic method that purports to provide mental health benefits by bringing painful memories – often associated with the scientifically dubious idea of repressed memories – into consciousness and emotionally reexperiencing those memories. This mechanism is hypothesized to allow an individual to let go of the repressed memory and thereby treat their difficult emotions or mental health problems. Often, the reexperiencing and discharging of intense emotions are exaggerated (notably, contemporary scientific therapies also rely on discussing painful memories but the concept of memory repression remains unsupported by science and potentially harmful; Loftus & Davis, 2006).

Freudian therapies dominated the psychotherapy landscape for the first half of the 20th century and many of the therapies developed in the second half incorporated similar ideas of catharsis and repressed memories. Primal scream therapy – with the help of a bestselling book (Janov, 1970) and high-profile patients including John Lennon and Yoko Ono – became popular by advocating loud screaming as a cathartic method to release repressed emotions and resolve psychological problems. Aside from strained vocal cords and wasted time, the harm from this treatment was minimal; however, the continued reliance on treating purportedly repressed memories, especially with cathartic means, has led to many more harms.

Nadean Cool, who visited a therapist in the 1990s to deal with a history of disordered eating, substance abuse, and mild depression, is an example of the harm caused by such treatments. Her therapist was adamant that she suffered from repressed traumatic memories due to horrific childhood abuse and employed techniques like hypnosis and guided imagery – now known to facilitate false memories (Loftus & Davis, 2006) – in therapy sessions lasting up to 15 hours. Nadean came to believe in horrific memories, including childhood satanic rituals, murder, and rape; however, when she eventually ended treatment after 5 years due to her worsening psychological health, she realized that none of these events actually happened. She eventually won a $2.4 million malpractice settlement for the harms she had suffered from her therapist's attempts to help (Lynn et al., 2003).

Nadean was not the only victim of such harmful interventions in her era as the 1980s and 1990s birthed a bitter debate about repressed and recovered memories. Hundreds of cases played out in the media and courtrooms as daycare workers were arrested, couples divorced, and therapists practicing recovered-memory techniques were sued (Lipton, 1999). Consequently, numerous lines of research have indicated that human memory is often re-constructed, that willful repression of memories is scientifically dubious, and memories are highly affected by suggestion, especially in therapy (Loftus & Davis, 2006). Despite the years people lost to wrongful incarceration, divorce, and family dissolution, the theory of repressed memories as the cause of psychological and mental health problems still permeates contemporary mental health practice. To wit, 8% of the U.S. population has worked with a therapist who discussed the possibility of repressed memories of abuse, while 4% has reported recovering memories of abuse in therapy for which they had no prior memory (Patihis & Pendergrast, 2019). And, as recently as 2021, a therapist was sentenced to prison for implanting false memories of abuse in a young girl (Otgaar et al., 2022).

Not to be confused with effective forms of augmentative communica-tion, facilitated communication (FC) is another example of the array of harms that can arise from a mental health intervention. Hailed by its developers as a revolutionary method for individuals to communicate, FC posited that many developmental disabilities (e.g., severe autism) were primarily a disorder of motor movement (Heinzen et al., 2014). Therefore, communication difficulties were due to motor problems rather than an intellectual disability. With a keyboard, a steady hand of an adult facili-tator – typically holding and guiding the hand of an individual with physical, cognitive, and communication impairments – and some training, the facilitator could overcome the limitations of the person with the dis-abilities by helping them type out their thoughts. Upon introduction, FC appeared to be a miracle approach allowing individuals that could never communicate effectively before to suddenly reveal a rich inner world. Some individuals even graduated college with coursework completed via FC.

Eventually, independent researchers began to question whether facilitators were the true authors of these messages as opposed to the individuals they were purportedly assisting. FC began to unravel as the experimental data was unequivocal, the facilitators were completely in control of the communication (Schlosser et al., 2014). For instance, when blinded from what each person in the pair could see (e.g., the individual unable to communicate sees an image of a car while the facilitator sees a dog), the facilitator could *never* assist in typing out what the other individual saw. It also became clear that the facilitators were generally operating with little to no conscious awareness of their own deception.

More harmful than the deception of FC, and akin to the consequence of recovered memory techniques, were the legal battles waged over the many fabricated cases of abuse stemming from FC (for review, see Lilienfeld et al., 2014a). Despite decades passing since FC was outrightly debunked, FC continues to be practiced and has led to more false accusations. In 2018, a father spent 35 days in jail and was barred from seeing his family for months because of false allegations of abuse levied by an elementary school teacher using FC with his 7-year-old son (Balko, 2018). Fortunately, investigators found the claims to be outlandish as the FC messages contained words and phrases unfamiliar to young children. Even more dangerous than such false accusations, however, is the history of crimes and abuses perpetrated by the facilitators. Perhaps most prominent is the case of Anna Stubblefield, who, in 2015 was sentenced to prison on two counts of first-degree aggravated sexual assault against a man who had cerebral palsy, could not speak, and was unable to stand independently or accurately direct movements of his body (Engber, 2015). Anna – a professor of philosophy at Rutgers University at the time – argued that consent was given while she provided FC to the victim. Despite the clear empirical data and the court record, FC practitioners can still be found, and FC training remains part of the School of Education at Syracuse University, where it was developed (Typing to Communicate - Center on Disability and Inclusion, n.d.). Moreover, FC has been successful in surviving through nominal rebranding as assisted typing, supported typing, spelling to communicate, rapid prompting, letterboarding, and informative pointing (Lilienfeld et al., 2014a; Travers, 2023).

Unfortunately, those most at risk for harmful treatments are also seemingly most in need of help as was exemplified by Jeane Newmaker, the mother of an adopted 10-year-old daughter named Candace. In 2000, Jeane sought help for Candace's behavioral problems and attended a retreat designed to strengthen their emotional bond. The set of interventions, falling under the umbrella of attachment therapies, provided to Candace included rebirthing therapy wherein therapists wrapped Candace in a flannel sheet, covered her with pillows, and instructed her to fight her way out to simulate the vaginal birthing process. With four adults holding her down, Candace fought and pleaded for her life for over an hour before dying from suffocation. Despite this tragedy, rebirthing, and other attachment treatments, continue to be practiced in some United States and elsewhere around the world.

Reexamining Lilienfeld's Original List of Potentially Harmful Treatments

Taking the prospect of harm from psychological interventions more seriously is a welcomed field-wide development that can be attributed to Scott Lilienfeld (2007), who developed a list of potentially harmful treatments (PHTs). Recovered memory techniques, FC, and attachment therapies were among the interventions included in Lilienfeld's PHTs. To build on this work, we recently reexamined Lilienfeld's PHTs using novel techniques that quantitatively capture the credibility we ascribe to – or the confidence we can feel about – a set of studies (Williams et al., 2021). Since many of the PHTs were never evaluated in randomized controlled trials, which is an indictment in its own right of their potential for mainstream benefit, we were limited to examining literatures for interventions that were subjected to rigorous tests of their efficacy. Among the interventions we were able to reexamine were critical incident stress debriefing (or more broadly psychological debriefing interventions) and Scared Straight interventions. While these interventions have long been debated about or outright discredited, all continue to be practiced today.

By recounting a potentially traumatic event shortly after it has occurred, critical incident stress debriefing (CISD) purports to prevent posttraumatic stress disorder in emergency responders. Nevertheless, research has indicated that CISD has the potential to increase posttraumatic symptoms (for reviews, see Gist, 2015; Lohr et al., 2015; Rose et al., 2002). Similarly, Scared Straight programs hope to deter criminal behavior by bringing adolescents who have run afoul of the law to adult prisons for vivid depictions of the dangers of prison life. However, empirical evaluations of Scared Straight suggest it may increase future criminal behavior (Petrosino et al., 2013).

Our re-analysis indicated that the evidence underlying many PHTs – the randomized controlled trials – is limited due to multiple important factors such as insufficient controls (e.g., randomization inconsistencies and overreliance on control groups that receive no treatment rather than more rigorous control groups), difficulty verifying the statistical results due to spartan reporting, use of sample sizes in trials that are too small for the plausible effect sizes expected from psychological interventions, and inflated rates of statistically significant results. Therefore, our findings indicate a *low level of credibility* for the data derived from these interventions. Additionally, we synthesized the data across trials for these PHTs to provide a range of possible effects ranging from potentially helpful to potentially harmful. Evidence for potential harm most clearly emerged for Scared Straight interventions and CISD.

For some, the idea of bringing teenagers who have gotten in trouble with the law into an actual prison is intuitively compelling. Have the inmates scream at them about the horrors of prison life and hope that the teens are so shocked that they turn away from a life of crime. This is not the first or last psychological intervention that takes a *tough love* approach to treatment. Still, whatever the therapeutic merits of putting the encounters on television (if any), it is fair to assume most people involved in administering Scared Straight programs believed they were helping wayward adolescents. Similarly, CISD is well-intentioned, and providing resources for people to receive help following a potentially traumatic event is a worthwhile endeavor. But as we have seen so far in this chapter, good intentions are a dime-a-dozen, and rarely good enough. Rather, scientific evidence is needed to identify potential benefits and potential harms. Our analyses corroborate previous concerns and indicate a lack of data for benefit from these interventions and some potential for harm.

A major caveat to our estimates of harm and benefit, however, is that much of the literatures for these PHTs demonstrated poor credibility. As a result, a proponent of CISD or Scared Straight may accurately point out that since our assessment of credibility was low, to draw a conclusion about harm or benefit is inappropriate. Perhaps proponents of these interventions may throw up their hands and profess to not know whether CISD or Scared Straight helps or harms. But considering the ethical obligation of non-maleficence, this argument (e.g., "we don't know enough about this intervention to know whether it helps or hurts people but let's continue to use it") is, conversely, an argument *against* using that intervention. As we attempt to highlight throughout this chapter, the pursuit to do good should not outweigh the pursuit to do no harm.

Given the probability for harm indicated in our review, Scared Straight and CISD are the most deserving candidates for *psychotherapy reversal* (see Sakaluk et al., 2019; Williams et al., 2022); that is, to have their use ceased and to be replaced by potentially more helpful – and potentially less harmful – alternatives. Despite the scientific reservations surrounding these PHTs – including our own work – each continues to be used. CISD continues to be an active and available intervention option with a professional and training organization (e.g., see https://icisf.org/), and has been promoted on popular podcasts (Rogan, 2020). And the *Beyond Scared Straight* television series (Shapiro & Coyne, 2011) lasted nine seasons, concluding in 2015.

Our review was limited to interventions that had accumulated rigorous randomized controlled trials. However, some treatments are so obviously harmful to people and the general scientific community that they lack any rigorous scientific evidence yet continue to be practiced. Perhaps the exemplar for this category of treatments are sexual orientation change therapies. Also known as reparative or conversion therapy, the harm from these interventions has been well documented and no rigorous scientific efforts (e.g., randomized controlled trials) have been attempted to show efficacy (for review, see Przeworski et al., 2021). In fact, most major health organizations have deemed it unethical (American Academy of Pediatrics, 1993); American Psychiatric Association, 2000; American Psychological Association, 2009) and about half of U.S. states have banned this treatment for minors. Nevertheless, licensed therapists can be found in most states that are willing to try to change the sexual orientation of their adult patients.

Broadly, psychotherapies are effective (e.g., Munder et al., 2019), but some therapies, if applied as a universal remedy for all individuals, can show harm (see Britton et al., 2021 for one example). Also, approximately one-third of empirically supported treatments – given therapies for given mental health problems that are supported by randomized controlled trials – have credible evidence that they help some clients (Sakaluk et al., 2019), but have not been assessed for their potential to cause harm among underrepresented groups, such as Indigenous clients in the United States and Canada (Wendt et al., 2022). Broadly, if psychotherapy research is primarily based on unrepresentative samples, there is potentially an increased risk of harm for these groups.

Summary and Conclusion

Throughout human history, adverse effects from treatments are often overlooked. Despite the perceptions from the media, like all health treatments, mental health interventions can lead to harmful outcomes. Moreover, mental health interventions need to be critically examined by researchers, clinicians, and consumers to identify the benefit-harm ratio. Harms can be as serious as death, but also include exacerbation of symptoms, abuses from the therapist, and false accusations. And even when client impact is minimal, harm can take on a more structural form, as opportunity costs of ineffective treatments rob the public of their time, energy, and money, while delaying their pursuit of effective treatments. Perhaps most importantly, it appears that humans have a short memory allowing debunked harmful therapies to linger well beyond their expiration date, and even make comebacks when rebranded in the "right" way.

Our assumption is that most clinicians that provide harmful treatments do so with the intention for beneficence. Since good intentions are not good enough, it is key to understand why practitioners continue to rely on harmful treatments. Since therapists are also humans, they are susceptible to the same cognitive and social biases, and these biases affect the ability of therapists to assess accurately ineffective and harmful therapies (Lilienfeld et al., 2014b). Perhaps adopting competency-based training methods, especially increasing scientific competence, could reduce the use of ineffective and harmful therapies (Cooper et al., 2020). However, until a dramatic shift is seen in clinical training, practice, and oversight; clinicians must be vigilant of harmful treatments.

Seemingly more people than ever are discussing mental health. The promotion of better mental health, though, needs to stay linked to scientific evidence. History is replete with harmful treatments due to a reliance on eminence rather than evidence. Relying on evidence-based treatments and practices is likely to provide clinicians with a more effective and ethical framework for treatment selection, especially for identifying ineffective and harmful treatments. For example, in our re-analysis of PHT trials (Williams et al., 2021), grief therapy – despite similar debates over harm due to the potential subversion of the normal grieving process (debated in Bonanno & Lilienfeld, 2008 and Larson & Hoyt, 2007) – showed credibility by some metrics with evidence of benefit and lacked evidence of harm. If clinicians relied on science-based treatments – as opposed to pseudoscientific treatments such as those that incorporate the concept of repressed and recovered memories – while weighing the efficacy data for different interventions, and then additionally examining the credibility of the efficacy data, clinicians would be much more likely to adhere to their ethical obligation for *both* beneficence and nonmaleficence. This is what all individuals seeking mental health treatment, present and future, deserve.

Yevgeny Botanov, PhD, is a clinical psychologist and assistant professor at Pennsylvania State University– York.

Alexander J. Williams, PhD, is a clinical psychologist and assistant teaching professor at the University of Kansas.

John K. Sakaluk, PhD, is a social psychologist and assistant professor at Western University.

Robyn E. Kilshaw, MS, is a doctoral candidate in clinical psychology at the University of Utah.

References

American Academy of Pediatrics (1993). Homosexuality and adolescence. *Pediatrics*, 92(4), 631–634.

American Psychiatric Association (2000). Position statement on therapies focused on attempts to change sexual orientation (reparative or conversion therapies). Retrieved from http://www.psychiatry.org/File%20Library/Advocacy%20and %20Newsroom/Posit ion%20Statements/ps2000_Reparative Therapy.pdf

American Psychological Association, Task Force on Appropriate Therapeutic Responses to Sexual Orientation (2009). Report of the American Psychological Association Task Force on appropriate therapeutic responses to sexual orientation. Retrieved from http://www.apa.org/pi/lgbc/publications/therapeutic-resp.html

Angermeyer, M. C., Van Der Auwera, S., Carta, M. G., & Schomerus, G. (2017). Public attitudes towards psychiatry and psychiatric treatment at the beginning of the 21st century: a systematic review and meta-analysis of population surveys. *World Psychiatry, 16*(1), 50–61.

Balko, R. (2018, March 8). Junk science leads to father's wrongful arrest, false accusation of raping his son: The Florida dad couldn't see his family for months before he was cleared. *Washington Post.*

Bonanno, G. A., & Lilienfeld, S. O. (2008). Let's be realistic: When grief counseling is effective and when it's not. *Professional Psychology: Research and Practice, 39,* 377–378.

Britton, W. B., Lindahl, J. R., Cooper, D. J., Canby, N. K., & Palitsky, R. (2021). Defining and measuring meditation-related adverse effects in mindfulness-based programs. *Clinical Psychological Science, 9*(6), 1185–1204.

Cooper, L. D., Bertagnolli, A., Botanov, Y., Jun, J. J., Valenstein-Mah, H., Washburn, J. J., & Teisler, D. (2020). Training competencies for master's programs in Health Service Psychology. *The Behavior Therapist, 43*(4), 118–126.

Crews, F. (2017). *Freud: The making of an illusion.* London: Profile Books.

Donaldson, I. M. L. (2016). van Helmont's proposal for a randomised comparison of treating fevers with or without bloodletting and purging. *Journal of the Royal College of Physicians of Edinburgh, 46*(3), 206–213.

Engber, D. (2015). The strange case of Anna Stubblefield. *The New York Times Magazine.* Retrieved on June 14, 2023, from https://www.nytimes.com/2015/ 10/25/magazine/the-strange-case-of-anna-stubblefield.html

Farreras, I. G. (2019). History of mental illness. *General psychology: Required reading,* 246.

Fried, S. (2019). *Rush: Revolution, Madness, and Benjamin Rush, the Visionary Doctor Who Became a Founding Father.* New York: Crown.

Gist, R. (2015). Psychological debriefing. In R. L. Cautin, & S. O. Lilienfeld (Eds.), *The encyclopedia of clinical psychology* (Vol. 4, pp. 2303–2308). Hoboken, NJ: Wiley.

Gump, W. (2010). Modern induced skull deformity in adults. *Neurosurgical Focus, 29*(6), E4.

Heinzen, T., Lilienfeld, S., & Nolan, S. A. (2014). *The Horse That Won't Go Away.* New York: Macmillan Higher Education.

Hyson, J. M. (2005). Leech therapy: a history. *Journal of the History of Dentistry, 53*(1), 25–27.

Janov, A. (1970). *The primal scream: Primal therapy: The cure for neurosis*. New York: Dell.

Kushner, D. S., Verano, J. W., & Titelbaum, A. R. (2018). Trepanation procedures/outcomes: comparison of prehistoric peru with other ancient, medieval, and american civil war cranial surgery. *World Neurosurgery, 114,* 245–251.

Larson, D. G., & Hoyt, W. T. (2007). What has become of grief counseling? An evaluation of the empirical foundations of the new pessimism. *Professional Psychology: Research and Practice, 38,* 347–355.

Lilienfeld, S. O. (2007). Psychological treatments that cause harm. *Perspectives on Psychological Science, 2*(1), 53–70.

Lilienfeld, S. O., Marshall, J., Todd, J. T., & Shane, H. C. (2014a). The persistence of fad interventions in the face of negative scientific evidence: Facilitated communication for autism as a case example. *Evidence-Based Communication Assessment and Intervention, 8*(2), 62–101.

Lilienfeld, S. O., Ritschel, L. A., Lynn, S. J., Cautin, R. L., & Latzman, R. D. (2014b). Why ineffective psychotherapies appear to work: A taxonomy of causes of spurious therapeutic effectiveness. *Perspectives on Psychological Science, 9*(4), 355–387.

Lipton, A. (1999). Recovered memories in the courts. In S. Taub (Ed.), *Recovered memories of child sexual abuse: Psychological, social, and legal perspectives on a contemporary mental health controversy* (pp. 165–210). Illinois: Charles C Thomas Publisher.

Loftus, E. F., & Davis, D. (2006). Recovered memories. *Annual Review of Clinical Psychology, 2,* 469–498.

Lohr, J. M., Gist, R., Deacon, B., Devilly, G. J., & Varker, T. (2015). Science and non-science based treatments for trauma related stress disorders. In S. O. Lilienfeld, S. J. Lynn, & J. M. Lohr (Eds.), *Science and pseudoscience in clinical psychology* (2nd ed., pp. 277–321). New York, NY: The Guilford Press.

Lynn, S. J., Loftus, E. F., Lilienfeld, S. O., & Lock, T. (2003). Memory recovery techniques in psychotherapy. *Skeptical Inquirer, 27*(4), 40–46.

Munder, T., Flückiger, C., Leichsenring, F., Abbass, A. A., Hilsenroth, M. J., Luyten, P., ... & Wampold, B. E. (2019). Is psychotherapy effective? A re-analysis of treatments for depression. *Epidemiology and Psychiatric Sciences, 28*(3), 268–274.

Otgaar, H., Curci, A., Mangiulli, I., Battista, F., Rizzotti, E., & Sartori, G. (2022). A court ruled case on therapy-induced false memories. *Journal of Forensic Sciences, 67*(5), 2122–2129.

Patihis, L., & Pendergrast, M. H. (2019). Reports of recovered memories of abuse in therapy in a large age-representative US national sample: Therapy type and decade comparisons. *Clinical Psychological Science, 7*(1), 3–21.

Petrosino, A., Turpin-Petrosino, C., Hollis-Peel, M. E., & Lavenberg, J. G. (2013). 'Scared Straight' and other juvenile awareness programs for preventing juvenile delinquency. *Cochrane Database of Systematic Reviews.* 10.4073/csr.2013.5

Przeworski, A., Peterson, E., & Piedra, A. (2021). A systematic review of the efficacy, harmful effects, and ethical issues related to sexual orientation change efforts. *Clinical Psychology: Science and Practice, 28*(1), 81–100.

Robison, R. A., Taghva, A., Liu, C. Y., & Apuzzo, M. L. (2012). Surgery of the mind, mood, and conscious state: an idea in evolution. *World Neurosurgery*, 77(5–6), 662–686.

Rogan, J. (Host). (2020, July 30). Nancy Panza #1517 [Audio podcast episode]. In *The Joe Rogan Experience*. https://open.spotify.com/episode/01A5ICPmRS5 edQeMIB71wn

Rose, S. C., Bisson, J., Churchill, R., & Wessely, S. (2002). Psychological debriefing for preventing post traumatic stress disorder (PTSD). *Cochrane Database of Systematic Reviews*. 10.1002/14651858.CD000560

Sakaluk, J. K., Williams, A. J., Kilshaw, R. E., & Rhyner, K. T. (2019). Evaluating the evidential value of empirically supported psychological treatments (ESTs): A meta-scientific review. *Journal of Abnormal Psychology*, 128(6), 500.

Shapiro, A. (Producer), & Coyne, P. (Producer) (2011). Beyond Scared Straight [Television Series]. USA: A&E.

Schlosser, R. W., Balandin, S., Hemsley, B., Iacono, T., Probst, P., & von Tetzchner, S. (2014). Facilitated communication and authorship: A systematic review. *Augmentative and Alternative Communication*, 30(4), 359–368.

Travers, J. C. (2023). Autism spectrum and intellectual disability. In S. Hupp, & R. Wiseman (Eds), *Pseudoscience in Therapy: A Skeptical Field Guide*. Cambridge University Press.

Typing to Communicate - Center on Disability and Inclusion. (n.d.). Syracuse University. https://disabilityinclusioncenter.syr.edu/communication/typing/

Van Dam, N. T., Van Vugt, M. K., Vago, D. R., Schmalzl, L., Saron, C. D., Olendzki, A., ... & Meyer, D. E. (2018). Mind the hype: A critical evaluation and prescriptive agenda for research on mindfulness and meditation. *Perspectives on Psychological Science*, 13(1), 36–61.

Wendt, D. C., Huson, K., Albatnuni, M., & Gone, J. P. (2022). What are the best practices for psychotherapy with indigenous peoples in the United States and Canada? A thorny question. *Journal of Consulting and Clinical Psychology*, 90(10), 802.

Williams, A. J., Botanov, Y., Kilshaw, R. E., Wong, R. E., & Sakaluk, J. K. (2021). Potentially harmful therapies: A meta-scientific review of evidential value. *Clinical Psychology: Science and Practice*, 28(1), 5–18.

Williams, A. J., Botanov, Y., Giovanetti, A. K., Perko, V. L., Sutherland, C. L., Youngren, W., & Sakaluk, J. K. (2022). A metascientific review of the evidential value of acceptance and commitment therapy for depression. *Behavior Therapy*. 10.1016/j.beth.2022.06.004

8 Energy Medicine

Jon Guy, Melanie Trecek-King,
Ruth Ann Harpur, and Jonathan N. Stea

One of the most important first tasks when researching any discipline is to define the object of study accurately and precisely. Defining "energy medicine" (EM) is a difficult undertaking, given the myriad definitions offered by EM proponents, as well as the sheer number of proposed EM modalities (e.g., Colquhoun, 2007; Gorski, 2019; Reddy, 2014; Terms Related to Complementary and Integrative Health, 2022; Wang et al., 2010). It is generally understood that EM is a blanket term which encompasses a vast number of healing nostrums, including Reiki, therapeutic touch, earthing, chakra balancing, chiropractic, anthroposophic medicine, psychic healing, crystal therapy, magnet therapy, traditional Chinese medicine (TCM), Feng Shui, acupuncture, Qigong, Ayurveda, homeopathy, bioenergy healing, and many more (Ernst, 2019; Hall, 2011; Singh & Ernst, 2008).

Examining the Claims

"Energy" is a fundamental component of our universe and exists in several different forms, including heat, light, mechanical, and electrical. Physicists measure energy in units of Joules, where energy is defined as the capacity to perform work (Ernst, 2019). Importantly, the "energies" of EM, or "putative energies" as they're called (see below), have never been empirically demonstrated (Baldwin & Hammerschlag, 2014) and "are based on pre-scientific and, in some cases, superstitious understandings of disease and human physiology" (Gorski, 2019, p. 310; Rosa et al., 1998), such as "vitalism" or "innate intelligence." Not only are putative energies vague and undefined by their supporters, so too are the symptoms they supposedly treat. According to its proponents, EM can treat (and even prevent) a multitude of ailments, including but not limited to physical injury, pain, emotional distress, mental disorders, and increase overall "wellness and peak performance." EM is also claimed to "stimulate immune function, relieve headaches, release stress, improve memory, enhance digestion, relieve

DOI: 10.4324/9781003259510-11

arthritis, neck, shoulder, and low back pain, and [help one] cope with electromagnetic pollution" (Eden, 2021, para. 4).

The National Center for Complementary and Integrative Health (NCCIH), a branch of the U.S. Department of Health and Human Services, defines "energy healing therapy" as:

> A technique that involves channeling healing energy through the hands of a practitioner into the client's body to restore a normal energy balance and, therefore, health. Energy healing therapy has been used to treat a wide variety of ailments and health problems, and it is often used with other alternative and conventional medical treatments.
>
> (Terms Related to Complementary and Integrative Health, 2022)

However, the NCCIH also states that there is "no scientific evidence supporting the existence of [putative] energy" (NCCIH, 2018, para. 3), which adds to the confusion and compounds an additional problem of understanding source credibility. The NCCIH recognizes two different kinds of energy ostensibly involved in EM: *veritable* energies, and *putative* energies. Veritable energies are energies which have known measurable properties, such as electrical or potential energy. By contrast, putative energies are energies which cannot be measured or have "yet to be measured," such as the human vital force, biofields, or subtle energies (Hall, 2015).

Using precise language to describe phenomena is foundational to the pursuit of scientific knowledge and advancement, "because everyday language can cause confusion when precision is needed" (Guy, 2022, p. 269). Scientific claims must be testable, and evidence must be observable, measurable, and repeatable. It is well understood that vague, unfalsifiable claims are a hallmark of pseudoscience (Guy, 2022, pp. 226–27); but because they cannot be disproven, evidence that appears to support a claim is veridically meaningless. EM claims about "removing electromagnetic pollution" or "stimulating immune function" sound "sciencey" and profound, but without clear definitions or the ability to observe the phenomena, are hollow and unscientific.

That said, the lack of consistency or clear definitions among EM proponents hasn't stopped scientists from investigations. But as with any scientific investigation, operational definitions must be established for there to be a clear end point to their research. Thus, researchers have defined the alleged "healing" involved in EM as "the direct interaction between the healer and a sick individual with the intention of bringing about an improvement or cure of the condition" (Abbot et al., 2001; Hodges & Scofield, 1995). Healing is purportedly achieved by several means, including by tapping, pinching, twisting, or burning specific energy points beneath the skin, by waving or swirling the hands over alleged energy pathways, by performing energy-enhancing exercises or postures, by focusing the mind on specific energies, and by surrounding oneself with positive energies. In the case of distance or remote healing, energy is purportedly transferred remotely from the practitioner to the patient, with the aim of restoring energy balance and flow by activating natural healing energies which have become disturbed or are imbalanced.

One would be hard pressed to find an EM proponent who doesn't use the terms "positive" and "negative" energy, but what do those terms mean? To be sure, the EM literature hasn't settled on precise definitions, leaving the serious researcher left with an array of vague terms which lack precise meaning. Thus, these terms merely serve as marketing buzz words for unscrupulous snake oil salespeople who hawk bogus products and treatments on the less informed. However, from both a logical as well as a scientific standpoint, these terms are rather problematic.

For one, EM proponents are fallaciously reifying that energies themselves are not inanimate products of nature, but conscious forces with sentience and intentionality. (Note that virologists do not speak about pathogens as positive or negative viruses.) Since there's no evidence that these energies exist in the first place, the idea that someone without any relevant expertise can definitively identify an energy as positive or negative stretches credulity to its limits. For two, EM proponents are committing what we're calling the fallacy of added complexity (i.e., taking something that's complex and lacking in evidentiary support such as putative energy), and explaining it by adding more layers of complexity for things that lack evidentiary support (i.e., positive and negative energies). However improbable the existence of putative energy is, one cannot explain it by invoking something more complex and thus more improbable.

Energy Medicine in Popular Culture

Despite its broad claims and lack of evidentiary support, EM enjoys widespread popularity in the eyes of the public. For example, a 2017 survey showed that nearly half of Americans have tried some form of energy-based alternative medicine (Funk et al., 2017), and a 2018 report showed that around 42% of American adults believe that spiritual energy exists in physical objects (Gecewicz, 2018).

Oftentimes, EM is amplified by celebrities and TV personalities who have no scientific training and rely exclusively on anecdotes as valid forms of evidence. For example, the American socialite Kim Kardashian has been outspoken about visiting energy healers (Corinthios, 2019). Singer-songwriters Adele and Katy Perry, English fashion designer and former Spice Girl Victoria Beckham, and Australian model Miranda Kerr have all claimed that carrying crystals boosts their performance, creates positive energy, and has the power to attract and soothe men (Boscamp, n.d.). Additionally, host of the TV show *Dr. Oz*, Dr. Mehemet Oz is well known for promoting EMs such as therapeutic touch, reflexology, homeopathy, and Reiki (Oz, 1998; Schwarcz, 2022); actress Gwyneth Paltrow, through her company Goop, suggests that her products have extraordinary healing powers that restore one's natural energies (Caulfield, 2015); and Oprah Winfrey has a long history fraught with promoting various forms of EM, such as manifesting, and psychic healing (Gorski, 2018). Examples of celebrities using alternative medicine abound, and when people look to celebrities for guidance, they undermine science-based medicine and place their health in the hands of those who are unqualified to give health advice (Ernst & Pittler, 2006).

Regrettably, support for EM isn't limited to celebrities and socialites, and demonstrating the prevalence of EM has proven to be a difficult task (Posadzki et al., 2013). Although EM practitioners are often not medically qualified, and the entire field of EM is devoid of any established training or ethical protocols, estimates have shown that the United Kingdom has roughly 14,000 spiritual healers. In the United States, various forms of EM are taught in at least 75 institutions and universities and many thousands of EM practitioners are scattered throughout the country (Ernst et al., 2008, p. 350). Even more troubling, some health insurance providers cover multiple EM treatments, such as acupuncture and chiropractic (Chiropractic services, n.d.). This unfortunate reality legitimizes EM in the minds of the public, who are rightfully confused as to its effectiveness.

Examining the Evidence for Energy Medicine

One of the most glaring problems with EM is that it makes incredible claims – unobservable forces producing physical effects – that violate diverse fields of well-established science, from physics and chemistry to biology and pharmacology. For example, physicists using extremely sensitive electromagnetic detectors, electron microscopes, and particle accelerators can measure minute energies such as the strength of an electron's magnetic field (i.e., the magnetic dipole moment) to one part in ten billion. Nevertheless, even with the help of our most advanced energy detecting technologies, all attempts to detect putative energies have been wholly unsuccessful (Stenger, 1999), and there remains zero scientific evidence for their existence (Ernst et al., 2008, pp. 291–361). As the late particle physicist Victor Stenger put it, "No carefully controlled, replicable experiment has ever produced data requiring us to postulate additional components to organic matter, whether material or spiritual, living or non-living" (Stenger, 1998, p. 4). Therefore, it takes no stretch of the imagination to conclude that the "energies" of EM are indistinguishable from "absolutely nothing."

Another problem is that no mechanism of action has ever been established for putative energies. The literature on EM has no shortage of claims related to healing just about every ailment known to exist (nor are EM proponents shy about inventing ailments in order to sell their clients novel treatments). However, what cannot be found within that body of literature are any details of how EM modalities are thought to work at a chemical, biological, or molecular level which comport with scientific standards of evidence. As one example, therapeutic touch practitioners claim that by waving their hands over a patient's body, they can detect and manipulate the patient's bioenergy field in a manner that reduces symptoms or cures a host of ailments. But this sort of literal handwaving is fanciful at best, and therapeutic touch practitioners have never demonstrated on a physical level any connection between manipulating bioenergy fields and biological processes. To put it a different way, therapeutic touch raises far more questions than it answers, such as: What is a bioenergy field? How is it being manipulated? What electro-chemical processes are taking place? And how does the body respond to those processes? Until EM proponents can answer basic questions about their nostrums, they are certainly not pursuing evidence-based medicine.

Despite all of its discoveries, science is not without a large number of "still unknowns," so it's possible that scientists may one day propose a theoretical framework for the existence of putative energies. But as it stands, EM proponents have never established any such framework. Yet even if putative energies exist, since they are alleged to have biological effects, it is safe to assume that researchers would be able to measure, quantify, and incorporate them into science-based medicine.

But what about its purported effects on patients? Edzard Ernst – physician, researcher, and author of Chapter 12 – specializes in investigating complementary and alternative medicine and has conducted more research on the topic than any other person in history. Ernst has said that EM is an "undefined" and "imagined" pseudoscientific paranormal healing practice, the benefits of which exist only in the minds of its proponents (Ernst, 2022). After conducting a review of studies by the NCCIH, Ernst concluded that, of the randomized controlled trials (RTCs) that suggested an effect of EM, they all "either applied statistics inappropriately, confounded the effects of energy healing by adding unrelated interventions to the experimental condition, or failed to design or blind equivalent placebo controls. Their results are thus wide open to bias" (Ernst & Seip, 2011, p. 109). Furthermore, Ernst and his colleagues have conducted multiple RCTs to test the effects of EM and have failed to find any positive effects (e.g., Abbot et al., 2001; Harkness et al., 2000).

More recently, a team of researchers conducted a systematic review on whether Reiki, therapeutic touch, healing touch, and polarity therapy had any measurable effect on anxiety, depression, mood, fatigue, quality of life, comfort, well-being, neurotoxicity, pain, and nausea in 1,375 patients with cancer. Replicating the findings of Ernst and colleagues, they found that, of the studies that were of moderate quality (and included significant methodological limitations), short-term improved outcomes were found for nausea, pain, and quality of life (readers will note that all three measures are entirely subjective experiences and therefore likely due to the placebo response), though no long-term outcomes were detected. However, of the high-quality studies examined, none of them found "any difference between bioenergy therapies and active (placebo, massage, [relaxation response therapy], yoga, meditation, relaxation training, companionship, friendly visit) and passive control groups (usual care, resting, education)" (Hauptmann et al., 2022, para. 4).

EM proponents like pointing to studies that appear to support their claims. Yet we can always find "evidence" that supports our beliefs if we're looking hard enough (e.g., the existence of Bigfoot, the power of witchcraft, or the omnipotence of Thor). However, cherry-picking low-quality studies and relying on anecdotes is insufficient evidence for the incredible claims of EM. And when it comes to the research, the better the study design, the worse the evidence for EM. In addition, even well-designed studies can show statistically significant outcomes simply due to chance (Guy, 2022, pp. 67–68). Therefore, it is prudent to favor quality meta-analyses and systematic reviews over individual studies.

The Most Likely Explanations for Energy Medicine's Claims

A common refrain amongst EM proponents (and even alternative medicine proponents, more broadly) is that they "know the treatment works," because it "worked for them." While most people trust their personal experiences, anecdotes are insufficient forms of evidence (Trecek-King, 2021) because no one can fool us like we can. Science is successful in large part because it recognizes and corrects for our flawed perceptions and cognitions. And as stated in the previous section, in carefully controlled, randomized, double-blinded studies designed to reduce bias and control for confounding variables, EM is no more effective than a placebo.

Like most forms of alternative medicine, EM's purported benefits can be explained by a suite of cognitive biases and logical fallacies, the most likely of which is the *placebo response*. The placebo response is real, yet often misunderstood (Novella, 2017). Although placebos lack the ability to produce clinical results (Guy, 2022, pp. 58–59), the act of being "treated" with one can result in an improvement in subjective symptoms, such as pain, nausea, and fatigue (Hróbjartsson & Gøtzsche, 2001). (Astute readers will notice these are often the symptoms EM claims to treat.) Clearly, symptom reduction is important, but it's important to keep in mind that placebos only affect symptoms, not the underlying condition. They may make the patient feel better, but they do not "treat" or "heal."

Another possible explanation is regression to the mean, in which abnormal or extreme events tend to be followed by more moderate ones. For example, self-limiting illnesses, such as colds or headaches, go away on their own, while cyclical diseases, such as irritable bowel syndrome or rheumatism, intensify and diminish over time. In either case, patients often seek treatment when their symptoms are at their worst, and mistakenly assume the treatment was the reason their condition improved.

Confirmation bias almost certainly plays a role as well. One of the most pervasive biases, confirmation bias is the tendency to give greater weight to information that confirms our beliefs, and to ignore, suppress, and discount information that conflicts with our beliefs. If a patient believes EM is effective, they're more likely to perceive improvements from their treatment and overlook symptoms they're experiencing afterwards. They're also more likely to only remember the times EM "worked" and forget the times it didn't (a phenomenon known as the *Jeane Dixon effect*). Closely related to confirmation bias is the emotionally-biased search for justifications to support desired beliefs. The more a patient wants to believe that EM is effective, the more motivated they will be to search for supporting evidence.

Occam's razor can be a helpful tool for comparing alternative explanations. Named after William of Ockham (1285–1347), Occam's razor states that, when evaluating competing explanations, the one that requires the fewest number of assumptions is the most likely to be true. The explanation that EM is effective requires us to make giant new assumptions; namely, that putative energies exist (and have evaded detection by experts who study energies), that EM practitioners can "feel" and manipulate those energies, and that they produce biological effects (with no plausible mechanism). The explanation that EM is a placebo requires no new assumptions, and has ample scientific evidence (Ernst & Seip, 2011). Therefore, Occam's razor would favor the placebo explanation over the putative energy explanation.

As a final note, it's likely that some EM practitioners aren't trying to con patients – many of them almost certainly believe in what they're promoting. However, EM proponents not only make incredible claims, but they also bear the burden of proof to provide evidence which supports them. Scientists are open to all claims, but proportion their acceptance of claims to the available evidence. Since EM proponents have, despite their best efforts, failed to meet the high standards of scientific evidence for the existence of putative energies and their effects, EM remains an unlikely explanation for healing. The good news is that the process of science is available to all – if EM proponents truly believe in putative energies and their effects, they are encouraged to provide evidence (and win a Nobel Prize!).

Possible Harms Associated with Energy Medicine

A 1989 Associated Press article retells the story of a man named E. Frenkel, a psychic who believed he had the power to stop moving bicycles, automobiles, and streetcars (Stenger, 1999, p. 58). Frenkel believed in his powers so deeply that he put them to the ultimate test when he attempted to stand in front of a moving freight train and stop it using the powers of his mind. With his arms raised, body clenched, and head lowered, Frenkel stood on the tracks and was tragically killed by the oncoming train (Stenger, 1999).

Thankfully most effects of EM aren't as extreme (Hauptmann et al., 2022). Yet one might be tempted to argue that, because direct harms are minimal and EM sessions might be enjoyable or relaxing for patients, there's no need to debunk EM claims. Should healthcare providers be concerned about EM? In this section we consider the effects of EM for people who experience mental disorders.

It's not unusual for patients with mental health concerns to consult practitioners of complementary and alternative medicine (CAM). Some studies have estimated that 43% of patients with anxiety disorders use CAM therapies (Bystritsky et al., 2012), and use of CAM seems to be more common in patients with mental health problems compared to those with physical illnesses (Mamtani & Cimino, 2002).

The most commonly recommended treatments for mental disorders, including depression, anxiety, posttraumatic stress disorder, psychotic disorders and bipolar disorder fall into two main categories: psychotropic medication and psychological therapies. Psychotropic medications can be unpopular due to their potential side effects and some patients' dislike of using prescriptions long term. About a third of patients withdraw from antidepressant medication due to side effects (Arroll et al., 2009). Additionally, psychological therapies are often viewed as preferable by patients (Prins et al, 2008), but availability may be limited and no therapy is effective for all patients.

Challenges in tolerating medication, difficulties in accessing effective psychological therapies, and/or gaining insufficient benefit from treatments all likely contribute to seeking CAM treatments for mental disorders. A study found that a fifth of patients with depression or anxiety visit a CAM therapy provider with 2.8% patients with anxiety and 5.4% patients with depression choosing an "energy therapy" (Kessler et al., 2001).

Whilst often seen as harmless, if ineffectual, Lilienfeld and colleagues (2014) highlight two key ways in which pseudoscientific treatments cause indirect harm: depriving time and financial resources from supported treatments, and undermining trust in scientific professionals that employ their use.

However, clinically, we would like to propose another way in which EM and other pseudosciences may have deleterious effects on patients who experience mental disorders. Psychological therapies foster self-understanding and disrupt unhelpful patterns of thoughts, feelings and behaviors. For example, behavioral activation for depression aims to break the cycle of patients becoming depressed, experiencing inertia, becoming increasingly inactive, and consequently more depressed by encouraging them to engage in personally meaningful activities (Dimidjian et al., 2011). Similarly, cognitive-behavioral therapy for obsessive-compulsive disorder (OCD) is based on an understanding that people with OCD interpret intrusive thoughts as a sign that something is wrong. For example, the thought that they have said or done something inappropriate, that their food may be contaminated, or that something bad may happen to someone they love is interpreted as an indication that something bad has happened or is about to happen. As a result, they may engage in rituals to neutralize the thought and keep themselves safe (Bream et al., 2017). A key component of effective therapy is exposure and response prevention, in which people with OCD expose themselves to their intrusive thoughts to build confidence that a thought is "just a thought" and not a sign of imminent danger (Law & Boisseau, 2019).

In contrast, EM relies on magical thinking, and as such, may prevent patients' understanding of and ability to manage their psychiatric symptoms. Some studies have suggested that magical thinking may be one factor that mediates a link between obsessive-compulsive beliefs and obsessive-compulsive symptoms (Fite et al., 2020; Goods et al., 2014) and may play a role in OCD and generalized anxiety disorder (Einstein & Menzies, 2004; West & Willner, 2011).

Whilst we were unable to find any studies which examined the impact of engaging in energy therapies on magical thinking and psychiatric symptomatology, it seems plausible that endorsing magical thinking may deny patients a realistic explanation for their difficulties, preventing them from building a sense of their own autonomy and independence. There may be a risk too, that rituals associated with energy medicine practices could be incorporated as "safety behaviors" designed to "neutralize" thoughts which are perceived as threatening, thereby maintaining inaccurate and unhelpful beliefs that fuel patients' anxiety. While not the extreme harm experienced by E. Frenkel, encouraging magical thinking may limit patients' ability to self-manage their condition and potentially prolong the suffering experienced by people going through mental illness.

Summary and Conclusion

Energy medicine is based on a type of "energy" that has never been identified and almost certainly doesn't exist. Further, nonexistent energy cannot produce a biological response. When tested with proper controls, EM performs no better than a placebo. While EM proponents claim their "treatments" are scientific, EM bears many hallmarks of pseudoscience, such as unfalsifiable claims, "sciencey" language, and lack of scientific plausibility. Unfortunately, instead of providing evidence for their claims, EM proponents often brand criticism from the scientific community as a conspiracy. Patients deceived by EM's claims face possible harms, such as financial costs, delaying effective treatment, and losing trust in evidence-based practices.

Jon Guy is an independent researcher and science communicator who writes about critical thinking, pseudoscience, logic, psychology, and related topics. He is the author of *Think Straight: An Owner's Manual for the Mind*.

Melanie Trecek-King, MA, is the creator of Thinking is Power and an associate professor of biology at Massasoit Community College.

Ruth Ann Harpur, PhD DClinPsych, is a clinical psychologist in independent practice in London, United Kingdom.

Jonathan N. Stea, PhD, RPsych, is a registered clinical psychologist and adjunct assistant professor of psychology at the University of Calgary in Canada. He is currently writing another book about mental health misinformation and pseudoscience to be published in 2025 by Penguin Random House Canada, Oxford University Press, and Audible.

References

Abbot, N. C., Harkness, E. F., Stevinson, C., Marshall, P. F., Conn, D. A., & Ernst, E. (2001). Spiritual healing as a therapy for chronic pain: a randomized, clinical trial. *Pain, 91*(1–2), 78–89.
Arroll, B., Elley, C. R., Fishman, R., Goodyear-Smith, F. A., Kenealy, T., Blashki, G., Kerse, N., & MacGillicray, S. (2009). Antidepressants versus placebo for depression in primary care. *Cochrane Database of Systematic Reviews, 3.*

Retrieved from Cochrane.org: https://www.cochranelibrary.com/cdsr/doi/10.1002/14651858.CD007954/full

Baldwin, A. L., & Hammerschlag, R. (2014). Biofield-based Therapies: A Systematic Review of Physiological Effects on Practitioners During Healing. *Explore, 10*(3), 150–161.

Boscamp, E. (n.d.). *9 Celebs Who Swear By The Healing Effects Of Crystals.* Retrieved from mindbodygreen.com: https://www.mindbodygreen.com/0-25945/9-celebs-who-swear-by-the-healing-effects-of-crystals.html

Bream, V., Challacombe, F., Palmer, A., & Salkovskis, P. (2017). *Cognitive behaviour therapy for obsessive-compulsive disorder.* Oxford University Press.

Bystritsky, A., Hovav, S., Sherbourne, C., Stein, M. B., Rose, R. D., Campbell-Sills, L., Golinelli, D., Sullivan, G., Craske, M. G., Roy-Byrne, P. P. (2012). Use of complementary and alternative medicine in a large sample of anxiety patients. *Psychosomatics, 53*(3), 266–272.

Caulfield, T. A. (2015). *Is Gwyneth Paltrow wrong about everything?: When celebrity culture and science clash.* Canada: Penguin.

Colquhoun, D. (2007). Science degrees without the science. *Nature, 446,* 373–374.

Corinthios, A. (2019, April 26). *See Kim Kardashian's Reaction as a Local Healer Repeatedly Burps in Her Face in Bali.* Retrieved from people.com: https://people.com/tv/kim-kardashian-bali-spiritual-healer-burping/

Dimidjian, S., Barrera Jr, M., Martell, C., Munoz, R. F., & Lewinsohn, P. M. (2011). The origins and current status of behavioral activation treatments for depression. *Annual Review of Clinical Psychology, 7,* 1–38.

Eden, D. (2021). *Energy Medicine Institute.* Retrieved from Energy Medicine: What is it and how does it work?: https://energymedicineinstitute.org/energy-medicine-what-is-it-and-how-does-it-work/

Einstein, D. A., & Menzies, R. G. (2004). The presence of magical thinking in obsessive compulsive disorder, *Behaviour Research and Therapy, 42*(5), 539–549.

Ernst, E. (2019). *Alternative medicine: A critical assessment of 150 modalities.* Cambridge, UK: Springer.

Ernst, E. (2022, October 8). *Energy healing for cancer?* Retrieved from edzardernst.com: http://edzardernst.com/

Ernst, E., & Pittler, M. H. (2006). Celebrity-based medicine. *Medical Journal of Australia, 185,* 680–681.

Ernst, E., & Seip, R. (2011). An independent review of studies of 'energy medicine' funded by the US National Center for Complementary and Alternative Medicine. *Focus on Alternative and Complementary Therapies, 16*(2), 106–109.

Ernst, E., Pittler, M. H., Wider, B., & Boddy, K. (Eds.). (2008). *The desktop guide to complimentary and alternative medicine: An evidence-based approach* (Second ed.). Mosby International Ltd.

Fite, R. E., Adut, S. L., & Magee, J. C., (2020) Do you believe in magical thinking? Examining magical thinking as a mediator between obsessive-compulsive belief domains and symptoms. *Behavioural and Cognitive Psychotherapy, 48*(4), 454–462.

Funk, C., Kennedy, B., & Hefferon, M. (2017, February 2). *Vast Majority of Americans say benefits of childhood vaccines outweigh risks.* Retrieved from Pew Research Center: https://www.pewresearch.org/science/2017/02/02/americans-health-care-behaviors-and-use-of-conventional-and-alternative-medicine/

Gecewicz, C. (2018, October 1). *'New Age' beliefs common among both religious and nonreligious Americans.* Retrieved from Pew Research Center: https://www.pewresearch.org/fact-tank/2018/10/01/new-age-beliefs-common-among-both-religious-and-nonreligious-americans/

Gorski, D. (2018, January 9). *Oprah Winfrey for President? Does anyone remember all the pseudoscience and quackery she's promoted?* Retrieved from Respectful Insolence: https://www.respectfulinsolence.com/2018/01/09/oprah-winfrey-president-anyone-remember-pseudoscience-quackery-shes-promoted/#:~:text=Besides%20her%20support%20of%20faith%20healing%20and%20antivaccine,on%20her%20show%20than%20I%20care%20to%20remember.

Gorski, D. H. (2019). "Integrative" Medicine: Integrating Quackery with Science-Based Medicine. In A. B. Kaufman, & J. C. Kaufman (Eds.), *Pseudoscience: The conspiracy against science* (First MIT paperback edition ed., pp. 309–329). The MIT Press.

Goods, N. A., Rees, C. S., Egan, S. J., & Kane, R. T. (2014). The relationship between magical thinking inferential confusion and obsessive-compulsive symptoms. *Cognitive Behavioural Therapy, 43*(4), 342–350.

Guy, J. (2022). *Think straight: An owner's manual for the mind.* Prometheus.

Hall, H. (2015, November 26). *Science Based Medicine: Lecture 7: Energy Medicine.* Retrieved from YouTube: https://www.youtube.com/watch?v=ISoL8qc2xHw&list=PL8MfjLNsf_miVcNu6eJMNigAMNwQkk_B9&index=8

Hall, H. (2011, January 1). *Energy Medicine and Fantasy Physics: How Real Physics has been Kidnapped by Alternative Medicine Practitioners.* Retrieved from SkepDoc: https://www.skepdoc.info/energy-medicine-and-fantasy-physics-how-real-physics-has-been-kidnapped-by-alternative-medicine-practitioners/

Harkness, E. F., Abbot, N. C., & Ernst, E. (2000). A randomized trial of distant healing for skin warts. *The American Journal of Medicine, 108*(6), 448–452.

Hauptmann, M., Kutschan, S., Hübner, J., & Dörfler, J. (2022). Bioenergy therapies as a complementary treatment: a systematic review to evaluate the efficacy of bioenergy therapies in relieving treatment toxicities in patients with cancer. *Journal of Cancer Research and Clinical Oncology.* doi: 10.1007/s00432-022-04362-x

Hodges, R. D., & Scofield, A. M. (1995). Is spiritual healing a valid and effective therapy? *Journal of the Royal Society of Medicine, 88*(4), 203–207. Retrieved from https://www.ncbi.nlm.nih.gov/pmc/articles/PMC1295164/?page=1

Hróbjartsson, A., & Gøtzsche, P. C. (2001). Is the placebo powerless? An analysis of clinical trials comparing placebo with no treatment. *New England Journal of Medicine, 24, 344*(21), 1594–1602. doi: 10.1056/NEJM200105243442106

Kessler, R. C., Soukup, J., Davis R. B., Wilkey, S. A., Van Rompay, M. I., & Eisenberg, D. M., (2001). The use of complementary and alternative therapies to treat anxiety and depression in the United States. *American Journal of Psychiatry, 158*(2), 289–294.

Law, C., & Boisseau, C. L. (2019). Exposure and response prevention in the treatment of obsessive-compulsive disorder: Current perspectives. *Psychology Research and Behavior Management, 12*, Article 1167–1174.

Lilienfeld, S. O., Lynn, S. J., & Lohr, J. M. (2014). *Science and Pseudoscience in Clinical Psychology (2nd ed.)*. New York: The Guilford Press.

Mamtani, R. & Cimino, A. (2002). A primer of complementary and alternative medicine and its relevance in the treatment of mental health problems. *Psychiatric Quarterly, 73*(4), 267–381.

National Center for Complementary and Integrative Health (NCCIH (2018). Reiki. Retrieved https://www.nccih.nih.gov/health/reiki

Novella, S. (2017, November 15). *Placebo Myths Debunked*. Retrieved from Science-Based Medicine: https://sciencebasedmedicine.org/placebo-myths-debunked/

Oz, M. (1998). *Healing from the Heart*. New York: Plume.

Posadzki, P., Watson, L. K., Alotaibi, A., & Ernst, E. (2013). Prevalence of use of complementary and alternative medicine (CAM) by patients/consumers in the UK: systematic review of surveys. *Clinical Medical Journal, 13*(2), 126. doi: 10.7861/clinmedicine.13-2-126

Prins, M. A., Verhaak, P. F., Bensing, J. M., van der Meer, K., (2008). Health beliefs and perceived need for mental health care of anxiety and depression - the patients' perspective explored. *Clinical Psychology Review, 28*(6), 1038–1058.

Reddy, S. (2014, April 21). *A Top Hospital Opens Up to Chinese Herbs as Medicines*. Retrieved from wsj.com: https://www.wsj.com/articles/SB10001424052702303626804579509590048257648

Rosa, L., Rosa, E., Sarner, L., & Barrett, S. (1998). A Close Look at Therapeutic Touch. *Journal of the American Medical Association, 279*(13), 1005–1010.

Schwarcz, J. (2022, February 18). *Dr. Oz's Sad Trip Down the Rabbit Hole*. Retrieved from McGill Office for Science and Society: https://www.mcgill.ca/oss/article/pseudoscience/dr-ozs-sad-trip-down-rabbit-hole

Singh, S., & Ernst, E. (2008). *Trick or Treatment: The Undeniable Facts About Alternative Medicine*. New York: W. W. Norton & Company, Inc.

Stenger, V. J. (1998). The Energy Fields of Life. *Skeptical Briefs, 8*(2), 4, 12. Retrieved from skepticalinquirer.org: https://skepticalinquirer.org/newsletter/energy-fields-of-life/

Stenger, V. J. (1999). Energy Medicine. In D. Ramey, *Consumer's Guide to Alternative Therapies in the Horse* (pp. 55–66). New York: Howell Book House.

Terms Related to Complementary and Integrative Health. (2022, August 28). Retrieved from National Center for Complimentary and Integrative Health: https://www.nccih.nih.gov/health/providers/terms-related-to-complementary-and-integrative-health

Trecek-King, M. (2021). *Four ways your personal experiences can lead you astray*. Thinking Is Power. https://thinkingispower.com/four-ways-your-personal-experiences-can-lead-you-astray/

Wang, C., Schmid, C. H., Rones, R., Kalish, R., Yinh, J., Goldenberg, D. L., ... McAlindon, T. (2010). A Randomized Trial of Tai Chi for Fibromyalgia. *New England Journal of Medicine, 363*, 743–754.

West, B., & Willner, P. (2011). Magical thinking in obsessive-compulsive disorder and generalized anxiety disorder. *Behavioural and Cognitive Psychotherapy, 39*(4), 399–411.

9   Purple Hat Therapies

Eve A. Rosenfeld and Carmen P. McLean

Unlike other chapters in this book, the notion of a purple hat therapy is a metaphor rather than being a specific type of therapy. First described by Rosen and Davison (2003), it refers to an intervention that combines evidence-based treatment components with a new component of questionable scientific plausibility. The positive treatment effects of purple hat therapies are attributed to the unique aspect of the treatment rather than the evidence-based components. Proponents of a purple hat therapy purport that the unique component of the intervention (i.e., wearing a purple hat) is the component responsible for therapeutic improvement. To illustrate the distinction between a standard therapy and a purple hat therapy, imagine you have a headache and a doctor recommends taking ibuprofen. In standard practice, the alleviation of headache pain would be attributed to taking the ibuprofen. In a purple hat therapy, a practitioner might recommend taking ibuprofen while wearing a purple hat, with great importance placed on the wearing of the hat. The reduction in headache pain might then be attributed in whole or in part to the wearing of a purple hat, rather than to the consumption of ibuprofen. And now that this doctor is on to something, she might start charging other doctors to get trained in, and even certified in, this new purple hat therapy.

Evidence showing that purple hat therapies can reduce symptoms of various mental and physical health problems is often mistaken as evidence supporting the clinical value of the purple hat component specifically. Explanations for how the purple hat component works often reference neuropsychological phenomena and/or theories from Eastern philosophies. As such, proponents often explain disconfirming evidence by pointing to the inability of Western science to understand or capture change generated by the unique component of the intervention.

Examining the Claims

In a purple hat therapy, positive treatment response is misattributed to a purported unique or novel component (the purple hat), rather than the

DOI: 10.4324/9781003259510-12

evidence-based components that are shared with existing approaches. Despite the use of evidence-based techniques, champions of purple hat therapies often minimize and at times ignore the potential effect of these evidence-based components on outcomes. This is the defining feature of a purple hat therapy – the use of evidence-based techniques as a backdrop against which a novel purple hat component is centered. Proponents of purple hat therapies attribute treatment effects to the purple hat component with little to no empirical evidence and sometimes lack of scientific plausibility. To demonstrate this pattern, we will critically examine three purple hat therapies: eye movement desensitization and reprocessing therapy (EMDR), energy psychology, and binaural beats.

In evaluating purple hat therapies, it is important to note that studies designed to compare the overall effect of a purple hat therapy relative to various control conditions such as waitlist, treatment-as-usual, or other active therapies, cannot speak to whether the purple hat component itself has an impact on treatment outcomes. Dismantling studies designed to compare the effects of the therapy with and without the purple hat component included (e.g., Fox & Malinowski, 2013) may be slightly more helpful in assessing the impact of the purple hat component, but these designs still do not control for demand characteristics or therapist bias. The true test of a purple hat therapy is a sham placebo-controlled design. In this design, both the therapist and the patient are blind to the specific procedures used in the purple hat component (Herbert & Gaudiano, 2005). A sham placebo condition that closely mimics the purple hat therapy allows researchers to control for all treatment effects (e.g., expectancy, therapeutic alliance, treatment credibility) except for the effect attributable to the specific technique or process that comprises the purple hat component.

Only sham placebo-controlled designs can yield evidence of *specific efficacy* (Lilienfeld, 2011) of the purple hat component. For example, while many studies show that EMDR is effective for treating PTSD relative to various control conditions, it is, at best, unclear whether the eye movement component has anything to do with the observed effects. Thus, EMDR lacks specific efficacy supporting its defining feature, despite considerable evidence supporting its overall efficacy.

Eye Movement Desensitization and Reprocessing Therapy (EMDR)

EMDR is a psychotherapeutic intervention that was originally developed to target traumatic memories and PTSD symptoms (Shapiro, 1989; Valiente-Gómez et al., 2017). In EMDR, a therapist leads the client through sequences of eye movements while thinking about the most salient aspect of a traumatic memory. Purportedly, the eye movement component of the intervention is a key component that is crucial for the patient to achieve reductions in PTSD symptoms (e.g., hyperarousal, re-experiencing, sleep disturbance) and to facilitate trauma processing and changes in cognitions (Shapiro, 1989).

Because EMDR involves the evidence-based strategy of imaginal exposure throughout the treatment, critics have questioned the incremental value of the eye movements. In the context of PTSD treatment, traditional imaginal exposure involves revisiting and recounting a traumatic memory and is a core feature of several evidence-based treatments for PTSD (e.g., Foa et al., 2019; Sloan et al., 2012). Imaginal exposure in EMDR differs from traditional imaginal exposure in that it is brief, non-sequential, not narrated, and involves dual attention (Rogers & Silver, 2002). However, it is nevertheless, a form of imaginal exposure. Thus, EMDR includes a highly effective intervention component grounded in science and a purple hat – i.e., eye movements – which introduces confusion. In fact, the very term "purple hat therapy" was coined by Rosen and Davison (2003) to describe EMDR. Rosen and Davison (2003) argued that treatment effects in EMDR are better explained by the cognitive and behavioral techniques such as exposure, rather than the eye movements.

The necessity of the eye movement component of EMDR remains controversial. There are now numerous reviews of dismantling studies that have concluded that there is very little evidence to support the clinical utility of the eye movements, or any form of dual attention task, relative to exposure alone (Boudewyns et al., 1993; Boudewyns & Hyer, 1996; Cahill et al., 1999; Lohr et al., 1999). Although Cahill et al. found that for PTSD, there was some evidence that eye movements reduced within-session distress, there were no clear differences in clinical outcomes between exposure with and without eye movements.

Consistent with findings from these reviews, a meta-analysis by Davidson and Parker (2001) found that, across populations, there was no significant incremental benefit on outcomes due to eye movements. In contrast, a meta-analysis by Lee and Cuijpers (2013) of 15 studies across populations found that effect sizes were larger when eye movements were used. However, it is important to note that most studies in this analysis used non-clinical samples and several had relatively small sample sizes. Moreover, in a subsequent meta-analysis, Cuijpers et al. (2020) did not replicate this finding. The more recent analysis examined 10 dismantling studies of clinical PTSD samples and did not find an advantage for EMDR relative to exposure without eye movements. Overall, the evidence from clinical trials indicates that eye movements are not a critical component of treatment.

Analogue studies have more often found an effect for eye movements on outcomes (see Jeffries & Davis, 2013) and there is some evidence, particularly from studies of non-clinical samples, that eye movements affect certain process variables during treatment (e.g., imagery vividness; Lee & Cuijpers, 2013). One of several proposed mechanisms of action for EMDR is that eye movements tax working memory, thereby attenuating the vividness and emotionality of the traumatic memory during exposure (see Wadji et al., 2022). Possibly such an effect could impact the tolerability of exposure therapy. However, dropout rates for EMDR are similar to other trauma-focused treatments (e.g., Hoppen et al., 2022; Lewis et al., 2020), which suggests that any effect of eye movements on tolerability is likely small and may not be clinically important.

Energy Psychology

Energy psychology is an umbrella term for a collection of treatments, including Thought Field Therapy™, the Emotional Freedom Technique™, the Tapas Acupressure Technique®, and dozens of other variations that are purported to yield rapid and lasting relief from a range of psychological and physical health conditions. Energy psychology proponents claim that psychological disorders and other health conditions are associated with disturbances in the body's "energy fields" (Feinstein, 2008). Energy psychology treatments typically combine imaginal exposure and other cognitive-behavioral techniques and supportive therapy approaches with "energy field manipulation" techniques, such as tapping specific areas of the body, referred to as "acupoints" that purportedly correspond to "energy fields" (Callahan & Callahan, 2000).

Energy psychology treatments also include a combination of imaginal exposure and other supported techniques. As such, studies showing that energy psychology treatments are efficacious relative to various control treatments are unsurprising and do not inform the question of whether energy manipulation has any therapeutic impact. Only two randomized controlled trials of energy psychology have tested "sham" tapping controls (Pignotti, 2005; Waite & Holder, 2003). In the first study, Waite and Holder (2003) compared the Emotional Freedom Technique with two sham conditions tapping on non–Emotional Freedom Technique points on the body and tapping on a doll, as well as a waitlist condition. There were no differences between the three active conditions, suggesting that tapping on specific areas of the body has no therapeutic benefit. In the second study, Pignotti (2005) compared tapping following a sequence of meridian points used in Thought Field Therapy and tapping in randomly selected sequences. There were no differences in outcome between the two conditions.

Thus, contrary to claims that energy psychology works by stimulating specific acupoint locations in specific sequences, sham placebo-controlled trials suggest that the location and sequence of tapping makes no difference, and thus could not be considered an active component of treatment. Incredibly, energy psychology proponents claim that sham tapping conditions are effective because therapists are inadvertently stimulating previously unidentified energy points on their own fingertips when tapping other points on the body or dolls (Feinstein, 2009), thus reinterpreting the null findings in support of energy psychology.

Binaural Sleep Sounds

A binaural beat is an auditory illusion in which an illusory modulating tone is perceived when two tones of different frequencies and shared amplitudes are presented separately, one tone to each ear; the fluctuation in the frequency of the illusory tone is perceived at midway between the frequency of the two stimulus tones (Jirakittayakorn & Wongsawat, 2017; Oster, 1973). Proponents of binaural beats as a therapeutic tool claim that they alter an individuals' brain waves through a process called *entrainment* or the *frequency following effect*, during which brainwaves align themselves with an outside frequency (Vernon et al., 2014). Based on this premise, binaural sleep sounds incorporate binaural beats into tracks of relaxing music to treat insomnia by matching the frequency of binaural beats to brainwaves involved in sleep and relaxation (Bogdan et al., 2009; Choi et al., 2020; Young et al., 2014).

Because binaural beats are a phenomenon of auditory perception that can be used to study how sound is processed in the brain (Oster, 1973; Vernon et al., 2014), they are not in and of themselves a purple hat therapy. However, extensions of binaural beats, such as binaural sleep sounds for insomnia, veer into pseudoscience. Evidence of the frequency following response to binaural beats is mixed (e.g., Jirakittayakorn & Wongsawat, 2017; López-Caballero & Escera, 2017; On et al., 2013; Orozco Perez et al., 2020; Vernon et al., 2014). Nevertheless, this purported effect has been used as rationale for using binaural sleep sounds in conjunction with relaxation techniques to treat insomnia. Given that meta-analyses have demonstrated that relaxing music improves sleep quality and sleep onset latency (De Niet et al., 2009; Feng et al., 2018), the integration of binaural beats (purple hat) into relaxing music (beneficial component) makes binaural sleep sounds for insomnia a purple hat therapy.

Evidence supporting the proposed mechanism of binaural beats (i.e., frequency following effect) is mixed, and, importantly, there is no evidence showing that binaural beats have any effect on insomnia over and above relaxing music. The only double-blind sham-controlled trial of binaural sleep sounds found that binaural beats did not improve sleep over pure music (Bang et al., 2019). Moreover, binaural beats have actually been found less effective than self-help insomnia interventions such as progressive muscle relaxation (Bogdan et al., 2009). Thus, there is limited support for the claim that binaural beats are an active treatment component in binaural sleep sounds interventions nor is there compelling evidence that the treatment package is particularly effective for treating insomnia.

Common Features of Purple Hat Therapies

Proponents of a purple hat therapy often make claims that go far beyond existing empirical evidence. Proponents are prone to drawing overstated conclusions from individual research studies, making bold claims that are unsubstantiated by research, and resisting disconfirming evidence. For example, claims about the efficacy of energy psychology lack any clear boundary conditions in terms of effects or treatment targets. These treatments are purported not to *reduce* symptoms but to *eliminate* or *cure* not only some problems, but seemingly almost all mental and physical health problems (Callahan, 1985, 2001). Similarly, purple hat therapies are often purported to be easier or more tolerable than mainstream alternatives. For example, EMDR is often pitched as having a much lower dropout rate than other trauma-focused therapies, but data suggest dropout rates are comparable across these treatments (e.g., Hoppen et al., 2022; Lewis et al., 2020).

Purple hat therapies often rely on dubious posthoc explanations for a serendipitous observation that led to the discovery of the purple hat component. These posthoc explanations often involve complex neuropsychological phenomenon that lend an appearance of scientific credibility to the treatment and are not easily scrutinized by those who lack neuropsychological expertise. The posthoc explanations offered tend to be highly complex yet vague, lack a basis in theory or existing evidence, and "rest on assumptions outside the mainstream of science" (Rosen & Davison, 2003, p. 303). Furthermore, across purple hat therapies, purported mechanisms identified by pioneers of purple hat therapies often demonstrate their own misunderstandings or (more cynically) misrepresentations of scientific concepts appropriated from a distinct scientific field (e.g., neuropsychology). Whether deliberate or accidental, the effect is one that impedes critical evaluation of the legitimacy of purported mechanisms.

Consider, for example, the narrative of Shapiro's (1989) serendipitous observation that when her "eyes were involuntarily moving in a multisaccadic manner when the disturbing thoughts arose. The thoughts disappeared completely and, if deliberately retrieved, were no longer upsetting" (p. 212). This observation led Shapiro to integrate eye movements into traumatic memory processing with clients (Shapiro, 1989), which resulted in the eventual development of the EMDR protocol (Shapiro, 1995). In this protocol, an EMDR "therapist elicits the saccadic eye movements by having patients visually track a finger rapidly waved back and forth in front of their face" (Feeny et al., 2007). While this might immediately raise a red flag for ophthalmologists, a psychologist may not realize that the eye movements involved in EMDR would be classified as smooth pursuit rather than saccadic, as saccadic eye movements are characterized as movements that occur in the absence of a moving visual stimulus (Westheimer, 1954). This likely unintentional misnomer highlights that Shapiro lacked any strong grasp of the concepts used to provide a posthoc theoretical justification for eye movements as a critical treatment component. Indeed, Shapiro (1989) recognized that the "basis for the effectiveness [of eye movements in EMDR] is, however, unclear" (p. 216) and pontificated that perhaps saccadic eye movements during traumatic memory recall restore "the neural balance" and reverse "the neural pathology" (p. 216). Because the proposed mechanism is vague, this allows for a wide array of neuropsychological findings (both structural and functional) to be misused as evidence supporting the use of eye movements in EMDR (see Landin-Romero et al., 2018 for review).

Summary and Conclusion

Purple hat therapies, such as EMDR, energy psychology, and binaural beats, focus on a pseudoscientific component of treatment which is the defining feature of the therapy. Although purple hat therapies also include evidence-based components, therapeutic change is attributed to the purple hat component specifically. For example, evidence from clinical trials for the efficacy of a purple hat therapy is often mistaken as supporting the therapeutic value of the purple hat component. Purple hat therapies provide an appealing solution for problems that are often complex and challenging to address.

Given that most people with mental health problems don't receive minimally adequate evidence-based treatment, it is reasonable to ask whether purple hat therapies pose any harm. In other words, if they work, does it matter *how* they work? We suggest several potential harms that could arise from the proliferation of purple hat therapies. First, purple hat therapies make it more confusing for potential patients who are trying to identify the treatment option that is most likely to work for them. This is especially true given how purple hat therapies are often marketed as being better, faster, and easier than mainstream treatments. Second, patients who try purple hat therapies and do not benefit will have wasted time, effort, and financial and other resources that may have been more fruitfully devoted to a first-line treatment. Such individuals may lose confidence in the potential benefits of mental healthcare in general, deterring future treatment seeking. Finally, by focusing on implausible pseudoscientific components, purple hat therapies can damage the reputation of clinical science and undermine the public's trust of mental health care.

Existing treatments for many mental health problems leave considerable room for improvement. Clinical innovation is needed to identify therapies that are more effective, efficient, tolerable, and helpful for more people. At the same time, proposed therapeutic innovations must be evaluated critically. Skepticism of new therapies is particularly important when the scientific plausibility of the proposed therapy is low, as is the case with purple hat therapies.

Eve A. Rosenfeld, PhD, is an advanced postdoctoral fellow at the National Center for PTSD, Dissemination and Training Division, at the VA Palo Alto Health Care System and at the Department of Psychiatry and Behavioral Sciences, Stanford University.

Carmen P. McLean, PhD, is a licensed clinical psychologist at the National Center for PTSD, Dissemination and Training Division, at the VA Palo Alto Healthcare System and a clinical associate professor (affiliated) at the Department of Psychiatry and Behavioral Sciences, Stanford University.

References

Bang, Y. R., Choi, H. yun, & Yoon, I.-Y. (2019). Minimal effects of binaural auditory beats for subclinical insomnia: A randomized double-blind controlled study. *Journal of Clinical Psychopharmacology, 39*(5), 499–503. 10.1097/JCP.0000000000001097

Bogdan, V., Balazsi, R., Lupu, V., & Bogdan, A. (2009). Treating primary insomnia: A comparative study of self-help methods and progressive muscle relaxation. *Journal of Cognitive and Behavioral Psychotherapies, 9*(1), 67–82.

Boudewyns, P. A., & Hyer, L. A. (1996). Eye Movement Desensitization and Reprocessing (EMDR) as Treatment for Post-Traumatic Stress Disorder (PTSD). *Clinical Psychology & Psychotherapy, 3*(3), 185–195. 10.1002/(SICI)1099-0879(199609)3:3<185::AID-CPP101>3.0.CO;2-0

Boudewyns, P. A., Stwertka, S. A., Hyer, L. A., Albrecht, J. W., & Sperr, E. V. (1993). Eye movement desensitization for PTSD of combat: A treatment outcome pilot study. *The Behavior Therapist, 16,* 29–33.

Cahill, S. P., Carrigan, M. H., & Frueh, B. C. (1999). Does EMDR Work? And if so, Why?: A Critical Review of Controlled Outcome and Dismantling Research. *Journal of Anxiety Disorders, 13*(1), 5–33. 10.1016/S0887-6185(98)00039-5

Callahan, R. (1985). *Five Minute Phobia Cure: Dr. Callahanas Treatment for Fears, Phobias and Self-sabotage.* Wilmington: Enterprise Publishing.

Callahan, R. J., & Callahan, J. (2000). *Stop the Nightmares of Trauma: Thought Field Therapy, the Power Therapy for the 21st Century.* Parenting Press Inc.

Callahan, R. J. (2001). The impact of Thought Field Therapy on heart rate variability. *Journal of Clinical Psychology, 57*(10), 1153–1170. 10.1002/jclp.1082

Choi, H., Bang, Y., & Yoon, I. (2020). 0505 insomnia: Entrapment of binaural auditory beats on subjects with insomnia symptoms. *Sleep*, *43*(Supplement_1), A193. 10.1093/sleep/zsaa056.502

Cuijpers, P., Veen, S. C. van, Sijbrandij, M., Yoder, W., & Cristea, I. A. (2020). Eye movement desensitization and reprocessing for mental health problems: A systematic review and meta-analysis. *Cognitive Behaviour Therapy*, *49*(3), 165–180. 10.1080/16506073.2019.1703801

Davidson, P. R., & Parker, K. C. H. (2001). Eye movement desensitization and reprocessing (EMDR): A meta-analysis. *Journal of Consulting and Clinical Psychology*, *69*(2), 305–316. 10.1037/0022-006X.69.2.305

De Niet, G., Tiemens, B., Lendemeijer, B., & Hutschemaekers, G. (2009). Music-assisted relaxation to improve sleep quality: Meta-analysis. *Journal of Advanced Nursing*, *65*(7), 1356–1364. 10.1111/j.1365-2648.2009.04982.x

Feeny, N. C., Stines, L. R., & Foa, E. B. (2007). Posttraumatic stress disorder—clinical. In G. Fink (Ed.), *Encyclopedia of Stress (Second Edition)* (pp. 135–149). Academic Press.

Feinstein, D. (2008). Energy psychology: A review of the preliminary evidence. *Psychotherapy: Theory, Research, Practice, Training*, *45*(2), 199–213. 10.1037/0033-3204.45.2.199

Feinstein, D. (2009). Facts, paradigms, and anomalies in the acceptance of energy psychology: A rejoinder to McCaslin's (2009) and Pignotti and Thyer's (2009) comments on Feinstein (2008a). *Psychotherapy: Theory, Research, Practice, Training*, *46*, 262–269. 10.1037/a0016086

Feng, F., Zhang, Y., Hou, J., Cai, J., Jiang, Q., Li, X., Zhao, Q., & Li, B. (2018). Can music improve sleep quality in adults with primary insomnia? A systematic review and network meta-analysis. *International Journal of Nursing Studies*, *77*, 189–196. 10.1016/j.ijnurstu.2017.10.011

Foa, E., Hembree, E. A., Rothbaum, B. O., & Rauch, S. (2019). Prolonged Exposure Therapy for PTSD: Emotional Processing of Traumatic Experiences - Therapist Guide. In *Prolonged Exposure Therapy for PTSD*. Oxford University Press. http://www.oxfordclinicalpsych.com/view/10.1093/med-psych/9780190926939.001.0001/med-9780190926939

Fox, L., & Malinowski, P. (2013). Improvement in study-related emotions in undergraduates following emotional freedom techniques (EFT): A single-blind controlled study. Energy Psychology: Theory, Research, and Treatment. *Energy Psychology: Theory, Research, and Treatment*.

Herbert, J. D., & Gaudiano, B. A. (2005). Moving from empirically supported treatment lists to practice guidelines in psychotherapy: The role of the placebo concept. *Journal of Clinical Psychology*, *61*(7), 893–908. 10.1002/jclp.20133

Hoppen, T. H., Jehn, M., Holling, H., Mutz, J., Kip, A., & Morina, N. (2022). *Psychological interventions for adult PTSD: A network and pairwise meta-analysis of short and long-term efficacy, acceptability and trial quality* (p. 2022.05.03.22274616). medRxiv. 10.1101/2022.05.03.22274616

Jeffries, F. W., & Davis, P. (2013). What is the role of eye movements in Eye Movement Desensitization and Reprocessing (EMDR) for Post-Traumatic Stress

Disorder (PTSD)? A review. *Behavioural and Cognitive Psychotherapy*, 41(3), 290–300. 10.1017/S1352465812000793

Jirakittayakorn, N., & Wongsawat, Y. (2017). Brain Responses to a 6-Hz Binaural Beat: Effects on General Theta Rhythm and Frontal Midline Theta Activity. *Frontiers in Neuroscience, 11.* https://www.frontiersin.org/articles/10.3389/fnins.2017.00365

Landin-Romero, R., Moreno-Alcazar, A., Pagani, M., & Amann, B. L. (2018). How Does Eye Movement Desensitization and Reprocessing Therapy Work? A Systematic Review on Suggested Mechanisms of Action. *Frontiers in Psychology, 9,* 1395. 10.3389/fpsyg.2018.01395

Lee, C. W., & Cuijpers, P. (2013). A meta-analysis of the contribution of eye movements in processing emotional memories. *Journal of Behavior Therapy and Experimental Psychiatry, 44,* 231–239. 10.1016/j.jbtep.2012.11.001

Lewis, C., Roberts, N. P., Andrew, M., Starling, E., & Bisson, J. I. (2020). Psychological therapies for post-traumatic stress disorder in adults: Systematic review and meta-analysis. *European Journal of Psychotraumatology, 11*(1), 1729633. 10.1080/20008198.2020.1729633

Lilienfeld, S. O. (2011). Distinguishing scientific from pseudoscientific psychotherapies: Evaluating the role of theoretical plausibility, with a little help from Reverend Bayes. *Clinical Psychology: Science and Practice, 18*(2), 105–112. 10.1111/j.1468-2850.2011.01241.x

Lohr, J. M., Lilienfeld, S. O., Tolin, D. F., & Herbert, J. D. (1999). Eye Movement Desensitization and Reprocessing: An analysis of specific versus nonspecific treatment factors. *Journal of Anxiety Disorders, 13*(1–2), 185–207. 10.1016/S0887-6185(98)00047-4

López-Caballero, F., & Escera, C. (2017). Binaural Beat: A Failure to Enhance EEG Power and Emotional Arousal. *Frontiers in Human Neuroscience, 11.* 10.3389/fnhum.2017.00557

On, F. R., Jailani, R., Norhazman, H., & Zaini, N. M. (2013). Binaural beat effect on brainwaves based on EEG. *2013 IEEE 9th International Colloquium on Signal Processing and Its Applications,* 339–343. 10.1109/CSPA.2013.6530068

Orozco Perez, H. D., Dumas, G., & Lehmann, A. (2020). Binaural beats through the auditory pathway: From brainstem to connectivity patterns. *ENeuro, 7*(2), ENEURO.0232-19.2020. 10.1523/ENEURO.0232-19.2020

Oster, G. (1973). Auditory beats in the brain. *Scientific American, 229*(4), 94–102. 10.1038/scientificamerican1073-94

Pignotti, M. (2005). Thought field therapy voice technology vs. random meridian point sequences: A single-blind controlled experiment. *The Scientific Review of Mental Health Practice, 4*(1), 38–47.

Rogers, S., & Silver, S. M. (2002). Is EMDR an exposure therapy? A review of trauma protocols. *Journal of Clinical Psychology, 58*(1), 43–59. 10.1002/jclp.1128

Rosen, G. M., & Davison, G. C. (2003). Psychology Should List Empirically Supported Principles of Change (ESPs) and Not Credential Trademarked Therapies or Other Treatment Packages. *Behavior Modification, 27*(3), 300–312. 10.1177/0145445503027003003

Shapiro, F. (1989). Eye movement desensitization: A new treatment for post-traumatic stress disorder. *Journal of Behavior Therapy and Experimental Psychiatry*, 20(3), 211–217. 10.1016/0005-7916(89)90025-6

Shapiro, F. (1995). *Eye movement desensitization and reprocessing: Basic principles, protocols, and procedures. 398 Pages. Price: $40.00.* New York: Guilford Press. 10.1080/00029157.1995.10403197

Sloan, D. M., Marx, B. P., Bovin, M. J., Feinstein, B. A., & Gallagher, M. W. (2012). Written exposure as an intervention for PTSD: A randomized clinical trial with motor vehicle accident survivors. *Behaviour Research and Therapy*, 50(10), 627–635. 10.1016/j.brat.2012.07.001

Valiente-Gómez, A., Moreno-Alcázar, A., Treen, D., Cedrón, C., Colom, F., Pérez, V., & Amann, B. L. (2017). EMDR beyond PTSD: A systematic literature review. *Frontiers in Psychology*, 8. https://www.frontiersin.org/article/10.3389/fpsyg.2017.01668

Vernon, D., Peryer, G., Louch, J., & Shaw, M. (2014). Tracking EEG changes in response to alpha and beta binaural beats. *International Journal of Psychophysiology*, 93(1), 134–139. 10.1016/j.ijpsycho.2012.10.008

Wadji, D. L., Martin-Soelch, C. & Camos, V. (2022). Can working memory account for EMDR efficacy in PTSD? *BMC Psychol*, 10, 245. 10.1186/s40359-022-00951-0

Waite, W. L., & Holder, M. D. (2003). Assessment of the emotional freedom technique: An alternative treatment for fear. *The Scientific Review of Mental Health Practice: Objective Investigations of Controversial and Unorthodox Claims in Clinical Psychology, Psychiatry, and Social Work*, 2(1), 20–26.

Westheimer, G. (1954). Mechanism of saccadic eye movements. *A.M.A. Archives of Ophthalmology*, 52(5), 710–724. 10.1001/archopht.1954.00920050716006

Young, C.-W., Tsai, C.-Y., Wang, L.-P., Chen, H.-W., & Ay, C. (2014, May 21). Investigate the effect of EEG for relaxation using binaural beats. *7 th International Symposium on Machinery and Mechatronics for Agriculture and Biosystems Engineering (ISMAB)*. http://www.brainisohertz.it/p/nuovi/INVESTIGATE%20THE%20EFFECT%20OF%20EEG%20FOR%20RELAXATION%20USING%20BINAURAL%20BEATS.pdf

10 Animal-Assisted Therapies

Kitti Bessenyei, Igor Yakovenko,
Lindsey Snaychuk, and
Andrew (Hyounsoo) Kim

By definition, animal-assisted interventions (AAI) "intentionally include or incorporate animals as part of a therapeutic or ameliorative process or milieu" (Fine, 2020, p. 22) and "rely on interactions with animals as the primary context for facilitating developmental change" (Sandbank et al., 2020, p. 5). Since the earliest definitions of AAIs coined in the 1980s by the Delta Society, professionals have begun to differentiate structured therapies referred to as animal-assisted therapy (AAT) from informal interventions called animal-assisted activities (AAA) in clinical settings (Delta, 1996). In AAT, a specifically trained animal is systematically incorporated in the therapy plan by a trained therapist in comparison to AAA, which solely offers the opportunity for clients to engage with the animal, often facilitated by volunteers (Ratschen & Sheldon, 2019).

AATs are widely accepted and often promoted by professionals as mental health treatments (Berget & Grepperud, 2011; Berget et al., 2013; Black et al., 2011; Pinto et al., 2017). This chapter will examine the claim that AAT is an effective treatment of mental health problems by summarizing the evidence that supports and does not support this claim. The chapter will place a special focus on pseudoscientific practices that undermine the use of AAT in evidence-based care and will articulate recommendations to increase the scientific approach and to make AAT more evidence-based. AAAs – that are not structured therapies and thus are not considered as mental health treatments – will not be discussed in this chapter.

Examining the Claims

The idea that human-animal interactions can affect health and wellbeing can be traced back to ancient Egypt (Fine, 2020). Despite a long-standing history of singular uses of animals in health, the first therapeutic use of animals is usually linked to Boris Levinson, a child psychologist in the 1960s (Levinson, 1969). While giving therapy to a withdrawn child,

DOI: 10.4324/9781003259510-13

Levinson observed that the child opened up and talked to his dog, Jingles. Consequently, he suggested the use of animals in psychotherapeutic settings and called for research on the benefits of using animals in psychotherapy (Levinson, 1978). As a follow-up, Sam and Elizabeth Corson at Ohio State University in the 1970s found that interactions with dogs made it easier for patients to communicate with others (Corson et al., 1977). These early experiments opened the door to consider the interactions with animals as being valuable in therapeutic environments and include animals in therapy sessions, which later led to the application of AAT in a wide array of settings, populations, and purposes (Fine, 2020).

AATs can be differentiated with respect to the animal incorporated in the therapy. While a variety of animals are used in AATs, dogs (canine-assisted therapy) and horses (equine-assisted therapy) are the most frequent (Ratschen & Sheldon, 2019; Veling et al., 2018). In addition, there are interventions that use virtual reality (Veling et al., 2018) or robots (Banks et al., 2008) to resemble the human-animal interaction.

Treatment for Specific Populations and Disorders

Across the variety of different kinds of populations and individuals targeted with AAT, older adults are perceived by some to benefit the most from AATs due to having less social opportunity and physical contact than other populations (Chang et al., 2021). Interventions for older adults often intend to improve loneliness, depression, cognitive and social functioning, with a special focus on people living in institutions (Chang et al., 2021; Jain et al., 2020). Children are another common target group for AATs mostly because of the belief that human-animal interactions may facilitate learning and development (Hoagwood et al., 2017). Benefits are usually expected in cognitive, social, and behavior domains of children and adolescents, with interventions often being delivered in educational settings (Hoagwood et al., 2017; Jones et al., 2019).

Of the various mental health problems for which AAT is used, the most popular targets include depression (Ambrosi et al., 2019), anxiety and stress (Ein et al., 2018), and trauma (M. E. O'Haire et al., 2015). There is also special interest in using AATs for autism in children (O'Haire, 2017; Sandbank et al., 2020) and for significant cognitive decline among older adults (Lai et al., 2019).

Research on the Efficacy of Animal-Assisted Therapies

Research on AATs has increased steadily in recent years (Charry-Sánchez et al., 2018; M. O'haire et al., 2015). Despite this, systematic reviews of the literature highlight major methodological limitations in the field

(Kamioka et al., 2014). Randomized controlled trials (RCTs) on AAT are limited, and few are considered high quality (Kamioka et al., 2014). Reviews on AAT across populations conclude that findings are mixed with highly variable effect sizes (Marino, 2012). It is also particularly difficult to draw broad conclusions when many studies do not have follow up data to determine if the effects were sustained. Despite low study quality, meta-analyses suggest that AATs overall appear to be deemed "generally favourable" (Charry-Sánchez et al., 2018; Kamioka et al., 2014).

There are some areas of support for AATs among children including autism spectrum disorder (ASD) (Borgi et al., 2016; O'Haire, 2017). One of the commonly assessed outcomes in children with ASD attending equine therapy is social interaction, which tends to increase in intervention groups exposed to AAT (O'Haire, 2017). However, notable limitations of this area of literature include the lack of formal ASD diagnosis amongst many samples, the lack of control groups, and the lack of randomization, which all impact study quality. Comparably, the use of canine therapy for trauma has been shown as one of the most promising outcomes (Hoagwood et al., 2017). However, results of studies on AATs for trauma are highly variable and the effects are unclear.

AAT for depressive symptoms tends to produce promising effects across various populations (Jain et al., 2020; Jones et al., 2019). The use of AAT with older adults is generally supported, with one study finding a large effect of canine-assisted therapy on depressive symptoms (Ambrosi et al., 2019). However, as many critics have highlighted, some degree of the effect may be simply related to participants' positive perceptions of animals (O'Haire et al., 2015). Engagement with animals is also associated with prosocial behavior (Jones et al., 2019), which has also been linked to reduced depressive symptoms (Flynn et al., 2015). Further, improvements may simply be attributed to behavioral activation rather than the use of an animal in therapy. Therefore, the claims that AAT have a direct effect on minimizing depressive symptoms may be inflated.

Multiple studies that evaluated the impact of AAT on depressive symptoms also measured symptoms of anxiety and results are mixed. One review suggests up to moderate sized effects for AAT on anxiety (Virués-Ortega et al., 2012), but in other studies, there were no changes in anxiety following AAT (Ambrosi et al., 2019).

One of the more novel forms of AAT is dolphin-assisted therapy (DAT), which has gained considerable media exposure (Marino & Lilienfeld, 2007). Despite strong claims, studies on the efficacy of DAT are highly variable and yield mixed results similar to other forms of AAT (Marino & Lilienfeld, 2007, 2021).

There are a number of alternative explanations to consider when examining the effects of AAT. One possible explanation for positive overall outcomes associated with AAT is that the animal may simply increase engagement with therapy. For example, one systematic review of AAT suggested high rates of participant retention (Jones et al., 2019). Further, research suggests that the use of an animal in treatment may foster a stronger therapeutic alliance (Spattini, 2018), which is one of the strongest predictors of favorable therapeutic outcomes (Flückiger et al., 2018).

Issues in the Development and Practice of Animal-Assisted Therapies

The mixed evidence for AAT may be due in part to the difficulties in developing and carrying out this type of therapy compared to therapies that do not involve animal welfare. One major issue in creating an AAT is choosing the appropriate animal (Fine et al., 2019). The process involves a variety of barriers that must be considered such as getting the animal certified physically and behaviorally (Fine et al., 2019). Much like with humans, a veterinarian who completes such an examination must be familiar not only with animal welfare, but also with the potential stressors and demands the animal may face as part of the therapy (Binfet et al., 2018). Therapy animal selection protocols have also highlighted that during development, handlers and therapists must ensure that the animal is not merely healthy and obedient, but that it seeks interaction with strangers and enjoys it without showing signs of fear or stress (Mongillo et al., 2015). As a result of the high standards recommended for the process of AAT, some researchers have emphasized that the practice of AAT deviates from the ideal since animals are often selected based on those that are available rather than those that meet a predetermined job description and behavioral criteria (Fine et al., 2019).

During the treatment itself, there are a variety of impacts on the animal that must be monitored. For example, some studies have reported increased signs of stress such as high cortisol levels in dogs after being used in therapy (King et al., 2011). Such stress may be due to a number of factors that must be all examined, such as who the handler is, the environment where the therapy occurs, and the therapeutic interaction itself (Fine, 2020). The multitude of practical issues that must be monitored and adhered to ensure a harmonious environment for the use of animals in therapy may present an untenable standard for most clinics or research studies, ultimately impacting the efficacy of the therapy or its scientific ethics.

The issues in the development and practice of AAT may also involve what most research ethical organizations would deem unscientific. Although there is no widespread evidence of unscientific practices and harms associated with AAT, the delivery and provision of animals for AAT has recently become a large business (Serpell et al., 2020). A recent large survey of 28 organizations who procure animals for AAT has found that the practices concerning animal welfare within them are highly variable and often border on alarming (Serpell et al., 2020). For example, only about half of the organizations surveyed imposed a time limit on the length of visits, suggesting that dogs could be made to engage in therapy for as long as needed without considering welfare. In addition, only a small minority of the survey responders protected the animals from disease transmission by prohibiting raw meat feeding and treats during AAT. While the evidence for it is limited, such unscientific and unethical practices combined with difficult issues in the development and application of AAT highlight why this type of therapy may be particularly challenging to practice safely and effectively.

Methodological Issues in the Research of Animal-Assisted Therapies

Systematic reviews and meta-analyses consistently cite the overall poor quality of the AAT literature and call for future studies to include a greater degree of methodological rigor. Despite the recommendations for stronger studies over the last decade (Kamioka et al., 2014; Marino, 2012; O'Haire et al., 2015), AAT research still suffers from a number of limitations and is generally deemed low quality (Hüsgen et al., 2022; Kamioka et al., 2014; Lai et al., 2019). Notably, one recent systematic review of canine-assisted therapy for children with behavioral and developmental disorders found only 3 studies out of the 14 included adhered to the quality guidelines laid out by the International Association of Human-Animal Interaction Organizations (IAHAIO) (Hüsgen et al., 2022), which are intended to protect the well-being of both the humans and animals involved in AAT.

While there is a general lack of RCTs evaluating AATs, even reviews focusing exclusively on AAT RCTs suggest that they are generally poor quality and subject to numerous limitations including threats to validity and weak study designs (H. Kamioka et al., 2014; Lai et al., 2019). Biases also exist in research on AAT, including performance bias, detection bias, and reporting bias, all of which were identified in 50–100% of studies included in a systematic review of RCTs on AAT for patients with significant cognitive decline (Lai et al., 2019).

The lack of a comparison group, or poorly designed comparison group (Waite et al., 2018), is another major limitation of many AAT studies. In one review of AAT for trauma, O'Haire and colleagues (2015) found that several studies relied solely on pre-post designs, and only half of studies utilized a comparison group. Given that some research suggests positive outcomes in both the intervention and control condition (Banks et al., 2008), findings from studies without a comparison group suggesting favorable results from AAT should be interpreted with caution as they could be at least partially attributed to placebo effects.

Additional limitations of the AAT research include a lack of theoretical framework (Marino & Lilienfeld, 2021), poor descriptions of the intervention (Hüsgen et al., 2022), and small sample sizes (Ein et al., 2018). It is also worth noting that even studies suggesting large effects of AAT tend to lack follow-up data and include interventions that are limited in scope (Waite et al., 2018). Together, these marked limitations call into question both the certainty and the validity of the observed effects of AAT (Marino, 2012).

Possible Harms

Direct harms associated with AAT are rarely reported in the literature. Kamioka and colleagues (Kamioka et al., 2014) found that the majority of RCTs on AAT did not provide any mention of whether any adverse events occurred. However, there are several considerations that are often overlooked. For example, animals used for AAT are not always well-regulated or trained, which may result in direct harm to the client (Bert et al., 2016). One review of AATs for older adults found that many studies did not indicate whether the animal involved in the intervention was properly certified (Chang et al., 2021). Bert and colleagues (2016) reviewed risk associated with AATs in hospital settings specifically and found that the primary adverse events were allergies, infections, and animal-related accidents. Despite this, most risk can be mitigated by proper and consistent hygiene protocols following each therapy session and animals involved in AAT should undergo regular examinations and health screenings (Bert et al., 2016).

Another consideration of potential harms associated with AAT is animal welfare, as more recent literature has called attention to the importance of ethical obligations (Fine & Griffin, 2022). Potential ethical concerns that may arise in animal welfare can include mistreatment of the animal from clients or staff, limited access to water, and high room temperatures (Hatch, 2007). These issues can ultimately lead to poorer outcomes for the client (O'Haire et al., 2015) and deterioration of the animal's health (Glenk, 2017). One review on AAT with dogs specifically found that there were a number of correlates associated with animal welfare such as the duration and frequency of AAT sessions and familiarity with the therapy recipient (Glenk, 2017). In other forms of AAT that use non-domesticated animals, such as DAT, the ethics of taking the dolphins from the wild and holding them captive are called into question (Marino & Lilienfeld, 2021). Fine and Griffin (2022) highlight the importance of adhering to ethical guidelines when working with AATs and have laid out specific models for clinicians to consider prior to initiating AAT.

Beliefs about Animal-Assisted Therapies

AATs have shown a steady growth in usage over the past several decades, reflecting an increasing popularity and acceptability among professionals (Linder et al., 2017). Existing evidence demonstrates that AATs are widely accepted by practitioners in different fields, including a variety of geographic locations such as Italy (Pinto et al., 2017), Norway (Berget & Grepperud, 2011; Berget et al., 2013), the United States (Thew et al., 2015), Spain (Perea-Mediavilla et al., 2014), and Australia (Black et al., 2011). For example, responding to an Italian survey, 94% of medical practitioners who knew of AATs supported the use with their patients (Pinto et al., 2017). Based on Norwegian data, almost 9 out of 10 mental health practitioners endorse that AAT should be used more in psychiatric treatment (Berget et al., 2013); between 56% and 87% believe to some or a high degree that AAT is effective depending on type of disorder and category of treatment effect (Berget & Grepperud, 2011). Similarly, 79% of students in American Psychological Association accredited clinical and counseling psychology programs in the United States endorse AAT as a legitimate adjunct to treatment, and 39% report being somewhat likely to very likely to practice AAT if properly trained (Thew et al., 2015).

Although most professionals see AATs as beneficial, psychologists who hold positive attitudes toward AAT tend to share the beliefs that it enhances the therapeutic relationship and is effective (Black et al., 2011); and psychology students also note that AAT may facilitate rapport and support client retention (Thew et al., 2015). Research studies also show that therapists' positive attitudes toward AAT are related to their personal experience with pets (Berget & Grepperud, 2011; Berget et al., 2013; Perea-Mediavilla et al., 2014; Pinto et al., 2017). Their positive beliefs also likely contribute to the positive bias in research that often leads to low-quality research results threatening the validity of conclusions that could be drawn based on research evidence (Lai et al., 2019). When asked, many professionals seem to lack awareness of the research evidence regarding AAT's efficacy (Black et al., 2011), while those who are aware of the lack of such evidence regard it as one of the obstacles for accepting AAT (Thew et al., 2015).

Understanding Beliefs

If AAT is not an evidence-based treatment for mental health problems, why do so many think it is or unequivocally believe that it can effect therapeutic change in mental health? The answer is a combination of lack of awareness of evidence and an emphasis on intuition and experience over science.

A series of well-established thinking errors known as cognitive biases and heuristics primarily contribute to the proliferation of dubious practices such as AAT (Garb & Boyle, 2015). Such biases include confirmatory bias (looking only at evidence that supports the belief that AAT works, but ignoring other evidence); overconfidence in one's opinion; and the availability heuristic, which describes the phenomenon of recalling only certain details clinically, which do not adequately describe the full experience (e.g., remembering only the positive effect of a dog in AAT and ignoring the neutral or negative effects). An additional complicating factor is that feedback about the scientific validity of one's practice and therapy is often non-existent in the real world – mental health professionals often do not receive feedback on the impact of their choices and decisions for therapy (Garb & Boyle, 2015). This is because getting such feedback would require collecting outcome and longitudinal data, which is often not practical in most therapeutic settings. Consequently, it is exceedingly easy for practitioners of AAT to never find out or know whether their patients recover or improve as a result of the therapy outside of the sessions or long term.

Lastly, some data have been published revealing that part of the explanation for the belief in AAT is simply lack of accurate knowledge and understanding of this type of therapy. A recent study from Canada of over 100 healthcare practitioners and a comparable group (comprised of the general public) reported that most of the participants had limited knowledge of AAT and how it works (Gardiner, 2021). In addition, there were no group differences on measures of understanding AAT or attitudes toward AAT between the healthcare practitioner group and the general public group. This limited data highlight that laypersons and medical professionals alike may simply not know much about AAT.

Summary and Conclusion

The chapter presented an overview of the history of animal-assisted interventions (AAIs) and the evidence for the efficacy of the structured version of such treatments called animal-assisted therapy (AAT). The reviewed data generally do not support AAT as an evidence-based therapy for mental health problems and at this stage, the practice risks entering pseudoscience territory. The existing evidence is fraught with methodological issues, and the positive findings from key areas such as AAT with older adults are overshadowed by bias and inconclusive evidence in most other areas. Compounding the issue is the potential for big ethical oversights and difficult practical barriers in employing animals in therapy, many of which are not adequately addressed in the field. Yet, AAT continues to be thought of by some as a positive and effective treatment for mental health problems, one that ought to be delivered alongside evidence-based treatments. The reasons for this are multifaceted, but may be due to lack of knowledge about AAT by both the general public and the healthcare providers, as well as cognitive errors and mental shortcuts prevalent in all clinicians who ignore evidence and leave them vulnerable to dubious practices. Perhaps the most prudent message on this topic is that animal companions often do inherently seem joyful and helpful, but the scientific and clinical mental health communities must remain vigilant in separating evidence-based treatment versus supportive, but ultimately unhelpful therapies.

Kitti Bessenyei, MA, is a clinical psychology doctoral student in the Department of Psychology and Neuroscience at Dalhousie University in Canada.

Igor Yakovenko, PhD, RPsych, is an assistant professor of clinical psychology and psychiatry in the Department of Psychology and Neuroscience and the Department of Psychiatry at Dalhousie University in Canada.

Lindsey Snaychuk, BA, is a clinical psychology master's student in the Department of Psychology at Toronto Metropolitan University in Canada.

Andrew (Hyounsoo) Kim, PhD, CPsych, is an assistant professor in the Department of Psychology at Toronto Metropolitan University in Canada. He is also an adjunct scientist at the University of Ottawa Institute of Mental Health Research at The Royal.

References

Ambrosi, C., Zaiontz, C., Peragine, G., Sarchi, S., & Bona, F. (2019). Randomized controlled study on the effectiveness of animal-assisted therapy on depression, anxiety, and illness perception in institutionalized elderly. *Psychogeriatrics,* 19(1), 55–64. 10.1111/psyg.12367

Banks, M. R., Willoughby, L. M., & Banks, W. A. (2008). Animal-assisted therapy and loneliness in nursing homes: use of robotic versus living dogs. *J Am Med Dir Assoc,* 9(3), 173–177. 10.1016/j.jamda.2007.11.007

Berget, B., & Grepperud, S. (2011). Animal-Assisted Interventions for psychiatric patients: Beliefs in treatment effects among practitioners. *European Journal of Integrative Medicine,* 3(2), e91–e96. 10.1016/j.eujim.2011.03.001

Berget, B., Grepperud, S., Aasland, O. G., & Braastad, B. O. (2013). Animal-Assisted Interventions and Psychiatric Disorders: Knowledge and Attitudes among General Practitioners, Psychiatrists, and Psychologists. *Society & Animals,* 21(3), 284–293. 10.1163/15685306-12341244

Bert, F., Gualano, M. R., Camussi, E., Pieve, G., Voglino, G., & Siliquini, R. (2016). Animal assisted intervention: A systematic review of benefits and risks. *Eur J Integr Med*, *8*(5), 695–706. 10.1016/j.eujim.2016.05.005

Binfet, J.-T., Silas, H. J., Longfellow, S. W., & Widmaier-Waurechen, K. (2018). When Veterinarians Support Canine Therapy: Bidirectional Benefits for Clinics and Therapy Programs. *Veterinary Sciences*, *5*(1), 2.

Black, A. F., Chur-hansen, A., & Winefield, H. R. (2011). Australian psychologists' knowledge of and attitudes towards animal-assisted therapy. *Clinical Psychologist*, *15*(2), 69–77. 10.1111/j.1742-9552.2011.00026.x

Borgi, M., Loliva, D., Cerino, S., Chiarotti, F., Venerosi, A., Bramini, M., Nonnis, E., Marcelli, M., Vinti, C., De Santis, C., Bisacco, F., Fagerlie, M., Frascarelli, M., & Cirulli, F. (2016). Effectiveness of a Standardized Equine-Assisted Therapy Program for Children with Autism Spectrum Disorder. *J Autism Dev Disord*, *46*(1), 1–9. 10.1007/s10803-015-2530-6

Chang, S. J., Lee, J., An, H., Hong, W.-H., & Lee, J. Y. (2021). Animal-Assisted Therapy as an Intervention for Older Adults: A Systematic Review and Meta-Analysis to Guide Evidence-Based Practice. *Worldviews on Evidence-Based Nursing*, *18*(1), 60–67. 10.1111/wvn.12484

Charry-Sánchez, J. D., Pradilla, I., & Talero-Gutiérrez, C. (2018). Animal-assisted therapy in adults: A systematic review. *Complement Ther Clin Pract*, *32*, 169–180. 10.1016/j.ctcp.2018.06.011

Corson, S. A., Arnold, L. E., Gwynne, P. H., & Corson, E. O. L. (1977). Pet dogs as nonverbal communication links in hospital psychiatry. *Comprehensive Psychiatry*, *18*(1), 61–72. 10.1016/S0010-440X(77)80008-4

Delta, S. (1996). *Standards of practice for animal-assisted activities and animal-assisted therapy*. Delta Society.

Ein, N., Li, L., & Vickers, K. (2018). The effect of pet therapy on the physiological and subjective stress response: A meta-analysis. *Stress Health*, *34*(4), 477–489. 10.1002/smi.2812

Fine, A. H. (2020). Handbook on animal-assisted therapy: foundations and guidelines for animal-assisted interventions. http://www.credoreference.com/book/estoat

Fine, A. H., Beck, A. M., & Ng, Z. (2019). The state of animal-assisted interventions: Addressing the contemporary issues that will shape the future. *International journal of environmental research and public health*, *16*(20), 3997.

Fine, A. H., & Griffin, T. C. (2022). Protecting Animal Welfare in Animal-Assisted Intervention: Our Ethical Obligation. *Semin Speech Lang*, *43*(01), 008–023.

Flückiger, C., Del Re, A. C., Wampold, B. E., & Horvath, A. O. (2018). The alliance in adult psychotherapy: A meta-analytic synthesis. *Psychotherapy (Chic)*, *55*(4), 316–340. 10.1037/pst0000172

Flynn, E., Ehrenreich, S. E., Beron, K. J., & Underwood, M. K. (2015). Prosocial Behavior: Long-Term Trajectories and Psychosocial Outcomes. *Soc Dev*, *24*(3), 462–482. 10.1111/sode.12100

Garb, H. N., & Boyle, P. A. (2015). Understanding why some clinicians use pseudoscientific methods: Findings from research on clinical judgment.

Gardiner, H. M. (2021). *How Animal-Assisted Therapy Is Understood and Perceived by Health Care Providers and the General Public in Canada* University of Windsor (Canada)].

Glenk, L. M. (2017). Current Perspectives on Therapy Dog Welfare in Animal-Assisted Interventions. *Animals: an open access journal from MDPI, 7*(2). 10.3390/ani7020007

Hatch, A. (2007). The View from All Fours: A Look at an Animal-Assisted Activity Program from the Animals' Perspective. *Anthrozoös, 20*(1), 37–50. 10.2752/089279307780216632

Hoagwood, K. E., Acri, M., Morrissey, M., & Peth-Pierce, R. (2017). Animal-Assisted Therapies for Youth with or at risk for Mental Health Problems: A Systematic Review. *Applied developmental science, 21*(1), 1–13. 10.1080/10888691.2015.1134267

Hüsgen, C. J., Peters-Scheffer, N. C., & Didden, R. (2022). A systematic review of dog-assisted therapy in children with behavioural and developmental disorders. *Advances in Neurodevelopmental Disorders*, 1–10.

Jain, B., Syed, S., Hafford-Letchfield, T., & O'Farrell-Pearce, S. (2020). Dog-assisted interventions and outcomes for older adults in residential long-term care facilities: A systematic review and meta-analysis. *Int J Older People Nurs, 15*(3), e12320. 10.1111/opn.12320

Jones, M. G., Rice, S. M., & Cotton, S. M. (2019). Incorporating animal-assisted therapy in mental health treatments for adolescents: A systematic review of canine assisted psychotherapy. *PloS one, 14*(1), e0210761–e0210761. 10.1371/journal.pone.0210761

Kamioka, H., Okada, S., Tsutani, K., Park, H., Okuizumi, H., Handa, S., Oshio, T., Park, S.-J., Kitayuguchi, J., & Abe, T. (2014). Effectiveness of animal-assisted therapy: A systematic review of randomized controlled trials. *Complementary therapies in medicine, 22*(2), 371–390.

Kamioka, H., Okada, S., Tsutani, K., Park, H., Okuizumi, H., Handa, S., Oshio, T., Park, S. J., Kitayuguchi, J., Abe, T., Honda, T., & Mutoh, Y. (2014). Effectiveness of animal-assisted therapy: A systematic review of randomized controlled trials. *Complement Ther Med, 22*(2), 371–390. 10.1016/j.ctim.2013.12.016

King, C., Watters, J., & Mungre, S. (2011). Effect of a time-out session with working animal-assisted therapy dogs. *Journal of Veterinary Behavior, 6*(4), 232–238.

Lai, N. M., Chang, S. M. W., Ng, S. S., Stanaway, F., Tan, S. L., & Chaiyakunapruk, N. (2019). Animal-assisted therapy for dementia. *The Cochrane Database of Systematic Reviews, 2019*(1), CD013243. 10.1002/14651858.CD013243

Lai, N. M., Chang, S. M. W., Ng, S. S., Tan, S. L., Chaiyakunapruk, N., & Stanaway, F. (2019). Animal-assisted therapy for dementia. *Cochrane Database of Systematic Reviews*(11).

Levinson, B. M. (1969). *Pet-oriented child psychotherapy*. Thomas.

Levinson, B. M. (1978). Pets and personality development. *Psychological Reports, 42*(3, Pt 2), 1031–1038. 10.2466/pr0.1978.42.3c.1031

Linder, D. E., Siebens, H. C., Mueller, M. K., Gibbs, D. M., & Freeman, L. M. (2017). Animal-assisted interventions: A national survey of health and safety policies in hospitals, eldercare facilities, and therapy animal organizations. *American journal of infection control, 45*(8), 883–887. 10.1016/j.ajic.2017.04.287

Marino, L. (2012). Construct Validity of Animal-Assisted Therapy and Activities: How Important Is the Animal in AAT? *Anthrozoös, 25*(sup1), s139–s151. 10.2752/175303712X13353430377219

Marino, L., & Lilienfeld, S. O. (2007). Dolphin-Assisted Therapy: More Flawed Data and More Flawed Conclusions. *Anthrozoös, 20*(3), 239–249. 10.2752/089279307X224782

Marino, L., & Lilienfeld, S. O. (2021). Third time's the charm or three strikes you're out? An updated review of the efficacy of dolphin-assisted therapy for autism and developmental disabilities [10.1002/jclp.23110]. *Journal of Clinical Psychology, 77*(6), 1265–1279. 10.1002/jclp.23110

Mongillo, P., Pitteri, E., Adamelli, S., Bonichini, S., Farina, L., & Marinelli, L. (2015). Validation of a selection protocol of dogs involved in animal-assisted intervention. *Journal of Veterinary Behavior, 10*(2), 103–110.

O'Haire, M. (2017). Research on animal-assisted intervention and autism spectrum disorder, 2012-2015. *Applied developmental science, 21*(3), 200–216. 10.1080/10888691.2016.1243988

O'Haire, M., Guérin, N., & Kirkham, A. (2015). Animal-Assisted Intervention for trauma: a systematic literature review [Review]. *Frontiers in Psychology, 6.* 10.3389/fpsyg.2015.01121

O'Haire, M. E., Guérin, N. A., & Kirkham, A. C. (2015). Animal-Assisted Intervention for trauma: a systematic literature review. *Frontiers in Psychology, 6,* 1121. 10.3389/fpsyg.2015.01121

Perea-Mediavilla, M. A., López-Cepero, J., Tejada-Roldán, A., & Sarasola, J. L. (2014). Intervenciones asistidas por animales y calidad de vida: expectativas en estudiantes universitarios españoles. *Escritos de Psicología (Internet), 7,* 10–18. http://scielo.isciii.es/scielo.php?script=sci_arttext&pid=S1989-38092014000300002&nrm=iso

Pinto, A., De Santis, M., Moretti, C., Farina, L., & Ravarotto, L. (2017). Medical practitioners' attitudes towards animal assisted interventions. An Italian survey. *Complement Ther Med, 33,* 20–26. 10.1016/j.ctim.2017.04.007

Ratschen, E., & Sheldon, T. A. (2019). Elephant in the room: animal assisted interventions. *Bmj, 367,* l6260. 10.1136/bmj.l6260

Sandbank, M., Bottema-Beutel, K., Crowley, S., Cassidy, M., Dunham, K., Feldman, J. I., Crank, J., Albarran, S. A., Raj, S., Mahbub, P., & Woynaroski, T. G. (2020). Project AIM: Autism intervention meta-analysis for studies of young children. *Psychol Bull, 146*(1), 1–29. 10.1037/bul0000215

Serpell, J. A., Kruger, K. A., Freeman, L. M., Griffin, J. A., & Ng, Z. Y. (2020). Current standards and practices within the therapy dog industry: Results of a representative survey of United States therapy dog organizations. *Frontiers in veterinary science, 35.*

Spattini, L., Giorgio, M., Raisi, F., Ferrari, S., Pingani, L., & Galeazzi, Gian M. (2018). Efficacy of animal assisted therapy on people with mental disorders: an update on the evidence. *Minerva Psichiatr, 59*(1), 54–66. 10.23736/s0391-1772.17.01958-6

Thew, K., Marco, L., Erdman, P., & Caro, B. I. (2015). Assessing Attitudes Towards Animal Assisted Therapy among Students and Faculty in American Psychological Association Accredited Programs. *Human-Animal Interact. Bull, 3*, 11–27.

Veling, W., Sjollema, M. J., & Brada, B. C. (2018). Reducing Impact of Stress in Patients with Psychiatric Disorders: A Pilot Study on the Effects of Swimming with Wild, Free Dolphins in Virtual Reality. *International journal of child health and human development, 11*, 183.

Virués-Ortega, J., Pastor-Barriuso, R., Castellote, J. M., Población, A., & de Pedro-Cuesta, J. (2012). Effect of animal-assisted therapy on the psychological and functional status of elderly populations and patients with psychiatric disorders: a meta-analysis. *Health Psychology Review, 6*(2), 197–221. 10.1080/17437199.2010.534965

Waite, T. C., Hamilton, L., & O'Brien, W. (2018). A meta-analysis of Animal Assisted Interventions targeting pain, anxiety and distress in medical settings. *Complement Ther Clin Pract, 33*, 49–55. 10.1016/j.ctcp.2018.07.006

Part IV
Special Topics

11 Child and Adolescent Psychology

Jaden Sangoi, Keaira Cox, and
Stephen Hupp

For over a century, developmentalists have created theories about the stages of childhood. For example, the book *Investigating Pop Psychology* (Hupp & Wiseman, 2023) includes a chapter focused on critically examining Freud's stages of psychosexual development (Axelrod & Vriesema, 2023). Everyone from Erik Erikson to Jean Piaget followed suit by theorizing about discrete stages of development, and every once in a while, a specific notion about a stage really seems to have encapsulated many people's beliefs about human child development. One such belief is the idea that most two-year-olds go through a "terrible twos" stage in which new terrible behaviors emerge such as whining, temper tantrums, and aggression. This idea was promoted by Arnold Gesell, who is often described as the first school psychologist. In fact, Gesell suggested that age two-and-a-half was actually the peak of terribleness and "the most exasperating age in the preschool period" (Gesell et al., 1943, p. 177). Perhaps Gesell was influenced by the thinking of his academic mentor, G. Stanley Hall, who also argued that a specific time during development was filled with specific challenges. However, Hall's suggested age range of turmoil was adolescence, which he famously described as a period of "storm and stress" (Hall, 1904). Overall, this chapter will examine the claims that most children go through the terrible twos and that most adolescents experience storm and stress.

Examining the Claims

Claim #1: Most Children Go Through the "Terrible Twos"

For many parents, the phrase "terrible twos" is something that may instill fear, anxiety, or apprehension. Anyone who has spent time around young children has likely experienced some temper tantrums. Conversations with parents may include stories of late nights, dramatic meltdowns, screaming matches, or broken toys. So, what *are* the terrible twos? Are they really that bad? Does every child go through this stage in their lives?

DOI: 10.4324/9781003259510-15

For parents concerned about their child going through a terrible twos stage, a quick internet search of "terrible twos" yields a wide variety of results, from magazine articles and family blogs, to columns and informational guides on healthcare websites. Attention-grabbing headlines like "Tips to Help You Survive Your Toddler's 'Terrible Twos'" (Cleveland Clinic, 2021) and "Terrible Twos: What to Expect, Plus 9 Tips to Get You Through It" (Christiano, 2019) are among the first listed online, targeting parents who are looking for guidance and support. Many of these websites offer a background into the "terrible twos," including common behaviors and tips on how to manage those behaviors. According to "What are the Terrible Twos?" (Iannelli, 2022), tips for parents include keeping a consistent sleep schedule, keeping snacks on hand, and offering limited choices to the child, among others. This specific site also offers strategies for dealing with tantrums, including redirecting the child's attention, ignoring problem behavior, and using time-outs for serious behaviors. Many of these types of webpages are written or reviewed by pediatricians or therapists. Many also include references and citations to studies that provide data about temper tantrums and methods for managing difficult behaviors.

Online bookstores are also flooded with books about the terrible twos. A plethora of parenting books can be easily found and follow a similar format to online blog posts and articles. Many of the book titles include phrases like "parent's survival guide" and "simple parenting solutions." Not only were parenting books about the terrible twos found in online bookstores, but so were a number of books targeted toward children. One children's book, *Sophie's Terrible Twos,* describes a two-year old cartoon mouse, who "wakes up on the wrong side of the crib" and has a terrible start to her birthday. She doesn't like her birthday outfit, birthday breakfast, or birthday presents. It's not until her grandma takes her for a walk to a costume store that her day turns around – they find a tiger costume so that she can dress up and better express all her terribleness (Wells, 2014).

Jay Hoecker, a pediatrician, writes that the extreme feelings, inappropriate behavior, and tantrums associated with the terrible twos are all a normal part of child development. One of the major challenges of this developmental period, writes Hoecker, is that children around this age are able to comprehend more speech than they can express themselves, which contributes to the frustration they face when trying to express themselves without success (Hoecker, 2022). Another pediatrician, Mary Wong, writes that the "gap between desire and ability can cause frustration, unruly behavior (like biting other children) and tantrums" (Cleveland Clinic, 2021).

While these young children are rapidly gaining the skills to better understand the words we say to them, they are yet unable to express their wants and needs in the same manner, which can lead to the stereotypical "terrible" behavior. A recent study found that expressive language is significantly associated with temper tantrums (Manning et al., 2019). The researchers found that toddlers aged 12 to 38 months old with less expressive language demonstrated more severe temper tantrums. Additionally, toddlers identified as "late talkers" also had more severe temper tantrums.

However, there is no distinct timeline in which infants start immediately acting out on their second birthday and then immediately comply with all requests on their third birthday. Rather, research shows that temper tantrums often occur between the ages of one to four years and beyond (Daniels et al., 2012). More specifically, research has shown that nearly 20% of two-year-olds, 18% of three-year-olds, and 10% of four-year-olds have at least one tantrum each day (Grover, 2008). The percentages between two-year-olds and three-year-olds are very similar. Another study found that 87% of one-year-olds and 91% of two-year-olds have at least one tantrum per month, hardly a substantial difference (Potegal & Davidson, 2003). Yet another study found that one-and-a-half-year-olds and two-and-a-half-year-olds have the same have the same amount of negative emotionality (Janson & Mathiesen, 2008), thus discrediting Gesell's idea that two-and-a-half was particularly terrible. Taken together, these studies show that there is no meaningful difference in the "terribleness" based on year of life in young children. Instead, the phrase "terrible twos" likely sticks around because it's catchy and rolls off the tongue. In reality, the terrible twos are an exaggeration and simplification of some of the new behaviors that emerge during this multi-year span.

Some parents may see the "terrible twos" as a precursor to a potential behavioral or psychological issue. They may worry that their child's newfound stubbornness and outbursts could lead to oppositional defiant disorder (ODD). For parents who believe their child's behavior is extreme, research has identified certain signs and behaviors to look out for, including tantrums that consistently involve some form of physical aggression, tantrums that occur many times a day, tantrums that last a long time, and an inability of the child to calm themselves down during a tantrum (Belden et al., 2008). Fortunately for these parents, there are evidence-based approaches such a parent behavior therapy (Kaminski & Claussen, 2017).

Claim #2: Most Adolescents Experience "Storm and Stress"

The belief that adolescence is filled psychological turmoil has been long-standing among many parents, pediatricians, and psychologists. To be sure, adolescence is a time of many changes, and it would be fair to assume that adolescents will struggle with some of those changes. However, the claim that most adolescents experience consistent "storm and stress" is worth further consideration. In order to evaluate the validity of this claim, we will take a three-fold approach examining different stereotypes about adolescence.

Do Most Adolescents Experience Substantial Disturbances in Their Mood?

One stereotype about adolescents that is perhaps most common above others is that they are "moody" and "hormonal." Other common descriptors include lazy, oppositional, selfish, depressed, emotional, and unstable. Frequent mood swings and unpredictable emotions fall into this description of adolescence as well; they can be pleasant in one moment, and rude and irritable in the next. They may be lending a helping hand after dinner and then make an incredibly hurtful retort without blinking an eye. Some parents may not want to come near their adolescent with a ten-foot pole when they're "in one of their moods."

Do most adolescents experience substantial disturbances in their mood? The notion that adolescents are moody, anxiety-ridden, and angsty is widespread throughout media, books, and even popular psychology. Many of the most popular movies and TV series featuring adolescence tend to typecast the same roles for its characters, with perhaps a slight twist now and again. Many characters include a bad teen from the wrong side of the tracks, a teacher's pet, a dumb jock, a popular airhead, and a quiet punk rocker. These stereotypes are present in many forms through pop culture; however, they are perhaps most famously portrayed in the movie *The Breakfast Club* (Hughes, 1985). Throughout the course of the movie, we learn that these five adolescents are much more than their stereotypes, and are in fact complex individuals with much more to offer. We also learn that for each of these adolescents, their lives are filled with turmoil.

According to the National Institute of Mental Health (NIMH), 14% of adolescents in the United States are affected by a mood disorder such as a major depressive disorder (National Institute of Mental Health [NIMH]). The prevalence of mood disorders was also found to be higher among females (18%) than males (11%). On a global scale, the World Health Organization (WHO) says that about 14% of youth (ages 10–19) experience some sort of mental health condition. More specifically, roughly 4% of adolescents in this age range experience an anxiety disorder, and around 2% experience a depressive disorder. Taken together, this data suggests that the majority of adolescents actually do not meet the diagnostic criteria for a mood disorder.

While interpreting this data, it's also important to distinguish between *symptoms* of a mood disorder (e.g., feeling depressed) and a clinical *diagnosis* of a mental illness (e.g., major depressive disorder). The words and phrases adults may use to characterize an adolescent as "depressed" do not always equate to the severity of symptoms that must be present to warrant a full diagnosis. For example, parents and teachers may use words like *lazy*, *unmotivated*, and *hormonal* to describe a teenager they think is depressed. However, to receive a diagnosis of major depressive disorder, one must present a number of symptoms which potentially include depressed mood, loss of interest or pleasure in activities, weight gain/loss, and fatigue, among others. Symptoms must also have been present more days than not over a minimum of two weeks. Additionally, the symptoms must cause significant distress or impairment in functioning (American Psychological Association [APA], 2022). While it's true that these characterizations of *lazy* and *unmotivated* can be a warning sign of a mood disorder, it is likely not the case for many adolescents.

Do Most Adolescents Engage in High Rates of Risky Behavior?

A second stereotype is that most adolescents regularly engage in risky behavior. When we think of risky behavior in adolescence, alcohol, drugs, and sex comes to mind. Many also consider vandalism and petty crimes (e.g., shoplifting) typical of adolescent behavior. Parents may be worried about the "types of kids" their adolescents hang out with, fearing that peers may offer their otherwise innocent and protected child a joint, a flask, or the opportunity to spray paint a wall behind their school. Youth entering middle school and high school are often exposed to new groups of people and are spending lots of time making new friends; it's natural that many parents would want to keep an eye on their children and those that surround them.

In the last decade, social media platforms have made it incredibly easy for adolescents to connect, post pictures, and share funny videos. While these platforms have their benefits, they have also come under scrutiny from parents, politicians, and news outlets. Although videos on TikTok include fun dances, cooking tutorials, and fun life hacks, there are also a large number of trends and *challenges*. Some of these challenges can be dangerous and even potentially deadly. A recent news article highlighted the story of two young adolescents who died as a result of the "blackout challenge" in which participants are encouraged to hold their breath until they pass out, after which a "euphoric" feeling is said to take over. According to NBC News, the blackout challenge has actually been circulating the internet since 1995, but has recently resurfaced due to the popularity of TikTok (Pargas, 2022). This is just one example of a dangerous online trend that has been put under the microscope of news outlets; others include the "Tide Pod challenge," where participants eat a laundry detergent pod, and the "penny challenge," where participants put a penny between a partially plugged-in charger and an electrical socket, meant to create a shower of sparks. While the incidents of injury and death are rare, concerned parents have taken action and put forth several petitions and lawsuits against platforms like TikTok, fighting for better regulation, transparency, and control over their children's online content (Faheid, 2021).

Do most adolescents engage in high rates of risky behavior? Let's consider data from the National Youth Risk Behavior Surveillance System (YRBSS) conducted by the CDC, which aims to provide ongoing data on health behaviors among high-school-aged students in the United States. Data is collected and published every two years in a Data Summary and Trends report, which summarizes findings and reports on trends from the last 10 years. Many themes were highlighted in this report based on data from 2021, including sexual behavior and high-risk substance use (CDC, 2023).

Regarding sex, 30% of high school students reported having ever had sex, 21% were currently sexually active (reported having had sexual intercourse in the past three months), and 33% used effective hormonal birth control. Some trends were reported to be decreasing, as those who reported ever having had sex was down 17% and those currently sexually active were down 13% from the previous decade. In addition, 52% of high school students reported having used a condom during their last sexual intercourse, although condom use was down 8% in the last decade (CDC, 2023). On the whole, fewer high school students reported engaging in sexual activity over the last 10 years, and over half used a condom.

Regarding substance use, 18% of high school students reported using an electronic vaping product in the last 30 days, which was down 7% from 2015 (data was not collected prior). In addition, 16% of students reported using marijuana in the last 30 days, down 7% from the previous decade, and 13% reported ever using select illicit drugs, down 6.5%. The CDC also reported that 12% of students had ever misused prescription opioids, and 6% misused prescription opioids in the last 30 days, both 1% lower than a few years prior (data had not been collected prior to 2017). Relatedly, 23% of high school students reported having drank alcohol in the past 30 days. Taken together, these trends show that less high school students are consuming alcohol and using drugs less compared to 10 years ago, and for each type of substance, the majority of high school students are abstaining.

Do Most Adolescents Have a Strained Relationship with Their Parents?

A third stereotype is that most adolescents have a strained relationship with their parents. Maybe you even remember a time from your own adolescents years when there was a strain on your relationship with your parent. Parents and adolescents have plenty of opportunities to dispute, no doubt. Homework, grades, going out with friends, dating, arguments with siblings, and responsibilities at home are just a few of the topics which can potentially cause disagreement.

Depictions of strained parent-adolescent relationships have been prevalent throughout books, movies, and television for decades. One of the more recent examples comes from the hit series *Modern Family*. While the popular family sitcom includes a multitude of relatable characters and interconnecting family dynamics, one theme that is consistent throughout the show is the relationship tension between Claire Dunphy and her oldest daughter, Haley. At the beginning of the show, Haley is beginning high school and finding herself butting heads with her mom. In one particular scene, Haley's mom tells her to stop saying the word "like" in every sentence. Voices rise and tensions escalate until the two are screaming while Haley's friend sits quietly to the side (Levitan, 2010). For many parents, this representation of the parent-adolescent dynamic, or more specifically the mother-daughter dynamic, may ring true for their own relationships.

Do most adolescents have a strained relationship with their parents? One large study found that an estimated 8% to 18% of 12-year-olds experience frequent (i.e., 10 or more times in the past 12 months) conflict with their parents (Parra-Cardona et al., 2017). In the same study, 16 to 29% of 17-year-olds experienced frequent conflict with their parents. While the number of parent-adolescent dyads that experience elevated conflict seems to increase throughout the adolescent years, it's important to put the numbers into perspective – less than one in five young adolescents have frequent clashes with their parents, and less than one in three older adolescents have frequent clashes.

Fortunately, for parents concerned about their adolescent's mood and behavior, there are several evidence-based treatments available. For depression, both cognitive-behavioral therapy and interpersonal psychotherapy are both well-established treatments (Weersing et al., 2017). For youth involved in the juvenile justice system, multisystemic therapy and functional family therapy are both well-established (McCart et al., 2022). Finally, for adolescent substance use both cognitive-behavioral therapy and ecological family-based treatment are both well-established treatment options (Hogue et al., 2018). Further, many of these treatments involve working on the parent–adolescent relationship.

Summary and Conclusion

Claims about the terrible twos and adolescent storms have been around for decades. Claims like these are part of larger trend in the developmental literature to identify specific stages in life. The nugget of truth about the terrible twos is that new challenging behaviors do often emerge in two-year-olds. However, there's nothing uniquely terrible about the age of two that doesn't also show up in many one-year-olds and three-year-olds. All children demonstrate some challenging behaviors across all years of their life, and for children that do demonstrate more significant challenging behaviors, parent behavior therapy is a good option for treatment. The nugget of truth about adolescent storms is that many adolescents do experience mood disturbances, risky behaviors, and strained relationships with their parents. However, the majority of adolescents don't experience the high levels of storm and stress on a regular basis, and several different evidence-based treatments are available for the adolescents who need them. For more discussion of the terrible twos, see the book *Great Myths of Child Development* (Hupp & Jewell, 2015) and for more about adolescent storms, see the book *Great Myths of Adolescents* (Jewell et al., 2019).

Jaden Sangoi, MS, is a doctoral student in the Clinical Science in Child and Adolescent Psychology program at Florida International University.

Keaira Cox, BS, is a master's student in the Clinical Child and School Psychology program at Southern Illinois University Edwardsville.

Stephen Hupp, PhD, is a professor of psychology at Southern Illinois University Edwardsville. Along with Cara Santa Maria, he is co-editor of the book *Pseudoscience in Therapy: A Skeptical Field Guide.*

References

American Psychiatric Association (2022). *Diagnostic and Statistical Manual of Mental Disorders* (5th ed., Text Revision). Author.

Belden, A. C., Thomson, N. R., & Luby, J. L. (2008). Temper tantrums in healthy versus depressed and disruptive preschoolers: defining tantrum behaviors associated with clinical problems. *The Journal of pediatrics, 152*(1), 117–122. 10.1016/j.jpeds.2007.06.030

Broadbent, E. (2017, October 14). *7 reasons threenagers are worse than the terrible twos.* Mommyish. Retrieved July 21, 2022, from https://mommyish.com/threenagers-worse-terrible-twos/

Canady V. A. (2021). CDC data finds sharp rise in suicide attempts among teen girls amid COVID-19. *Mental Health Weekly, 31*(24), 1–3. 10.1002/mhw.32836

Centers for Disease Control and Prevention. (2023). *Youth risk behavior survey: Data summary & trends report 2011–2021.* U.S. Department of Health and

Human Services. https://www.cdc.gov/healthyyouth/data/yrbs/pdf/YRBS_Data-Summary-Trends_Report2023_508.pdf

Christiano, D. (2019, February 25). *Terrible twos: What to expect, plus 9 tips to get you through it.* Healthline. Retrieved July 21, 2022, from https://www.healthline.com/health/parenting/terrible-twos

Cleveland Clinic. (2021, December 17). *Tips to help you survive your toddler's 'terrible twos'.* Cleveland Clinic. Retrieved July 21, 2022, from https://health.clevelandclinic.org/tips-help-you-survive-your-toddlers-terrible-twos/

Coffey, J. K., Xia, M., & Fosco, G. M. (2022). When do adolescents feel loved? A daily within-person study of parent–adolescent relations. *Emotion, 22*(5), 861–873. 10.1037/emo0000767

Daniels, E., Mandleco, B., & Luthy, K. E. (2012), Assessment, management, and prevention of childhood temper tantrums. *Journal of the American Academy of Nurse Practitioners, 24,* 569–573. 10.1111/j.1745-7599.2012.00755.x

Faheid, D. (2021, July 29). Parents are asking TikTok for access to the videos kids are watching. *NPR.* https://www.npr.org/2021/07/29/1022442198/parents-send-a-letter-to-tiktok-demanding-to-see-what-their-kids-see

Gesell, A., Ilg, F. L., & Ames, L. B. (1943). *Infant and Child In The Culture Of Today: The Guidance Of Development In Home And Nursery School.* Harper & Row.

Gregston, M. (2020, February 6). How to repair a broken relationship with your teen. *Parenting today's teens.* https://parentingtodaysteens.org/blog/healthy-relationship-teen/

Grover, G. (2008). Temper tantrums. In C. Berkowitz (Ed.), *Pediatrics: A primary care approach.* (pp. 199–201). W. B. Saunders.

Hall, G. S. (1904). *Adolescence: Its psychology and its relations to physiology, anthropology, sociology, sex, crime, religion, and education.* Appleton.

Hoecker, J. L. (2022, February 23). *Toddler angst: Why are the twos terrible?* Mayo Clinic. Retrieved July 21, 2022, from https://www.mayoclinic.org/healthy-lifestyle/infant-and-toddler-health/expert-answers/terrible-twos/faq-20058314

Hogue, A., Henderson, C. E., Becker, S. J., & Knight, D. K. (2018). Evidence base on outpatient behavioral treatments for adolescent substance use, 2014–2017: Outcomes, treatment delivery, and promising horizons. *Journal of Clinical Child & Adolescent Psychology, 47*(4), 499–526. 10.1080/15374416.2018.1466307

Hughes, J. (Director). (1985). *The Breakfast Club.* [Motion picture]. Universal Pictures.

Hupp, S., & Jewell, J. (2015). *Great myths of child development.* Wiley.

Hupp, S. , & Wiseman, R. (2023). *Investigating pop psychology: Pseudoscience, fringe science, and controversies.* Routledge Press.

Iannelli, V. (2022, January 10). *Helpful tips to manage the terrible twos.* Verywell Family. Retrieved July 21, 2022, from https://www.verywellfamily.com/terrible-twos-and-your-toddler-2634394

Janson, H., & Mathiesen, K. S. (2008). Temperament profiles from infancy to middle childhood: development and associations with behavior problems. *Developmental Psychology, 44*(5), 1314–1328.

Jewell, J., Prinstein, M., Axelrod, M., & Hupp, S. (2019). *Great myths of adolescence*. Wiley.

Kaminski, J. W., & Claussen, A. H. (2017). Evidence base update for psychosocial treatments for disruptive behaviors in children. *Journal of Clinical Child & Adolescent Psychology*, 46(4), 477–499. 10.1080/15374416.2017.1310044

Levitan, S. (Writer) & Hudlin, R. (Director). (2010, March 3). Fears (Season 1, Episode 16) [TV series episode]. In S. Levitan & C. Lloyd (Executive Producers), *Modern Family*. ABC.

Mahan, B. (2022, April 30). How to heal a strained parent-teenager relationship. *Additude*. https://www.additudemag.com/parent-teenager-relationship-building-strategies/

Manning, B. L., Roberts, M. Y., Estabrook, R., Petitclerc, A., Burns, J. L., Briggs-Gowan, M., ... & Norton, E. S. (2019). Relations between toddler expressive language and temper tantrums in a community sample. *Journal of Applied Developmental Psychology*, 65, 101070. 10.1016/j.appdev.2019.101070

McCart, M. R., Sheidow, A. J., & Jaramillo, J. (2022). Evidence base update of psychosocial treatments for adolescents with disruptive behavior. *Journal of Clinical Child & Adolescent Psychology*, 1–28. 10.1080/15374416.2022.2145566

National Institute of Mental Health. (n.d.). *Any mood disorder*. https://www.nimh.nih.gov/health/statistics/any-mood-disorder

Pargas, S. (2022, July 10). Parents, beware of these 5 dangerous TikTok challenges on your child's 'for you' page. *NBC 6 South Florida*. https://www.nbcmiami.com/news/local/parents-beware-of-these-5-dangerous-tiktok-challenges-on-your-childs-for-you-page/2800166/

Parra-Cardona, Yeh, H.-H., & Anthony, J. C. (2017). Epidemiological research on parent-child conflict in the United States: subgroup variations by place of birth and ethnicity, 2002–2013. *PeerJ (San Francisco, CA)*, 5, e2905–e2905. 10.7717/peerj.2905

Pickhardt, C. (2013). *Surviving your child's adolescence: how to understand, and even enjoy, the rocky road to independence*. Wiley. Print.

Potegal, M., & Davidson, R. J. (2003). Temper tantrums in young children: 1. Behavioral composition. *Journal of Developmental & Behavioral Pediatrics*, 24(3), 140–147. 10.1097/00004703-200306000-00002

Rinaldi, C. M., & Howe, N. (2012). Mothers' and fathers' parenting styles and associations with toddlers' externalizing, internalizing, and adaptive behaviors. *Early Childhood Research Quarterly*, 27(2), 266–273. 10.1016/j.ecresq.2011.08.001

Rodgers, L. (2021, August 23). *How to handle the terrible twos*. What to Expect. Retrieved July 21, 2022, from https://www.whattoexpect.com/toddler-behavior/terrible-twos.aspx

Silva, K., Ford, C. A., & Miller, V. A. (2020). Daily Parent-Teen Conflict and Parent and Adolescent Well-Being: The Moderating Role of Daily and Person-Level Warmth. *Journal of youth and adolescence*, 49(8), 1601–1616. 10.1007/s10964-020-01251-9

Weersing, V. R., Jeffreys, M., Do, M. C. T., Schwartz, K. T., & Bolano, C. (2017). Evidence base update of psychosocial treatments for child and adolescent depression. *Journal of Clinical Child & Adolescent Psychology, 46*(1), 11–43. 10.1080/15374416.2016.1220310

Wells, R. (2014). *Sophie's Terrible Twos*. Penguin.

World Health Organization. (2021). *Adolescent mental health*. https://www.who. int/news-room/fact-sheets/detail/adolescent-mental-health

12 Alternative Medicine

Edzard Ernst

"Alternative medicine" is often described as "any of various systems of healing or treating disease (such as chiropractic, homeopathy, or faith healing) not included in the traditional medical curricula" (Merriam-Webster Dictionary, n.d.). For a comprehensive list of alternative medicine examples, see my book *Alternative Medicine: A Critical Assessment of 202 Modalities, 2nd Edition* (Ernst, 2022). For this chapter, I'll open with a brief description of a somewhat smaller number of examples:

- **Acupuncture** involves the insertion of needles into the skin and underlying tissues at acupuncture points for therapeutic or preventative purposes. Traditional acupuncture is mainly based on Taoist philosophy. Western acupuncturists believe that acupuncture is based on neurophysiological concepts.
- **Alexander technique** is a treatment that focusses on the patients' posture.
- **Anthroposophic medicine** is based on the mystical concepts of Rudolf Steiner. Various treatments are employed by anthroposophic doctors who use a holistic approach to understand disease.
- **Aromatherapy** employs "essential" oils usually combined with gentle massage; less commonly the oils are applied via inhalation.
- **Bach flower remedies** are based on the notion that all diseases are due to emotional imbalances which can be corrected with 1 of the 38 highly diluted remedies.
- **Bowen technique** involves manual mobilizations by a therapist, called "Bowen moves," over muscles, tendons, nerves, and fascia.
- **Chiropractic** was developed over a century ago by Daniel David Palmer. The hallmark therapy of chiropractors is spinal manipulation which, they believe, is necessary to adjust "subluxations."
- **Crystal healing** uses the alleged power of crystals to stimulate the self-healing properties of the body.

DOI: 10.4324/9781003259510-16

- **Cupping** originates from several cultures. Dry cupping involves one or more vacuum cups being applied over the intact skin; the vacuum is usually is strong enough to cause bruising. In wet cupping, the skin is scratched prior to applying the vacuum which allows blood to be sucked into the cup.
- **Detox** is an umbrella term for numerous approaches that allegedly rid the body of toxins.
- **Dowsing** is a method of problem-solving that uses a motor automatism, amplified through a pendulum, divining rod, or similar device. The best-known from of dowsing is probably water-divining (e.g., finding water wells with the help of a dowsing rod), but it is also used as a diagnostic technique.
- **Emotional Freedom Technique** is alleged to work by releasing blockages within the energy system which are thought to be the source of emotional intensity and discomfort. The treatment is similar to acupuncture but involves the use of fingertips rather than needles.
- **Energy healing** is an umbrella term for several approaches that rely on the use of "energy" (i.e., vital force). Examples include Reiki, Therapeutic Touch, and Johrei healing.
- **Gerson therapy** includes a starvation diet of raw foodstuff and coffee enemas and is used mostly, but not exclusively, to treat cancer.
- **Herbal medicine** (or phytotherapy) is the medicinal use of preparations that contain exclusively plant material.
- **Homeopathy** is a therapeutic method using extremely diluted substances whose effects, when administered to healthy subjects, correspond to the manifestations of the disorder in the individual patient.
- **Iridology** is a diagnostic method based on the belief that discolorations on specific spots of the iris of a patient provide diagnostic clues as to the health of organs.
- **Manual therapies** are treatments performed by therapists with their hands. Examples include chiropractic, massage, osteopathy, shiatzu, or Bowen technique.
- **Naturopathy** is a type of health care which employs what nature provides (e.g., herbal extracts, manual therapies, heat and cold, water, and electricity) for stimulating the body's ability to heal itself.
- **Osteopathy** is a manual therapy involving manipulation of the spine and other joints as well as mobilization of soft tissues.
- **Reflexology** employs manual pressure to specific areas of the body, usually the feet, which are claimed to correspond to internal organs with a view of generating positive health effects.
- **Reiki** is a Japanese approach where the therapist claims to channel life energy into the patient's body which allegedly stimulates self-healing abilities.

- **Shiatsu** is a Japanese approach where the therapists use their fingers to apply pressure to certain points of the body.
- **Spinal manipulation** is the term used for the manual adjustments of subluxations of the vertebrae often employed by chiropractors and osteopaths.
- **Therapeutic Touch** is a form of energy healing where the therapist claims to channel life energy into the patient's body which is said to stimulate self-healing abilities.
- **Traditional Chinese Medicine** is a diagnostic and therapeutic system based on the Taoist philosophy of Yin and Yang. It includes approaches that emerged from China, including acupuncture, herbal medicine, tui-na (Chinese massage), tai chi, and diet.

Examining the Claims

After having researched this area for more than 30 years, I consider "alternative medicine" a nonsensical term and I therefore tend to avoid it. If there is good evidence that a treatment or diagnostic method is effective, it clearly does not belong under this umbrella but must fall under the purview of evidence-based practice. If a treatment or diagnostic method does not work, it cannot possibly serve as an alternative to anything. The term "alternative medicine" is, however, commonly used and therefore cannot be easily abandoned completely. As a solution to this conundrum, I have long suggested a compromise and employ a term to account for this situation: So-called alternative medicine (SCAM; Ernst, 2018a).

As described above, the vast area of SCAM includes a diverse array of modalities. Currently, between 30% and 70% of the general population have used at least one type of SCAM during the preceding year; for patient populations, those figures can be considerably higher. One reason for this popularity is that powerful lobby-groups promote SCAM and advocate its further integration into conventional health care. Yet, the basic assumptions of many forms of SCAM are not plausible—that is, they contradict the laws of nature as we understand them today. The effectiveness of most forms of SCAM is unsupported by evidence, in some cases even disproven. Contrary to many claims by SCAM providers, most forms of SCAM are not free of risks.

In this chapter, I will focus on three issues: the ethics of SCAM, the risks of SCAM, and the integration of SCAM into conventional medicine. This involves the examination of the following, commonly-made claims: 1) SCAM is an ethical form of health care, 2) SCAM does not cause significant harm, and 3) integration of SCAM is in the interest of patient care.

Claim #1: SCAM Is an Ethical Form of Health Care

Medical ethics comprise a set of rules and principles which are essential for all aspects of medicine. The main issues are (Ernst & Smith, 2018):

- Respect for autonomy (e.g., patients must have the right to refuse or choose their treatments).
- Beneficence (e.g., researchers and clinicians must act in the best interest of the patient).
- Non-maleficence (e.g., the expected benefits of interventions must outweigh their risks).
- Justice (e.g., the distribution of health resources must be fair).
- Respect for persons (e.g., patients must be treated with dignity).
- Truthfulness and honesty (e.g., informed consent is an essential element in research and clinical practice).

While ethical principles have long been accepted in conventional health care, they are often neglected in SCAM. It is therefore timely to ask, how much of SCAM abides by the rules of medical ethics?

The subject is, of course, complex, but for the purpose of this chapter, I have selected three areas where ethical principles are violated with regularity: nonsensical research, the biased researcher, and informed consent.

Nonsensical Research

Nonsensical research is an investigation that lacks a plausible hypothesis. Arguably, most research into SCAM is of this nature. At best, nonsensical research is a waste of precious resources; at worst, it violates the beneficence principle. Both scenarios are unethical.

More often than not, nonsensical research takes the guise of a survey. For instance, SCAM researchers might opt to conduct a survey aimed at finding out how many mental health patients use SCAM. They put together a few questions and design a questionnaire. Subsequently, the investigators might get one or two hundred responses from patients attending various mental health clinics. They then calculate simple descriptive statistics and demonstrate that a particular percentage use SCAM. This finding eventually gets published in one of the many SCAM journals.

Such surveys possess none of the features that would render them sensible scientific investigations: They lack an accepted definition of what is being surveyed. There is no generally accepted definition of SCAM, and even if the researchers address specific therapies, they run into huge problems. The questionnaires used for such surveys are rarely validated which means that we cannot even be sure what precisely they evaluate. Enthusiastic researchers of SCAM usually use a small convenience sample of participants for their surveys. Consequently, there is no way the survey is representative of the population in question. The typical survey has a low or even unknown response rate. This means that selection bias would invalidate any findings. These investigations are thus regrettably counter-productive because:

- they tend to grossly over-estimate the popularity of SCAM,
- they distract money, labor, and attention from the truly important research questions in this field,
- they give a false impression of a buoyant research activity in SCAM,
- and their results are constantly misused.

The last point is important, as all too often the findings are used for SCAM promotion of pseudoscientific assessments and treatments. For example, findings might show that a large percentage of mental health patients use SCAM, pay for SCAM out of their own pockets, and are satisfied with it, leading to conclusions that SCAM is beneficial and should be made available to all mental health patients free of charge.

But there are many other ways to conduct nonsensical SCAM research to mislead the public. Take for instance the plethora of "pragmatic" trials which are currently popular in SCAM. They can be designed in such a way that their results must produce what the researchers intended to show; the "A+B versus B" study design is a prominent example of this type of abuse (Ernst & Lee, 2008). Or take the plethora of pilot studies that generate a seemingly positive outcome and are never followed up by a definitive trial (Ernst, 2018b). The list of ways of conducting nonsensical and hence unethical research in SCAM is endless.

Nonsensical research abuses the willingness of patients to participate by misleading them that it is a worthwhile sacrifice. In SCAM, it usually is little more than an attempt to generate findings that mislead us all into believing SCAM is fine. Moreover, it gives science a bad name and can lead to patients' unwillingness to take part in further important research. The damage done by nonsensical SCAM research projects can, in my view, not be overestimated.

The Biased Researcher

Nonsensical research would not be possible if it were not for such an abundance of deeply biased researchers investigating SCAM. These are in-dividuals who are foremost advocates of SCAM and employ research to promote it. On my blog (https://edzardernst.com/), I have created the (sar-castically named) "Hall of Fame." It is reserved for researchers who made a career out of investigating an area of SCAM and who, during their career, managed to publish nothing but positive results for their pet therapy. It might not come as a surprise that my "Hall of Fame" is densely populated.

If unbiased researchers test the efficacy of an intervention, they are bound to produce mixed results. This would be the case even if the treatment in question works well – no therapy works all the time in all situations and for all conditions. If a researcher who spent many years testing SCAM publishes nothing but positive findings, then this is a pseudoscientific warning sign, particularly if the assessment or treatment under investigation lacks scientific plausibility.

After observing many such cases, I have come to the conclusion that many SCAM researchers have a quasi-religious belief in SCAM. They therefore conduct their studies in order to confirm their convictions about the value of the therapy in question. This approach is, however, an unethical abuse of science; after all, science is not a tool for confirming opinions but one for testing hypotheses.

It is my view that SCAM researchers whose work is biased to the extent that it promotes untruth have either failed to enlighten themselves as to the facts, or have chosen to deliberately deceive. In either case, they are in breach of ethical standards that demand both truthfulness and awareness of the facts.

Informed Consent

Informed consent is an essential precondition for any health care practice. It requires the clinician giving the patient full information about the condition and the possible treatments. Amongst other things, the following information may be needed:

- the nature and prognosis of the condition,
- the evidence regarding the efficacy and risks of the proposed treatment,
- the evidence regarding alternative options.

Depending on the precise circumstances of the clinical situation, the patient's consent can be given either in writing or verbally. Not obtaining any form of informed consent is a violation of the most fundamental ethics of health care. However, in SCAM, informed consent is woefully neglected. This may have more than one reason:

- SCAM practitioners have frequently no adequate training in medical ethics,
- there is no adequate regulation and control of SCAM practitioners,
- SCAM practitioners have conflicts of interest and might view informed consent as commercially counter-productive.

To illustrate, I will briefly outline two hypothetical scenarios from the realm of "energy healing." Specifically, I will discuss the virtual case of a patient with depression consulting a Reiki healer for alleviation of their symptoms. I should stress that I have chosen Reiki merely as an example – the issues outlined below also apply to most other forms of SCAM.

Scenario 1. Our patient has experienced lethargy, anxiety, as well as depression and has heard from a friend that Reiki healers are able to help these kinds of mental health concerns. The patient consults a Reiki healer highly recommended in their local area. The practitioner has no medical or formal mental health training and has been taught that Reiki can help patients with any type of illness. The practitioner explains that Reiki uses a holistic approach. By allegedly channelling healing energy into the patient's body, they are confident they can stimulate healing, which will naturally ease the patient's problems. No conventional diagnosis is discussed, nor is there any mention of the prognosis, likelihood of benefit, risks of treatment, and alternative therapeutic options.

Scenario 2. Our patient consults a Reiki healer who had previously been trained as a nurse. The practitioner takes a medical history and conducts a thorough examination of our patient, suggesting that the patient might be suffering from depression and explains that this condition needs to be investigated and treated with conventional means and not with any form of SCAM. The practitioner thus writes a brief note and urges the patient to give it to his general practitioner.

One could think of many more scenarios but the two seem to cover a realistic spectrum of what a patient might encounter in real life. It seems clear, that the Reiki healer in scenario 1 failed dismally regarding informed consent. In other words, only scenario 2 describes a behavior that is ethically acceptable. But how likely is scenario 2? I fear that it would be an extremely rare turn of events. Even if well-versed in both medical ethics and scientific evidence, a SCAM practitioner might think twice about providing all the information required for informed consent – because, as scenario 2 demonstrates, fully informed consent essentially prevents a patient from agreeing to be treated by a SCAM practitioner. In other words, SCAM practitioners have a powerful conflict of interest that discourages them to adhere to the rules of informed consent.

Claim #2: SCAM Does Not Cause Significant Harm

Contrary to what is often claimed, the use of SCAM may cause direct harm to patients. As there is no system to monitor adverse events in SCAM, the frequency of adverse events caused by SCAM is unknown (Ernst, 2007). More importantly, SCAM regularly causes harm through patients choosing to forego evidence-based treatments. A topical example

Table 12.1 Direct Adverse Effects of Some Forms of SCAM

Treatment	Known Adverse Effects of a Serious Nature
Acupuncture	Pneumothorax, cardiac tamponade, infections, death
Aromatherapy	Allergic reactions
Chiropractic	Stroke, bone fracture, paralysis, disc prolapse, death
Cupping	Hematoma, infections
Gerson therapy	Malnutrition, loss of quality of life, death
Herbal medicine	Liver damage, other organ damage, cancer, death
Osteopathy	Stroke, paralysis, disc prolapse

would be the anti-vaccination views expressed by many SCAM practitioners (Li et al., 2018). The risks of SCAM are thus diverse (Ernst & Lee, 2008) and might be summarized as follows:

- direct harm due to adverse effects of SCAM (see Table 12.1);
- direct harm due to interactions of SCAM with prescribed medicines;
- direct harm through the use of bogus diagnostic techniques (Ernst & Hentschel, 1995);
- direct harm to animals by using ingredients taken from endangered species;
- indirect harm through incompetent advice such as recommendation to discontinue prescribed medications;
- indirect harm due to employing SCAM instead of an effective therapy for a serious mental health condition;
- indirect harm due to medicalizing trivial states of reduced well-being;
- indirect harm through reducing the public's confidence in evidence-based medicine;
- indirect harm caused by undermining rational thinking in society;
- indirect harm caused by inhibiting medical progress and research;
- financial harm due to the often considerable costs of SCAM.

Claim #3: Integration of SCAM Is in the Interest of Patients

In recent years, SCAM supporters have tried hard to include more and more SCAM into routine health care. They do this under the banner of integrated medicine (UK) or integrative medicine (US). One of the most prominent and influential defenders of integrated medicine (IM) is Charles III. In his 2006 address to the WHO, Charles explained: "We need to harness the best of modern science and technology, but not at the expense of losing the best of what complementary approaches have to offer. That is integrated health – it really is that simple."

There are several academic "definitions" of IM, and the original principle of "THE BEST OF BOTH WORLDS" has been modified considerably, for example:

- IM is a "comprehensive, primary care system that emphasizes wellness and healing of the whole person" (Bell et al., 2002, p. 134).
- IM "views patients as whole people with minds and spirits as well as bodies and includes these dimensions into diagnosis and treatment" (Rees & Weil, 2001, p. 119).
- IM is a "holistic, evidence-based approach which makes intelligent use of all available therapeutic choices to achieve optimal health and resilience for our patients" (College of Medicine and Integrated Health, 2015, para. 2).

All these "definitions" are, of course, highly problematic. For the purpose of this chapter, I would like to analyze merely the last one proposed by the UK College of Medicine and Integrated Health:

1 IM is holistic. Holism has always been at the core of any type of good health care. To state that IM is holistic misleads people into believing that conventional medicine is not holistic. It also pretends that health care might become more holistic through the addition of SCAM.
2 IM is evidence based. This assumption is simply not true. If we look what is being used under the banner of IM, we find no end of treatments that are not supported by good evidence, as well as several for which the evidence is squarely negative.
3 IM is intelligent. The erroneous implication here is that conventional medicine is unintelligent.
4 IM uses all available therapeutic choices. This is the crucial element of this definition, which allows IM proponents to employ anything they wish. This line of thinking is ethical flawed insofar as responsible health care is about applying the most effective therapies for the condition at hand, not recommending a limitless amount of therapies, some of which are pseudoscientific and inappropriate.
5 IM aims at achieving optimal health. Another straw-man; it implies that conventional health care professionals do not want to restore their patients to optimal health.

A critical evaluation of IM arrives at the following conclusions:

- Proponents of IM mislead us with their very own, nonsensical terminology and "definitions."
- They mainly promote two principles: use of SCAM and holism.

- Holism is at the heart of all good health care; IM is at best an unnecessary distraction.
- Using holism to promote SCAM is dishonest and counter-productive.
- The integration of SCAM will render health care not better but worse.
- IM flies in the face of common sense and medical ethics.
- IM is a disservice to patients.

So, on the basis of these mostly theoretical considerations, IM is a superfluous, misleading, and counterproductive distraction. But the most powerful argument against IM is an entirely practical one: namely the nonsensical, bogus, and potentially dangerous interventions that are happening every day in its name and under its banner.

If we look around us, go on the internet, read the relevant literature, or simply walk into an IM clinic within our neighborhood, we are sure to find behind the smoke screen of politically correct slogans of holism and "best of all worlds" the face of pure quackery. If you don't believe me, please go and look for yourself. I promise you will discover any unproven and disproven SCAM that you can think of, anything from crystal healing to Reiki, and from homeopathy to urine therapy. IM is a front of ill-defined concepts behind which boundless quackery and bogus treatments that are being promoted in the name of patient care.

Summary and Conclusion

In this chapter, I have briefly discussed three aspects of SCAM: ethics, harm, and integration. I have shown that, in the realm of SCAM, ethical standards often are flagrantly neglected. I have discussed that, contrary to common opinion, SCAM can cause significant harm in multiple ways. Finally, I have demonstrated that IM is little more than an attempt to bring more SCAM into routine health care which can ultimately undermine its effectiveness. The inescapable conclusion is that SCAM is not in the best interest of patients or consumers.

Edzard Ernst, MD, PhD, is an emeritus professor at the University of Exeter in the United Kingdom. He is author of the book, *Don't Believe What You Think: Arguments for and against SCAM.*

References

Bell, I. R., Caspi, O., Schwartz, G. E., Grant, K. L., Gaudet, T. W., Rychener, D., Maizes, V., & Weil, A. (2002). Integrative medicine and systemic outcomes research: issues in the emergence of a new model for primary health care. *Archives of Internal Medicine, 162*(2), 133–140.

College of Medicine and Integrated Health (2015). Seminar: Cardiovascular health from an integrated medicine perspective. Retrieved from https://collegeofmedicine.org.uk/seminar-cardiovascular-health-from-an-integrated-medicine-perspective/

Ernst E. (2007). 'First, do no harm' with complementary and alternative medicine. *Trends in Pharmacological Sciences, 28*(2), 48–50.

Ernst, E. (2018a). *SCAM: So-called Alternative Medicine.* Societas.

Ernst, E. (2018b). 'Pilot studies' of alternative medicine: incompetent, unethical, misleading and harmful. Retrieved from https://edzardernst.com/2018/04/pilot-studies-of-alternative-medicine-incompetent-unethical-misleading-and-harmful/

Ernst, E. (2022). *Alternative Medicine: A Critical Assessment of 202 Modalities.* 2nd Edition. Springer International Published.

Ernst, E., & Hentschel, C. (1995). Diagnostic methods in complementary medicine. Which craft is witchcraft? *The International Journal of Risk & Safety in Medicine, 7*(1), 55–63.

Ernst, E., & Lee, M. S. (2008). A trial design that generates only "positive" results. *Journal of Postgraduate Medicine, 54*(3), 214–216.

Ernst, E. & Smith, K. (2018). *More Harm Than Good? The Moral Maze of Complementary and Alternative Medicine.* Springer.

Li, B., Forbes, T. L., & Byrne, J. (2018). Integrative medicine or infiltrative pseudoscience? *The Surgeon: Journal of the Royal Colleges of Surgeons of Edinburgh and Ireland, 16*(5), 271–277.

Merriam-Webster Dictionary (n.d.). Alternative medicine. Retrieved from https://www.merriam-webster.com/dictionary/alternative%20medicine

Rees, L., & Weil, A. (2001). Integrated medicine. *BMJ (Clinical Research Ed.), 322*(7279), 119–120.

13   Neuropsychology

Isabella Hartley and Indre V. Viskontas

Encoding, storage, retrieval, wiring, hardware, and software: so many of the descriptions of brain function, particularly those of cognition, rely on the metaphor that brains are computers. Distinguishing hardware (or neuroanatomy) to software (or functional activation) suggests that, like a computer, the hardware of the brain is immutable, and any change in its function is merely the result of different activation patterns of neurons. This metaphor encourages the idea that the anatomy of the brain, and the "wiring," or connections between cells, once established, cannot change – entailing an injured brain cannot repair itself. It also suggests that changes in cognition, or other aspects of brain function, are somewhat less permanent, as activations of brain regions or the firing patterns of neurons are transient. At the core of neuropsychology is the assessment of brain function and cognition, and because the computer metaphor is so prevalent, critically examining related claims is a useful way of developing a more thorough and accurate understanding of the field (Dekker et al., 2012; Duque, 2007). In this chapter, we will examine four primary claims: 1) the brain is hardwired; 2) the programming of memories is a precise, objective, and permanent process; 3) we only use 10% of our brains; and 4) neurodiversity is the result of a broken brain. The brain is not like a computer. Its hardware does change with use and experience. We don't have extra RAM or reams of storage capacity unassigned in our brains, as is the case in our computers, and ultimately, memory is not simply a function of encoding, storage and retrieval, but rather a dynamic process involving the reconstruction of an experience – one that can change a memory trace or fail for a multitude of reasons.

Examining the Claims

Claim #1: The Brain Is Hardwired

One popular use of the computer metaphor is to distinguish hardwire, or neuroanatomy, from software, or function/activation. With the advent of

DOI: 10.4324/9781003259510-17

functional neuroimaging – a set of tools that allows neuroscientists to look into the activity of the brain non-invasively *in vivo* – a conversation emerged regarding the differences between volumetric or other measures of brain structure and activation or measures of brain function. For instance, a group of patients or other individuals may not be distinguishable from healthy counterparts with respect to structural differences, but there may be functional differences that map onto their abilities and impairments. Before neuroimaging, research in human neuropsychology relied heavily on patients with neurodegenerative diseases, brain injuries, and other structural changes to map out brain functions.

But neuropsychologists would be the first to note that brain regions, and the connections between them, are malleable; wiring is not finite, and because programming is not permanent, areas can be reassigned and injuries can be repaired. This capacity for remodeling is called neuroplasticity. Lived experiences affect the brain's neuroanatomy from the cellular to the systems level because use alters the strength of synaptic connections – or the efficiency with which neurons communicate (Mateos-Aparicio & Rodríguez-Moreno, 2019). Hebbian theory can be described by the rhyme popularized by Carla Shatz, "cells that fire together wire together," entailing that repeated activation of the same neurons causes them to link through biological processes – including dendritic growth and receptor upregulation (Hebb, 1964; Shatz, 1992, p. 64). Once associated, communication between neurons becomes more efficient, but if a set of synapses go silent for a while, they eventually atrophy and disconnect. The functional neuroanatomy of the brain is far from stagnant, and unlike the stable wiring of computers, changes in a use-dependent manner (Martin et al., 2000).

Although the majority of neuroplasticity occurs during child development (Leuner & Gould, 2010), there is growing evidence that the brain is capable of change throughout the lifetime at both the cortical and subcortical levels of the central nervous system (Zhao et al., 2008). As an illustration, London's "Black Cab" drivers have been shown to have better hippocampal function, as well as structurally larger hippocampi, compared to age and education-matched controls (Maguire et al., 2000). Researchers identified the catalyst of this increased hippocampal volume and efficiency to be the shaping of the hippocampus – which supports spatial memory and navigational processes – that occurred during training, as the drivers navigated London's roads (Maguire et al., 2000). In a similar example, researchers studying the brains of highly trained musicians found unique anatomical and functional markers, specific to the genre and musical instrument that the learner mastered (Gaser & Schlaug, 2003), and several neurophysiological and neuroimaging studies – utilizing both transcranial magnetic stimulation (TMS) and functional magnetic resonance imaging (fMRI) – have found that limb amputations result in reorganization of the sensory and motor cortices (Schwenkreis et al., 2000).

While these examples reflect changes to specific brain regions, other work has shown that the brain is capable of cross-modal plasticity: reorganization of its cortex, in which sensory functions are redistributed to different regions, usually due to the cessation of input from a sense (Bavelier & Neville, 2002). A compelling example of this kind of modification can be seen in the brains of individuals who are blind. Neuroimaging studies have revealed that the visual cortex (responsible for the integration and perception of visual stimuli) exhibits activation during nonvisual activities (such as tactile Braille reading) in individuals who are blind. Burton and colleagues (2002), also observed activation of the visual word form area, a region of the left hemsiphere involved in the identification of words and letters, which suggests that vision loss does not turn off the cortex normally assigned to vision, but rather, reassigns it to support other functions. These findings contradict the idea that once established, functional neuroanatomy is engrained for life (Burton, 2003).

If the brain were like a computer, traumatic brain injuries (TBIs) and infarctions from strokes would resemble damage to hardware: they would be permanent and calamitous to functioning. In actuality, rehabilitation and cortical reassignment make recovery possible for many patients. Melodic intonation therapy (MIT), an effective treatment method used in the rehabilitation of patients with non-fluent aphasia – a common symptom of left hemisphere strokes that affects speech production – can serve as an example of the brain's ability to rewire following injury (García-Casares et al., 2022).

MIT was developed following the discovery that people with aphasia often retain the ability to sing words that they cannot say, when those words are embedded in a familiar song. MIT teaches patients to articulate words and phrases in the context of a melody, which emphasizes the patterns and rhythms of sound, while tapping their left hand to denote syllables. Predominantly, language is lateralized to the left hemisphere, and there is a white matter tract that joins regions of the brain responsible for language comprehension with those necessary for speech production, called the arcuate fasciculus. In most individuals, the arcuate fasciculus is thicker on the left side of the brain, but in musicians, who excel in their ability to turn thoughts and feelings into sounds, this tract is thicker in the right hemisphere, when compared with non-musicians (Halwani et al., 2011). There is evidence that the arcuate fasciculus in the right hemisphere thickens with therapeutic training, providing a potential mechanism for the rewiring that underlies the patient's rehabilitation (Schlaug et al., 2009). In their meta-analysis, García-Casares and colleagues (2022) also noted that for individuals with limited left hemisphere damage, MIT resulted in recruitment of the left perilesional areas – located outside of the speech production regions – and noted that the mechanisms by which MIT rewires the brain depends on the patient, and their loci of injury.

In a computer, hardware and software determine what it can do, but in the human brain, anatomy dictates function, but function also shapes anatomy. With training, individuals can reassign parts of the brain and rewire connections to bypass regions that were irretrievably damaged. The brain is not hardwired like the hardware of a computer; rather, it changes with use and disuse, and training can shape the brain, enabling the person to accomplish what once seemed impossible.

Claim #2: The Programming of Memories Is a Precise, Objective, and Permanent Process

It has become nearly impossible to detail memory function without the vocabulary of computers, but the computer metaphor neglects aspects of its complicated nature and encourages the flawed assumption that memories are precise, objective, and unchanging – like data encoded and stored on a computer chip. In truth, memories are not guaranteed permanence and can be unreliable, because they are influenced by a myriad of confounding factors, both during initial perception and with every recall. When computers encode new information, they do not alter their wiring or hardware, but the human brain does. Learning and memory are enacted through brain changes that range from large-scale network modifications to tiny alterations of cell membranes (Mayford et al., 2012). Cognition – how perceptions are converted into actions – does not behave like a computer program, which creates internal representations that are then manipulated in accordance with a set of rules. In contrast to the tangible writing of data on a chip, internal states – including memories and representations – do not have a permanent, physical basis in the brain. Instead, memories are constructed from experiences and then reconstructed upon recall (Josselyn & Tonegawa, 2020).

Historically, memory formation has been discussed as a three-stage process that consists of encoding, storage, and retrieval (Melton, 1963). Encoding entails amassing information in the brain, while storage warrants the holding and reorganization of information in long-term memory (LTM), and retrieval denotes pinpointing information and bringing it back into active use (Tulving & Thomson, 1973). In reality, this technologically inspired model is very different from human memory.

When you experience an event, a population of neurons are activated. During sleep, those neurons replay the day's activities, so upon waking, this pattern of activity has been stabilized and can be reactivated more efficiently. Some memories, however, are culled during this process, meaning details that the brain determines to be insignificant are excluded from the trace and therefore not retained (Rasch & Born, 2013). The more you ponder a memory, the more ingrained its representative pattern becomes, but damage to this part of the brain can result in memory loss if consolidation – a time-dependent process where recent experiences are remodeled and stabilized into long-term memories – has not been completed (McGaugh, 2000).

Every time a person recalls a memory, it is rewritten: the event is often remembered as it was last recalled, not as originally witnessed. Instead of simply pulling out the file, reading it as written, and storing it as it was, the brain reconstructs the memory, and as a consequence of this process, information can be influenced by the current environment (Loftus, 2005). Northwestern Medicine's "telephone game" study demonstrated that, every time a memory is recalled, there is potential for it to be distorted. Bridge and Paller (2012) asked participants to memorize 180 object locations and then employed a test of recall on days two and three. Memories recalled on day three were shown to be influenced by the second day's recollection. When recalling objects' locations on day three, those who misremembered day two were inclined to recall objects' locations as closer to their inaccurate, second day memories, as opposed to their original memory (Bridge & Paller, 2012).

Remembering an event in a novel environment, at a different time, or during dissimilar emotions can result in new information being integrated into old memories. Memory is context-dependent, denoting that the location and state in which information is first learned affects future recall. For example, Godden and Baddeley (1975) determined that revisiting the context in which a memory was learned makes reminiscing easier. Participants included divers who learned a list of words on land or underwater, and in a later test of free recall, it was discovered that participants could remember more words when recalling them in the same place they were learned (Godden & Baddeley, 1975).

In addition to environmental influences, intrusion errors – the altering of memories by unrelated prior knowledge – can lead to assumptions that are not stated, and therefore, unobjective. In Brewer and Treyens' (1981) "Schema Theory" experiment, 87 participants were asked to wait in an office without direction, after which they were prompted to describe the objects they had observed. Of note, the majority of participants recalled objects that were not present but likely would be in a typical office, such as books, and were likely to forget the presence of unusual items, such as a skull – though this error decreased when participants were provided with a list of objects in the room (Brewer & Treyens, 1981).

Brewer and Treyens's (1981) exploration of memory formation reveals the influence of schematic knowledge in both encoding and recall.

Schemata are knowledge structures that arise from past experiences (Tse et al., 2007). New information must be related to previous knowledge, and so, novel input is compared against enduring schemas to determine how it should be organized. The brain is geared for efficiency, and therefore, schemata "fill in the blanks" and inform us of what is typical when we experience holes in our understanding (Rumelhart, 1978).

These organizational models allow the brain to quickly turn sensations into rich perceptions, but they can also mistakenly provide more information than is actually present in a given situation. The human brain is therefore prone to mistakes that computers are not, because technology has the ability to consider every possibility from an unweighted perspective, unlike the brain, which predicts the future using models built on past experiences that may or may not be accurate in the present situation (Baldwin, 1992; Gilboa & Marlatte, 2017). What's more, we tend to seek information that confirms our schemas (Trope & Thompson, 1997) and remember information that affirms, rather than contradicts them, leading us to succumb to confirmation bias (Stangor & McMillan, 1992).

The precision and accuracy of computers can appear unattainable when evaluating the biases of the human brain, but in a study that can inspire hope, Craik and Tulving (1975) found that deep processing – meaningful consideration that involves actively working with information – enhances memory recall. Participants' memories were found to significantly improve when they were directed to consider words in meaningful sentences, rather than passively look for capitalizations or rhymes. This evidence indicates that the brain reflects upon knowledge in a distinct way that does not resemble the dependability and impartiality of pre-programmed computer software, but with consideration, human biases can be reduced (Craik & Tulving, 1975).

Claim #3: We Only Use 10% of Our Brains

In 2013, a study by The Michael J. Fox Foundation for Parkinson's Research discovered that 65% of Americans believe we use just 10% of our brains, despite research demonstrating this claim a myth (McDougle, 2014). Neuroimaging studies, however, have provided evidence that the brain accomplishes its functions through vast networks of interconnected neurons, which expand across the entirety of the brain. Even at rest, there is ample activity throughout the brain (Raichle et al., 2001; Smith et al., 2009). While the exact origin of this myth remains murky, numerous events and individuals have been implicated in its proliferation. William James – often referred to as the "Father of American Psychology" – suggested that most people realize just a fraction of their mental potential. Though he never specified a percentage, James proposed that a large portion of our psychological resources remain unemployed, and it is likely that a journalist set this percentage to 10% (James, 1911; James, 1987; James & Myers, 1992).

Then, in 1980, Roger Lewin published a case study by John Lorber, a professor and neurologist who specialized in treating hydrocephalus (Lewin, 1980). In this condition, cerebrospinal fluid (CSF) builds up, which can enlarge the ventricles it is usually contained in and damage the surrounding brain tissue (Greitz, 2004; National Institute of Neurological Disorders and Stroke, 2020). In the article published in *Science*, Lewin reported that one of Lorber's patients with hydrocephalus "has an IQ of 126, has gained a first-class honors degree in mathematics, and is socially completely normal. And yet the boy has virtually no brain" (Lewin, 1980, p. 1232). While it is typical to have approximately 4.5 centimeters of brain tissue between the surface of the cortex and the ventricles, upon neuro-imaging, it was determined that Lorber's patient had only a thin layer of about a millimeter. Lewin then theorized that the brain must exhibit a "tremendous amount of redundancy or spare capacity" (Lewin, 1980; Nolte, 1981). As recently as 2007, cases of hydrocephalus have appeared to validate this idea. The brain scans of a 44 year old French man revealed that some 90% of his brain was missing, though he was not conspicuously impaired: his IQ was 84, below average but not by much, and he had a steady government job along with a wife and two kids (Feuillet et al., 2007). These examples likely fostered the misconception that humans can operate as usual, even if large portions of the brain are absent or damaged, because there are regions that we do not utilize. In truth, it is not that the brain can operate without key regions, but rather, that the brain can compensate for loss or injury by reassigning and redistributing functions to other areas. The compensation involved in these case studies was likely possible because hydrocephalus is slow in its progression or occurs in childhood, allowing for reorganization of function in the rest of the brain (Nudo, 2006).

Other neuroscientists have credited the misinterpretation that glial cells outnumber neurons 10:1 as the source of this myth. This ratio has per-petuated the miscommunication that neurons comprise just 10% of the brain's matter. In actuality, glial cells outnumber neurons at this ratio in only certain areas of the brain, whereas, in the gray matter of other regions – such as the cerebral cortex – glial cells outnumber neurons by a factor of less than two. And furthermore, glial cells in the cerebellum are themselves outnumbered 25:1 (Herculano-Houzel, 2009; Pelvig et al., 2008).

Localized brain regions – anatomically segregated areas determined to represent particular information – have been identified, but recent research has demonstrated that even brain regions with a specific function rarely operate solo (Lewis et al., 2015). Rather than acting as islands, brain regions are part of networks that can encompass millions of neurons and join together many specialized brain regions (Bressler & Menon, 2010; Menon, 2011). Brain scans demonstrate that even the most straightforward behaviors and cognitions require multiregional interactions: the collaboration of different, localized brain regions. The vast majority of thoughts and actions are represented by some combination of cortical and subcortical activation, rather than in isolated areas (Rodriguez et al., 1999; Varela et al., 2001). This widespread collaboration of neural networks, localized brain regions working in tandem, supports the fact that we use far more than 10% of our brains at any given time.

Claim #4: Neurodiversity Is the Result of a Broken Brain

People interact with and interpret information in various ways. The lenses through which we see the world are based on a myriad of factors that can range from genetics to lived experience (Antinori et al., 2017). With computers, hardware must be wired in a certain layout for the computer to function as intended, or at all, for that matter, but there is no one way to connect neurons across the human brain, and no single neural network mapping is "correct."

Diagnoses such as autism spectrum disorder (ASD) and dyslexia are subsumed under the umbrella of neurodiversity. Cognitive distinctions exist but are present on a continuum even within individuals who are given a diagnosis. These divergences are not categorical deficits (Armstrong, 2015; Charlton, 2013). Rather, some of these differences facilitate certain types of creativity, problem solving, and novel ways of thinking, experiencing, or interpreting the world. For example, Baron-Cohen and colleagues (2009) found that autistic people surpassed controls when asked to pinpoint tiny details in a complicated, systematic pattern. This finding suggests that some autistic people can exhibit particularly good attention to detail. fMRI neuroimaging studies have found that this heightened ability may result from differences in neural activation, with autistic people exhibiting comparatively higher levels of activation in the brain's visual systems than speech-processing systems, as compared with people who are neurotypical, or those without the diagnosis. This finding is further supported by research showing many autistic people score higher on the nonverbal Raven's Matrices test of intelligence – which requires analytical skills to solve a visual pattern – than on the verbal Wechsler Scales (Mottron, 2011).

Similarly, people with dyslexia – characterized by graphomotor challenges and difficulties determining written phonemes – have also been found to possess unique strengths. Several studies have found that individuals with dyslexia may have a special propensity for global visual-spatial understanding: comprehension of objects' locations in space (Habib, 2021). It is possible that these individuals are especially capable of comprehending visual-spatial information in a holistic manner (globally), rather than part by part (locally) (Von Karolyi et al., 2003). In addition, Sturm and colleagues (2021), found that children with dyslexia exhibit greater emotionality in their reactions and elevated emotional-facial behavior was correlated with higher scores on measures of social skills. While more research is needed, modern neuropsychology is moving towards a model in which neurodiversity is studied and characterized with respect to both challenges and strengths, and not simply focused on deficits.

There is also growing evidence that individuals with attention-deficit/ hyperactivity disorder (ADHD) also show distinctive strengths, and that accommodations made during their education can go a long way to helping them succeed. Recently, Climie and colleagues (2019) have argued for the adoption of a strengths-based approach to the diagnosis and education of children with ADHD, highlighting evidence that children with ADHD can show better than average verbal skills and logic and reasoning (Ek et al., 2007) and creativity (Fugate et al., 2013). Climie and colleagues (2019) further demonstrated that children with ADHD might be better skilled at managing their emotions, even when their understanding of emotions might not be as strong. Therefore, this is a growing movement among neurodiversity advocates to recognize these individuals as having brains that might be atypical, or different, but not broken or in need of fixing. Instead, they can make unique contributions and share diverse perspectives, which will ultimately enrich our society, and help us find innovative and effective solutions to the looming problems we face.

Summary and Conclusion

In significant ways, the brain does not function like a computer: it is not hardwired, and it is not an impartial processor of data. The brain does not remember things exactly as they happened, but it also does not remain unrepairable following damage. The human brain is malleable, and at times, unreliable, unlike the hard-wired, pre-programmed systems of a computer. There is also no right or wrong way to wire the brain, and programming can be undone, adapted, and altered throughout the lifetime. Susceptible to subconscious biases and change, the human brain does not function like a computer running a pre-programmed set of software.

Isabella Hartley, BA, is a recent graduate of the University of San Francisco, where she majored in psychology and minored in neuroscience.

Indre V. Viskontas, PhD, is an associate professor of psychology at the University of San Francisco, director of communications for the Sound

Health Network, and president-elect of the Society for the Neuroscience of Creativity. She also co-hosts the *Inquiring Minds* podcast.

References

Antinori, A., Carter, O. L., & Smillie, L. D. (2017). Seeing it both ways: Openness to experience and binocular rivalry suppression. *Journal of Research in Personality, 68*, 15–22. 10.1016/j.jrp.2017.03.005

Armstrong, T. (2015). The myth of the normal brain: Embracing neurodiversity. *AMA Journal of Ethics, 17*(4), 348–352. 10.1001/journalofethics.2015.17.4.msoc1-1504.

Baldwin, M. W. (1992). Relational schemas and the processing of social information. *Psychological Bulletin, 112*(3), 461–484. 10.1037/0033-2909.112.3.461

Baron-Cohen, S., Ashwin, E., Ashwin, C., Tavassoli, T., & Chakrabarti, B. (2009). Talent in autism: hyper-systemizing, hyper-attention to detail and sensory hypersensitivity. *Philosophical Transactions of the Royal Society B: Biological Sciences, 364*(1522), 1377–1383. 10.1098/rstb.2008.0337

Bavelier, D., & Neville, H. J. (2002). Cross-modal plasticity: Where and how? *Nature Reviews Neuroscience, 3*(6), 443–452. 10.1038/nrn848

Bressler, S. L., & Menon, V. (2010). Large-scale brain networks in cognition: Emerging methods and principles. *Trends in Cognitive Sciences, 14*(6), 277–290. 10.1016/j.tics.2010.04.004

Brewer, W. F., & Treyens, J. C. (1981). Role of schemata in memory for places. *Cognitive Psychology, 13*(2), 207–230. 10.1016/0010-0285(81)90008-6

Bridge, D. J., & Paller, K. A. (2012). Neural correlates of reactivation and retrieval-induced distortion. *Journal of Neuroscience, 32*(35), 12144–12151. 10.1523/jneurosci.1378-12.2012

Burton, H. (2003). Visual cortex activity in early and late blind people. *The Journal of Neuroscience, 23*(10), 4005–4011. 10.1523/jneurosci.23-10-04005.2003

Burton, H., Snyder, A. Z., Conturo, T. E., Akbudak, E., Ollinger, J. M., & Raichle, M. E. (2002). Adaptive changes in early and late blind: A fmri study of Braille Reading. *Journal of Neurophysiology, 87*(1), 589–607. 10.1152/jn.00285.2001

Charlton, B. (2013). *Defining my Dyslexia*. The New York Times. https://www.nytimes.com/2013/05/23/opinion/defining-my-own-dyslexia.html

Climie, E. A., Saklofske, D. H., Mastoras, S. M., & Schwean, V. L. (2019). Trait and ability emotional intelligence in children with ADHD. *Journal of attention disorders, 23*(13), 1667–1674. 10.1177/10870547177022

Craik, F. I., & Tulving, E. (1975). Depth of processing and the retention of words in episodic memory. *Journal of Experimental Psychology: General, 104*(3), 268–294. 10.1037/0096-3445.104.3.268

Dekker, S., Lee, N. C., Howard-Jones, P., & Jolles, J. (2012). Neuromyths in education: Prevalence and predictors of misconceptions among teachers. *Frontiers in Psychology, 3*. 429. 10.3389/fpsyg.2012.00429

Duque, P. (2007). *Understanding the brain: The Birth of a Learning Science.* OECD.

Ek, U., Fernell, E., Westerlund, J., Holmberg, K., Olsson, P. O., & Gillberg, C. (2007). Cognitive strengths and deficits in schoolchildren with ADHD. *Acta Paediatrica, 96,* 756–761. 10.1111/ j.1651-2227.2007.00297.x

Feuillet, L., Dufour, H., & Pelletier, J. (2007). Brain of a white-collar worker. *The Lancet, 370*(9583), 262. 10.1016/s0140-6736(07)61127-1

Fugate, C. M., Zentall, S. S., & Gentry, M. (2013). Creativity and working memory in gifted students with and without characteristics of attention deficit hyperactive disorder: Lifting the mask. *Gifted Child Quarterly, 57,* 234–246. 10.1177/0016986213500069

García-Casares, N., Barros-Cano, A., & García-Arnés, J. A. (2022). Melodic intonation therapy in post-stroke non-fluent aphasia and its effects on brain plasticity. *Journal of Clinical Medicine, 11*(12), 3503. 10.3390/jcm11123503

Gaser, C., & Schlaug, G. (2003). Brain structures differ between musicians and non-musicians. *The Journal of Neuroscience, 23*(27), 9240–9245. 10.1523/ jneurosci.23-27-09240.2003

Gilboa, A., & Marlatte, H. (2017). Neurobiology of schemas and schema-mediated memory. *Trends in Cognitive Sciences, 21*(8), 618–631. 10.1016/ j.tics.2017.04.013

Godden, D. R., & Baddeley, A. D. (1975). Context-dependent memory in two natural environments: On land and underwater. *British Journal of Psychology, 66*(3), 325–331. 10.1111/j.2044-8295.1975.tb01468.x

Greitz, D. (2004). Radiological assessment of hydrocephalus: New theories and implications for therapy. *Neurosurgical Review, 27*(3). 10.1007/s10143-004-0326-9. 145–167.

Habib, M. (2021). The neurological basis of developmental dyslexia and related disorders: A reappraisal of the temporal hypothesis, twenty years on. *Brain Sciences, 11*(6), 708. 10.3390/brainsci11060708

Halwani, G. F., Loui, P., Rüber, T., & Schlaug, G. (2011). Effects of practice and experience on the arcuate fasciculus: Comparing singers, instrumentalists, and non-musicians. *Frontiers in Psychology, 2,* 1–9. 10.3389/fpsyg.2011.00156

Hebb, D. O. (1964). *The Organization of Behavior.* John Wiley and Sons Inc. 10.4324/9781410612403

Herculano-Houzel, S. (2009). The human brain in numbers: A linearly scaled-up primate brain. *Frontiers in Human Neuroscience, 3.* 10.3389/neuro.09.031. 2009. 31

James, W. (1911). The energies of men. In W. James, *On Vital Reserves: The Energies of Men, the Gospel of Relaxation* (pp. 3–39). Henry Holt and Company. 10.1037/11005-001

James, W. (1987). *William James: Writings 1902–1910.* Library of America.

James, W., & Myers, G. E. (1992). *William James: Writings 1878-1899.* The Library of America.

Josselyn, S. A., & Tonegawa, S. (2020). Memory engrams: Recalling the past and imagining the future. *Science, 367*(6473). eaaw4325. 10.1126/science.aaw4325

Leuner, B., & Gould, E. (2010). Structural plasticity and hippocampal function. *Annual Review of Psychology*, 61(1), 111–140. 10.1146/annurev.psych. 093008.10035

Lewin, R. (1980). Is your brain really necessary? *Science*, 210(4475), 1232–1234. 10.1126/science.7434023

Lewis, C. M., Bosman, C. A., & Fries, P. (2015). Recording of brain activity across spatial scales. *Current Opinion in Neurobiology*, 32, 68–77. 10.1016/j.conb. 2014.12.007

Loftus, E. F. (2005). Planting misinformation in the human mind: A 30-year investigation of the malleability of memory. *Learning & Memory*, 12(4), 361–366. 10.1101/lm.94705

Maguire, E. A., Gadian, D. G., Johnsrude, I. S., Good, C. D., Ashburner, J., Frackowiak, R. S., & Frith, C. D. (2000). Navigation-related structural change in the hippocampi of taxi drivers. *Proceedings of the National Academy of Sciences*, 97(8), 4398–4403. 10.1073/pnas.070039597

Martin, S. J., Grimwood, P. D., & Morris, R. G. (2000). Synaptic plasticity and memory: An evaluation of the hypothesis. *Annual Review of Neuroscience*, 23(1), 649–711. 10.1146/annurev.neuro.23.1.649

Mateos-Aparicio, P., & Rodríguez-Moreno, A. (2019). The impact of studying brain plasticity. *Frontiers in Cellular Neuroscience*, 13. 10.3389/fncel.2019. 00066

Mayford, M., Siegelbaum, S. A., & Kandel, E. R. (2012). Synapses and memory storage. *Cold Spring Harbor Perspectives in Biology*, 4(6). a005751. 10.1101/cshperspect.a005751

McDougle, S. (2014). *You already use way, way more than 10 percent of your brain*. The Atlantic. https://www.theatlantic.com/technology/archive/2014/07/you-already-use-way-way-more-than-10-percent-of-your-brain/374520/

McGaugh, J. L. (2000). Memory– a century of consolidation. *Science*, 287(5451), 248–251. 10.1126/science.287.5451.248

Melton, A. W. (1963). Implications of short-term memory for a general theory of memory. *Journal of Verbal Learning and Verbal Behavior*, 2(1), 1–21. 10.1016/S0022-5371(63)80063-8

Menon, V. (2011). Large-scale brain networks and psychopathology: a unifying triple network model. *Trends in Cognitive Sciences*, 15(10), 483–506. 10.1016/j.tics.2011.08.003

Mottron, L. (2011). The power of autism. *Nature*, 479(7371), 33–35. 10.1038/479033a

National Institute of Neurological Disorders and Stroke. (2020, April). *Hydrocephalus Fact Dheet*. National Institute of Neurological Disorders and Stroke. https://www.ninds.nih.gov/hydrocephalus-fact-sheet

Nolte, J. (1981). *The human brain: An introduction to its functional anatomy*. Mosby.

Nudo, R. J. (2006). Mechanisms for recovery of motor function following cortical damage. *Current opinion in neurobiology*, 16(6), 638–644. 10.1016/j.conb. 2006.10.004

Pelvig, D. P., Pakkenberg, H., Stark, A. K., & Pakkenberg, B. (2008). Neocortical glial cell numbers in human brains. *Neurobiology of Aging, 29*(11), 1754–1762. 10.1016/j.neurobiolaging.2007.04.013

Raichle, M. E., MacLeod, A. M., Snyder, A. Z., Powers, W. J., Gusnard, D. A., & Shulman, G. L. (2001). A default mode of brain function. *Proceedings of the National Academy of Sciences, 98*(2), 676–682. 10.1073/pnas.98.2.676

Rasch, B., & Born, J. (2013). About sleep's role in memory. *Physiological Reviews, 93*(2), 681–766. 10.1152/physrev.00032.2012

Rodriguez, E., George, N., Lachaux, J. P., Martinerie, J., Renault, B., & Varela, F. J. (1999). Perception's Shadow: Long-distance synchronization of human brain activity. *Nature, 397*(6718), 430–433. 10.1038/17120

Rumelhart, D. (1978). Schemata: The building blocks of cognition. In R. Spiro, B. Bruce, & W. Brewer (Eds.), *Theoretical Issues in Reading Comprehension* (1st ed., pp. 33–58). Routledge.

Schlaug, G., Marchina, S., & Norton, A. (2009). Evidence for plasticity in white-matter tracts of patients with chronic Broca's aphasia undergoing intense intonation-based speech therapy. *Annals of the New York Academy of Sciences, 1169*(1), 385–394. 10.1111/j.1749-6632.2009.04587.x

Schwenkreis, P., Witscher, K., Janssen, F., Dertwinkel, R., Zenz, M., Malin, J.-P., & Tegenthoff, M. (2000). Changes of cortical excitability in patients with upper limb amputation. *Neuroscience Letters, 293*(2), 143–146. 10.1016/s0304-3940(00)01517-2

Shatz, C. J. (1992). The developing brain. *Scientific American, 267*(3), 60–67. 10.1038/scientificamerican0992-60

Smith, S. M., Fox, P. T., Miller, K. L., Glahn, D. C., Fox, P. M., Mackay, C. E., Filippini, N., Watkins, K. E., Toro, R., Laird, A. R., & Beckmann, C. F. (2009). Correspondence of the brain's functional architecture during activation and rest. *Proceedings of the National Academy of Sciences, 106*(31), 13040–13045. 10.1073/pnas.0905267106

Stangor, C., & McMillan, D. (1992). Memory for expectancy-congruent and expectancy-incongruent information: A review of the social and social developmental literatures. *Psychological Bulletin, 111*(1), 42–61. 10.1037/0033-2909.111.1.42

Sturm, V. E., Roy, A. R. K., Datta, S., Wang, C., Sible, I. J., Holley, S. R., Watson, C., Palser, E. R., Morris, N. A., Battistella, G., Rah, E., Meyer, M., Pakvasa, M., Mandelli, M. L., Deleon, J., Hoeft, F., Caverzasi, E., Miller, Z. A., Shapiro, K. A., …Gorno-Tempini, M. L. (2021). Enhanced visceromotor emotional reactivity in dyslexia and its relation to salience network connectivity. *Cortex, 134*, 278–295. 10.1016/j.cortex.2020.10.022

Trope, Y., & Thompson, E. P. (1997). Looking for truth in all the wrong places? Asymmetric search of individuating information about stereotyped group members. *Journal of Personality and Social Psychology, 73*(2), 229–241. 10.1037/0022-3514.73.2.229

Tse, D., Langston, R. F., Kakeyama, M., Bethus, I., Spooner, P. A., Wood, E. R., Witter, M. P., & Morris, R. G. (2007). Schemas and memory consolidation. *Science, 316*(5821), 76–82. 10.1126/science.1135935

Tulving, E., & Thomson, D. M. (1973). Encoding specificity and retrieval processes in episodic memory. *Psychological Review*, *80*(5), 352–373. 10.1037/h0020071

Varela, F., Lachaux, J.-P., Rodriguez, E., & Martinerie, J. (2001). The brainweb: Phase synchronization and large-scale integration. *Nature Reviews Neuroscience*, *2*(4), 229–239. 10.1038/35067550

Von Karolyi, C., Winner, E., Gray, W., & Sherman, G. F. (2003). Dyslexia linked to talent: Global visual-spatial ability. *Brain and language*, *85*(3), 427–431. 10.1016/S0093-934X(03)00052-X

Zhao, C., Deng, W., & Gage, F. H. (2008). Mechanisms and functional implications of adult neurogenesis. *Cell*, *132*(4), 645–660. 10.1016/j.cell.2008.01.033

14 Forensic Psychology

Montana L. Ploe, David K. Marcus,
and John F. Edens

Forensic psychology applies psychological science to legal issues and helps inform decision-making in both criminal and civil cases. Although forensic psychologists are involved in a wide array of psycho-legal issues, their roles are largely misunderstood by the general public and commonly misrepresented by popular media. Forensic psychologists serve as expert witnesses in criminal and civil proceedings, perform psychological and risk assessments, consult with policymakers on criminal justice reform, and provide treatment to justice-involved individuals. For example, competency assessments in which psychologists help establish whether a criminal defendant is competent to stand trial, are the most common assessments conducted by forensic psychologists and the demand for these evaluations have been steadily increasing (Gowensmith, 2019). In contrast, the popular media often portrays forensic psychologists as "profilers" who investigate and solve crimes, a role that few, if any, real-life forensic psychologists play. This chapter will provide an overview of some of the controversies surrounding forensic psychology as well as some of the ways in which pseudoscientific beliefs have influenced forensic practice.

Examining the Claims

Claim #1: All Crime Scene Investigation Techniques Are Objective and Infallible

Forensic psychologists often serve as expert witnesses in legal cases along with experts from other disciplines. These various experts can provide evidence-based knowledge that may help judges and juries make more informed decisions. Unfortunately, it is not uncommon for pseudo-scientific findings or junk science to enter into purportedly scientific testimony. Before discussing pseudoscience in forensic psychology, it is worth noting some of the other areas in which junk science has been admitted under the guise of professional expertise.

DOI: 10.4324/9781003259510-18

In 2009, the National Research Council (NRC) of the National Academy of Sciences published a groundbreaking review that concluded that "little rigorous systematic research has been done to validate the basic premises and techniques in a number of forensic science disciplines" (p. 189). In fact, many of the procedures that are often featured in popular portrayals of forensic science, such as bite mark evidence, blood spatter analysis, and tire track matching are based on flimsy evidence (Bell et al., 2018; Bowers, 2019; NRC, 2009).

For example, although forensic dentistry can help determine the identity of bodies by matching teeth to dental records, bite mark analysts who claim to identify assailants by matching their teeth to the impressions left on their victim's skin have contributed to numerous wrongful convictions. Before DNA evidence exonerated Keith Harward, he spent 33 years in prison for rape and murder. His original conviction was largely driven by the testimony of a forensic dentist who claimed that the impression on the victim's body matched Harward's teeth (see Fabricant, 2022 for descriptions of this and other wrongful convictions based on bite mark analysis). According to the NRC (2009), the skin's elasticity along with swelling and changes over time can limit the validity and reliability of bite mark evidence. In other words, despite its scientific façade and claims of objectivity, matching bite marks to suspects' teeth is highly subjective. Even when following strict guidelines and using the same evidence, different experts can produce wildly different results (Bowers, 2019). Bite mark analysis often yields false positives (i.e., finding a match when there is not one), because analysts often work with law enforcement and prosecutors who share their theory of the case and may even encourage the analysts to find a match.

There are similar problems with a variety of other pattern matching techniques that claim the mantle of forensic science. Unlike in movies or television series where it is often portrayed as an objective and infallible method for matching perpetrators' vehicles to crime scenes, tire track matching is a subjective process (NRC, 2009). Evaluations for tire track impressions include identifying a known standard comparison and then assessing how this impression might deviate from the standard with features of wear and tear. These deviations are then used to identify tires with the same precise deviations from the known standard. However, there are no guidelines on how many individualized deviations must be present to make a positive identification (NRC, 2009). Tire tack evidence is unsubstantiated at best and greatly increases the chance of a false positive identification, especially if (as is often the case) investigators first inform the analyst that the vehicle belongs to the suspect.

Similarly, despite Dexter's ability to solve (and commit) crimes on TV, many of the conclusions reached by real-world blood spatter analysts far exceed the scientific basis of this endeavor. Although there are many professional societies for blood spatter analysis, only two of these organizations recommend any formal qualifications for conducting these analyses and both emphasize experience over formal education and a strong scientific foundation (NRC, 2009). The lack of strict guidelines and requirements surrounding this practice is problematic given the complexity involved with making claims that a blood spatter pattern is associated with a particular type of assault. Given the uncertainties associated with these analyses, experts should discuss any findings in a court of law with great care and clear transparency regarding any of these types of pattern analyses.

Claim #2: Forensic Psychological Testimony Is Objective and Unbiased

The NRC report did not focus on problems with forensic psychology, and it is important to underscore that evidence-based psychological testimony can provide valuable information to the courts. Still, forensic psychological testimony has its own controversies and unfortunately, some forensic psychological testimony can veer into the realm of pseudoscience. However, unlike bite mark and blood spatter analysts who appear to be more invested in promoting than in evaluating their purported sciences, forensic psychologists have often been at the forefront of investigating the reliability and validity of forensic psychological methods and of critiquing pseudoscientific and other controversial psychological testimony.

One noteworthy area of focus has been on the issue of adversarial allegiance (Boccaccini et al., 2017). Expert witnesses are supposed to serve as neutral and objective parties who are retained by either the prosecution or defense when evidence is technical or difficult to understand (Groscup et al., 2002). For experts who testify regarding forensic issues, this expectation means that how dangerous, psychopathic, or cognitively impaired a defendant is should, in principle, be the same regardless of whether that defendant was evaluated by a psychologist hired by the defense or the prosecution. Unfortunately, there are overt and subtle influences that may lead psychological experts to deviate from this ideal, with expert witnesses falling prey to adversarial allegiance, which is the tendency to be biased in favor of the side that retained them (Boccaccini et al., 2017).

For example, many states have enacted sexually violent predator (SVP) laws in which risk assessments are conducted on sex offenders who have completed their sentences to determine whether they should be civilly committed because they pose an ongoing danger to the public. These risk assessments are conducted by forensic psychologists using purportedly objective measures such as the *Psychopathy Checklist-Revised* (PCL-R; Hare, 2003). However, in a sample of 35 sex offenders, experts for the prosecution provided higher PCL-R scores (*M* = 24) indicating higher risk than did experts for the defense (*M* = 18) (Murrie et al., 2009). Because correlation cannot prove causation, other explanations besides adversarial allegiance might explain the findings from this naturalistic study. Therefore, in a true experiment, Murrie and colleagues (2013) had actual forensic evaluators score the same set of PCL-R protocols for an SVP evaluation, but half of the evaluators were led to believe that they were being hired by the prosecution and the other half believed that they were being hired by the defense. Evaluators who believed that they were working for the prosecution consistently provided higher PCL-R scores than those who thought that they were working for the defense.

Similarly, in 2002, the Supreme Court determined that it was unconstitutional to execute individuals who were intellectually disabled (*Atkins v. Virginia*). Consequently, psychological experts have testified about whether a capital defendant is intellectually disabled. Despite the widespread assumption that intelligence testing is an objective endeavor, a recent review of "Atkins cases," found that prosecution experts reported that the defendants had higher IQ scores (often above the threshold for an intellectual disability diagnosis), whereas defense experts reported lower IQ scores that were typically below the threshold needed for a diagnosis (Lambros, 2021).

Risk assessment instruments (e.g., the PCL-R) and intelligence tests are not inherently pseudoscientific. On the contrary, they are among the most studied and well-validated tools in clinical psychology. However, within the context of an adversarial system such as the American legal system, the findings from even these scientific tools can be distorted. Thus, when scoring the PCL-R, the same behavior may appear glib to a prosecution expert (earning 2 points), while appearing appropriately socially engaged to a defense expert and thus being scored a 0. Similarly, during an evaluation to assess whether a capital defendant is intellectually disabled (i.e., Atkins evaluation), the same definition of a word may earn 2 points when scored by a prosecution expert and only 1 point when scored by a defense expert. One way to reduce adversarial allegiance across a variety of psychological evaluations would be to use court appointed expert witnesses instead of relying on the prosecution or defense to hire their own. Unfortunately, this is not common practice in the United States.

Psychologists may also serve as experts in civil cases such as in lawsuits seeking monetary damages due to emotional distress, cases when various civil competencies are called into question (e.g., competency to execute a will or contract), or in child custody cases. Child custody evaluations have been especially controversial, and this is an area where psychological experts are at risk of engaging in pseudoscientific practices. These evaluations are typically conducted when the parents in a divorce cannot agree about the custodial arrangements. In these evaluations, the psychologist assesses both the parents and the children to determine what would be in the best interest of the child. Most custody evaluators use general psychological assessments that focus broadly on psychopathology rather than using measures that directly address issues relevant to child custody decisions such as parenting ability and the parent–child relationship (Valerio & Beck, 2017). Many of these general psychological instruments are well-validated measures of psychopathology that can serve a valuable role in diagnosis and treatment planning and in extreme cases may identify parents who are so severely psychologically impaired that they cannot function in a custodial role. In most instances, however, these instruments provide limited information about what arrangement would be in the best interest of the child. In other words, there is limited scientific support for their use in custody evaluations.

Consequently, mental health professionals have attempted to develop specialty instruments designed to inform what custodial arrangement would be in the best interests of the child. The use of these specialty instruments appears to be increasing among psychologists who conduct custody evaluations (Ackerman & Pritzl, 2011). Unfortunately, many of these custody instruments seem to be based on pseudoscientific principles and may not be valid measures of what is in the best interests of the child (Otto et al., 2000).

Consider the *Perception of Relationships Test* (PORT; Bricklin, 2014), which almost a third of child custody evaluators surveyed in 2008 reported using (Ackerman & Pritzl, 2011). This measure uses projective drawing by the children to determine which parent they are closer to. The PORT is based on the assumption that "that children's unconscious preferences are more important than their verbalized statements" (Otto et al., 2000, p. 324), an assumption that is not testable and that lacks any scientific support. More broadly, there is little evidence that any projective measures provide valid information for making custody recommendations (Erickson et al, 2007; for the pseudoscientific aspects of projective drawing, see the book *Investigating School Psychology* in this series). Unfortunately, measures that may not be relevant to determining the best interests of the child, either because they were not designed to address this issue or because they were based on pseudoscientific principles, remain a common feature of many child custody evaluations (Ackerman & Pritzl, 2011).

Claim #3: You Might Be a Psychopath If … .

One topic in forensic psychology that seems to be especially fascinating for the general public is psychopathy. Although there is debate among psychopathy researchers about the precise definition of psychopathy, most agree that psychopathy is characterized by callousness and a general lack of concern regarding the welfare of others, impulsiveness/disinhibition, and many psychopathy researchers also believe that fearlessness or bold-ness is also a component (Patrick, 2022). Because individuals high in psychopathic traits are responsible for a disproportionate amount of crime and are more likely to reoffend, forensic psychologists have devoted considerable research to examining the causes, measurement, and corre-lates of psychopathy.

The assessment of psychopathy is also a central component of many forensic assessments, including risk assessments. Although there is a well-established and growing science of psychopathy, the concept of psychop-athy has attracted quite a number of fringe theories and pseudoscientific beliefs, with popular media representations of psychopathy contributing to numerous misconceptions about what psychopathy is. Media accounts of scientific research findings in general have at best a checkered history of accuracy. In particular, it is often hard, if not impossible, to cram into a headline any degree of nuance regarding a complicated study's main results. Given this challenge, it is important to consider that what headlines say about "psychopaths" – and particularly what sorts of things are likely to make someone a psychopath – is likely to be an exaggeration or gross oversimplification of what the original scientific study actually found.

One of the most common misrepresentations in headlines is to state something categorically that actually is just a matter of degree: *"X Makes You Likely to Be a Psychopath!"* That certainly sounds like enticing clickbait, but more than likely what the study found was a statistically significant correlation between some measure of X and scores on some psychopathy assessment procedure (frequently a self-report question-naire). That does not mean that being high on whatever X is (e.g., enjoying mixed martial arts fights) puts someone in the range of severe psycho-pathy, it just means there is some – likely modest – relationship between being higher/lower on one and higher/lower on the other. Also, it is important to remember that in studies conducted on college students or community members, the odds of there being many extremely psycho-pathic people in the sample are quite low. It also does not mean that the magnitude of the association between the predictor variable X and psy-chopathy is very strong either. If a study includes 500 or more people, a "statistically significant association" can actually be quite small and of little practical significance at the level of trying to predict anything about a particular person – even if at the group-level there is a modest degree of overlap between the two that is scientifically useful to know.

The headline "Psychopaths Drink Their Coffee Black, Study Finds" (Maldonado, 2022) is a misrepresentation of an otherwise perfectly acceptable correlational study that found a weak association between people reporting that they liked the taste of bitter food and drinks and their scores on a four-item self-report psychopathic traits scale in two large samples of online survey participants (Sagioglou & Greitemeyer, 2016). Importantly, when participants were asked about *specific* foods that are bitter (for example, coffee, radishes, tonic water) there was *no* association with the four-item psychopathic traits scale – or any of the other scales (such as narcissism). This suggests that although there might be a modest association between enjoying bitter taste and self-reported psychopathic traits, it is not specific to drinking black coffee. Additionally, given that the study was correlational, it would be irresponsible to draw a causal conclusion between these variables.

Popular media has also implied that studying business might make someone a psychopath, despite the source article finding no significant effects (Collins, 2017; Vedel & Thomsen, 2017). This study looked at the majors of almost 500 Danish college students and compared their self-reported psychopathic traits on a nine-item scale. The findings from the original article suggest that the different majors did not significantly differ from each other in terms of how they rated themselves on psychopathy (Vedel & Thomsen, 2017). If anything, when the study authors looked more closely at their results, it seemed that psychology majors tended to rate themselves as somewhat lower than all the other majors on these traits. Although personality in general may have something to do with chosen college major, it cannot confirm whether someone can be labeled with psychopathy.

Additionally, headlines can attempt to invoke fear, which is especially relevant for psychopathy. Despite the headline, "Creative People Might Secretly Be Psychopaths, Scientists Warn" (Waugh, 2016), suggesting some covert operation that exposed an underworld of creative psychopaths, the original study simply reported a very modest overlap between self-reported creative accomplishments and a nine-item self-report psychopathy scale in a large on-line sample primarily composed of people from the Philippines (Galang et al., 2016). More specifically, there was actually a somewhat stronger correlation with a self-report narcissism scale – though it should not be surprising to find that more narcissistic people think they are also more accomplished than other people. The significance of creativity in being useful to diagnose someone as a psychopath, based on these findings, is negligible.

Similarly, Mental Floss posted the headline "Study Shows Psychopaths Don't Catch Yawns" (Ferro, 2015) citing a study that used the *Psychopathic Personality Inventory-Revised* (PPI-R) to measure self-reported psychopathic traits among 135 male and female college students who watched a video of people yawning and then had their own number of yawns recorded (Rundle et al., 2015). The PPI-R scale provides a total score and scores on three narrower traits, called Fearless Dominance, Self-Centered Impulsivity, and Coldheartedness. What the authors actually found was *no* differences in yawning for the PPI-R total psychopathy score, Fearless Dominance, or Self-Centered Impulsivity. There was a small statistically significant relationship between the scores on the Coldheartedness scale and the number of times people yawned. What this study likely suggests, if its findings can be replicated, is that there is some marginal correlation between contagious yawning and the level of empathy one expresses for other people but cannot be used to identify psychopathy.

Another study examining correlations between self-reported psychopathic traits and some other self-reported predictor variable in college and community samples was reported as "Study Says Night Owls More Likely to be Psychopaths" (Sreedhar, 2013). In this instance, the variable of interest was self-reported preferences regarding being a "morning person" versus an "evening person." The study did not directly measure whether participants who self-reported higher levels of psychopathic traits actually were "night owls" (Jonason et al., 2013). All the correlations reported were modest in magnitude, though statistically significant. Although this might suggest some correlation between time-of-day preferences and psychopathic traits, it likely can be attributed more to chance.

Headlines can also be deceiving given what we know about those with psychopathy. For example, the headline "Narcissists and Psychopaths Love to Stay Friends with Their Exes" (Tourjee, 2016), seems highly counter-intuitive, given all of the books written by individuals claiming to have been married to psychopaths who destroyed their lives. What the original study actually found, using a large university sample, was that students who got higher scores on self-reported Antagonism (that is, low agreeableness) and Extraversion scales and lower scores on the trait of Honesty-Humility were somewhat more likely to value staying friends for pragmatic reasons than were people with lower levels of Antagonism and Extraversion and higher levels of Honesty-Humility (Mogilski & Welling, 2017). The study did not directly assess psychopathy, narcissism, or even measure how long anyone actually stayed friends with their exes. Therefore, it does not even address the question of whether psychopaths "love" to stay friends with their exes in an absolute sense. It also did not assess whether they actually *do* stay friends for longer amounts of time than non-psychopaths.

"Playlist of the Lambs: Psychopaths May Have Distinct Musical Preferences" / "How to Spot a Psychopath: Music Taste Can Offer Clues" / "Study Says Psychopaths Love Rap Music" (Dovey, 2017; Sample, 2017; Study Says Psychopaths Love Rap Music, 2019): We list three separate headlines about this one study in part because they seem to show the *devolution* of the original findings as the headlines get further away from the original source (though props to *The Guardian* for working in a reference to a movie about a cannibalistic serial killer in the title of an article about a research study likely conducted on college students or the general public). We say "likely conducted on" because the original research itself as of this writing has not been published in a scientific journal and the sample is not described anywhere in any detail. Also, the study's lead author describes the findings as "preliminary" and not about genres of music but instead about specific songs, such as Eminem's "Lose Yourself."

Media headlines typically oversimplify the findings from otherwise competently conducted – but fairly complicated – studies. For example, the headline "How to Tell Whether a Child Might become a Psychopath, as Early as Five Weeks Old" (Goldhill, 2015) cited a study in which none of the children at any point in time during the study had been diagnosed as psychopaths (Kimonis et al., 2016). The study used ratings of several traits (e.g., callousness, lack of emotion) that tap into psychopathic-like traits among very young children. But at no point in the study was there any categorical statement that any child was or was not "a psychopath," which would have been inappropriate given their age. Second, the strength of the association was statistically significant only for boys in the study – not girls. Third, even for boys the correlation was modest in size. Finally, the "psychopath test" in question was actually just a ratio of how much time the infants gazed at a red ball in their visual field relative to how much time they spent looking at the research assistant who was holding them. Those boys who – relative to other boys – spent more time looking at the ball tended to be rated as somewhat more callous and unemotional a couple of years later by a parent (Kimonis et al., 2016). In short, this is perfectly fine research that suggests that visual attention during infancy may have some modest association with later parent ratings of quasi-personality traits evident among preschool boys. It has absolutely no practical usefulness at the moment in terms of diagnosis, however, though perhaps that could change once considerably more scientific research is completed.

Unlike the problematic headlines reviewed above, the headline "Can an On-line Quiz Spot a Psychopath?" is from a very good article in *The Guardian* that describes a number of quizzes out there on the web that purport to be able to tell you just how psychopathic someone is (Crockett & Viding, 2015). The quizzes that are available, as this article aptly notes, do not typically seem to have any scientific evidence to suggest they are of much if any real use. Some tests are just lists of adjectives that you have to decide whether they apply to someone. Some are bizarre projective-type tests that ask you to pick what you think different clouds look like.

Generally, the weirder the content of the test, the less informative the results will be. Some claim to be able to give you a score that corresponds to some percentile rank, though it is rarely if ever clear where any of the numbers come from or whether they actually mean anything.

Summary and Conclusion

Because of the many real-world consequences associated with the practice of forensic psychology, such as which parent gets primary custody of a child, whether a sex offender is involuntarily committed for an indeterminate amount of time, whether someone is labeled a psychopath, and even whether a capital murderer is executed, it is important that the practice of forensic psychology be grounded in science. Fortunately, the field has been introspective, using scientific methods to examine the practice of forensic psychology, including identifying the dangers of adversarial allegiance and the limitations of many forensic assessment instruments. Unfortunately, there are misconceptions about forensic psychology, many of which are fueled by inaccurate portrayals in the media (e.g., forensic psychologists are profilers who solve crimes, people who stay up late are psychopaths). Although forensic psychologists cannot control how the field is portrayed in the media (a movie about a profiler is more entertaining than a movie about a competency assessment), they should strive to only use assessment instruments that were validated to address the psycho-legal issue in question and be aware of how their conclusions may have been influenced by the people who paid for their services.

Montana L. Ploe, BA, is a doctoral student in the clinical psychology program at Washington State University.

David K. Marcus, PhD, is a clinical psychologist and professor and chair of the Department of Psychology at Washington State University.

John F. Edens, PhD, is a clinical psychologist and professor in the Department of Psychological and Brain Sciences at Texas A&M University.

References

Ackerman, M. J., & Pritzl, T. B. (2011). Child custody evaluation practices: A 20-year follow-up. *Family Court Review*, 49(3), 618–628.
Atkins v. Virginia, No. 00-8452 (Supreme Court of the United States 2002).
Bell, S., Sah, S., Albright, T. D., Gates Jr, S. J., Denton, M. B., & Casadevall, A. (2018). A call for more science in forensic science. *Proceedings of the National Academy of Sciences*, 115(18), 4541–4544.

Boccaccini, M. T., Marcus, D. K., & Murrie, D. C. (2017). Allegiance effects in clinical psychology research and practice (pp. 323–339). In S. O. Lilienfeld & I. D. Waldman (Eds.), *Psychological Science Under Scrutiny: Recent Challenges and Proposed Remedies*. John Wiley and Sons.

Bowers, C. M. (2019). Review of a forensic pseudoscience: Identification of criminals from bitemark patterns. *Journal of Forensic and Legal Medicine*, *61*, 34–39.

Bricklin, B. (2014). *Perception of Relationships Test*. Village Publishing.

Collins, T. (2017, May 4). *Did You Study Business or Economics? Then You Might be a Psychopath, Claim Scientists*. DailyMail. https://www.dailymail.co.uk/sciencetech/article-4473012/Studied-business-economics-psychopath.html

Crockett, M., & Viding, E. (2015, June 10). *Can an online quiz spot a psychopath?* The Guardian. https://www.theguardian.com/science/head-quarters/2015/jun/10/can-an-online-quiz-spot-a-psychopath

Devery, C. (2010). Criminal profiling and criminal investigation. *Journal of Contemporary Criminal Justice*, *26*(4), 393–409.

Dovey, D. (2017, September 26). *How to Spot a Psychopath: Music Taste Can Offer Clues*. Newsweek. https://www.newsweek.com/how-spot-psychopath-music-taste-can-offer-clues-671459

Erickson, S. K., Lilienfeld, S. O., & Vitacco, M. J. (2007). A critical examination of the suitability and limitations of psychological tests in family court. *Family Court Review*, *45*(2), 157–174.

Fabricant, M. C. (2022). *Junk Science and the American Criminal Justice System*. Akashic Books.

Ferro, S. (2015, August 21). *Study Shows Psychopaths Don't Catch Yawns*. Mental Floss. https://www.mentalfloss.com/article/67644/new-study-shows-psychopaths-dont-catch-yawns

Galang, A. J. R., Castelo, V. L. C., Santos III, L. C., Perlas, C. M. C., & Angeles, M. A. B. (2016). Investigating the prosocial psychopath model of the creative personality: Evidence from traits and psychophysiology. *Personality and Individual Differences*, *100*, 28–36.

Goldhill, O. (2015). *How to Tell Whether a Child Might Become a Psychopath, as Early as Five Weeks Old*. Quartz. https://qz.com/500496/how-to-tell-whether-a-child-will-become-a-psychopath-as-early-as-five-weeks-old

Gowensmith, W. N. (2019). Resolution or resignation: The role of forensic mental health professionals amidst the competency services crisis. *Psychology, Public Policy, and Law*, *25*(1), 1–14. 10.1037/law0000190

Groscup, J. L., Penrod, S. D., Studebaker, C. A., Huss, M. T., & O'Neil, K. M. (2002). The effects of Daubert on the admissibility of expert testimony in state and federal criminal cases. *Psychology, Public Policy, and Law*, *8*(4), 339–372.

Hare, R. D. (2003). *The Hare Psychopathy Checklist—Revised* (2nd ed.). Multi-Health Systems.

Jonason, P. K., Jones, A., & Lyons, M. (2013). Creatures of the night: Chronotypes and the Dark Triad traits. *Personality and Individual Differences*, *55*(5), 538–541.

Kimonis, E. R., Fanti, K. A., Anastassiou-Hadjicharalambous, X., Mertan, B., Goulter, N., & Katsimicha, E. (2016). Can callous-unemotional traits be reliably measured in preschoolers?. *Journal of Abnormal Child Psychology*, 44(4), 625–638.

Lambros, A. M. (2021). *The Role of Adversarial Allegiance in Atkins v. Virginia Cases* [Unpublished master's thesis]. Washington State University.

Maldonado, D. (2022). *Psychopaths Drink Their Coffee Black, Study Finds*. Indy100. https://www.indy100.com/viral/psychopaths-coffee-black-study

Mogilski, J. K., & Welling, L. L. (2017). Staying friends with an ex: Sex and dark personality traits predict motivations for post-relationship friendship. *Personality and Individual Differences*, 115, 114–119.

Murrie, D. C., Boccaccini, M. T., Guarnera, L. A., & Rufino, K. A. (2013). Are forensic experts biased by the side that retained them? *Psychological Science*, 24(10), 1889–1897.

Murrie, D. C., Boccaccini, M. T., Turner, D. B., Meeks, M., Woods, C., & Tussey, C. (2009). Rater (dis) agreement on risk assessment measures in sexually violent predator proceedings: Evidence of adversarial allegiance in forensic evaluation? *Psychology, Public Policy, and Law*, 15(1), 19–53.

National Research Council. (2009). *Strengthening Forensic Science in the United States: A Path Forward*. National Academies Press.

Otto, R. K., Edens, J. F., & Barcus, E. H. (2000). The use of psychological testing in child custody evaluations. *Family and Conciliation Courts Review*, 38, 312–340.

Patrick, C. J. (2022). Psychopathy: Current knowledge and future directions. *Annual Review of Clinical Psychology*, 18, 387–415.

Rundle, B. K., Vaughn, V. R., & Stanford, M. S. (2015). Contagious yawning and psychopathy. *Personality and Individual Differences*, 86, 33–37.

Sagioglou, C., & Greitemeyer, T. (2016). Individual differences in bitter taste preferences are associated with antisocial personality traits. *Appetite*, 96, 299–308.

Sample, I. (2017, September 26). *Playlist of the Lambs: Psychopaths May Have Distinct Musical Preference*. The Guardian. https://www.theguardian.com/science/2017/sep/26/playlist-of-the-lambs-psychopaths-prefer-rap-over-classical-music-study-shows

Sreedhar, A. (2013, August 7). *Study Says Night Owls More Likely to be Psychopaths*. Mic. https://www.mic.com/articles/58217/study-says-night-owls-more-likely-to-be-psychopaths#.T2G8MJGHG

Study says psychopaths love rap music. (2019, October 1). Iotwreport.com. Retrieved January 9, 2023, from https://iotwreport.com/study-says-psychopaths-love-rap-music/.

Tourjee, D. (2016, May 10). *Narcissists and Psychopaths Love to Stay Friends with Their Exes*. Vice. https://www.vice.com/en/article/ezjy3m/narcissists-and-psychopaths-love-to-stay-friends-with-their-exes

Valerio, C., & Beck, C. J. (2017). Testing in child custody evaluations: An overview of issues and uses. *Journal of Child Custody*, 14(4), 260–280.

Vedel, A., & Thomsen, D. K. (2017). The Dark Triad across academic majors. *Personality and Individual Differences*, *116*, 86–91.

Waugh, R. (2016, April 26). *Creative People Might Secretly be Psychopaths, Scientists Warn*. Metro. https://metro.co.uk/2016/04/26/creative-people-might-secretly-be-psychopaths-scientists-warn-5842431/

Part V

Conclusion

15 Science-Based Clinical Psychology

Stephen Hupp and Vyla Hupp

By now, you must surely be feeling disheartened about the scientific status of clinical psychology. Remember, though, that this book has been focusing on claims skewing toward the pseudoscientific end of the science-pseudoscience continuum. Fortunately, clinical psychology has plenty of reputable scientific findings as well, and this chapter creates a space for us to celebrate the science. In particular, several psychosocial treatments have strong research support, and so we'll first spend a little time defining what it means for an intervention to be characterized as a *well-established treatment*. Next, we'll provide a critique of this definition, and with an eye to the future we'll share some aspirational goals for identifying the most effective treatments.

Well-Established Treatments in Clinical Psychology

In the 1990s, the Society of Clinical Psychology (SCP; Division 12 of the American Psychological Association [APA]) created a Task Force on Promotion and Dissemination of Psychological Procedures to develop criteria for identifying which psychosocial treatments could be characterized as *empirically validated treatments* (EVTs; APA Task Force, 1995). Soon thereafter, the term EVTs was replaced by *empirically supported treatments* (ESTs; Chambless & Hollon, 1998), and since then the broader term of *evidence-based practices* (EBPs) has also been introduced (APA Presidential Task Force, 2006). Across these different ways of describing efficacious treatments, the definition of what would be called a *well-established treatment* (also called *efficacious*) has remained about the same. That is, a treatment is well established once it has two well-done randomized controlled trials (RCTs) by at least two different teams. That is, the research design for the RCT had to be strong, and replication by a second research team was required (APA Task Force, 1995; Chambless et al., 1998).

The characterization of well-established treatment was meant to be the highest level of support within this framework. Less stringent criteria for a

DOI: 10.4324/9781003259510-20

second level of EST support – *probably efficacious* – were also developed. Since then, criteria for additional (even lower) levels of support have also been developed and include *possibly efficacious, experimental,* and *questionable efficacy* (Silverman & Hinshaw, 2008). For the purposes of this chapter, however, we'll focus on the well-established treatments.

How many well-established treatments are there and what are they? Table 15.1 includes the well-established treatments for adults at the time of this writing (SCP, n.d.a.).

Table 15.1 Well-Established Psychosocial Treatments for Adults

Disorder/Issue	Well-Established Treatments
Attention-Deficit/Hyperactivity Disorder	Cognitive-Behavioral Therapy
Schizophrenia	Assertive Community Treatment
	Cognitive-Behavioral Therapy
	Cognitive Remediation
	Family Psychoeducation
	Social Learning/Token Economy Programs
	Social Skills Training
	Supported Employment
Bipolar Disorders	Psychoeducation (mania)
	Systemic Care (mania)
	Family-Focused Therapy (depression)
Depressive Disorders	Behavioral Activation
	Cognitive Therapy
	Cognitive-Behavioral Analysis System of Psychotherapy
	Cognitive-Behavioral Therapy (for people with diabetes)
	Interpersonal Psychotherapy
	Mindfulness-Based Cognitive Therapy
	Problem-Solving Therapy
	Self-Management/Self-Control Therapy
Anxiety Disorders	Cognitive and Behavioral Therapies (generalized anxiety)
	Cognitive-Behavioral Therapy (panic; social anxiety)
	Exposure Therapies (specific phobias)
Obsessive-Compulsive Disorder	Cognitive-Behavioral Therapy
	Exposure and Response Prevention
Posttraumatic Stress Disorder	Cognitive Processing Therapy
	Prolonged Exposure Therapy
	Seeking Safety (with substance use disorders)

(*Continued*)

Table 15.1 (Continued)

Disorder/Issue	Well-Established Treatments
Pain	Acceptance and Commitment Therapy (chronic)
	Cognitive-Behavioral Therapy (back; head; irritable bowel)
	Multi-Component CBT (fibromyalgia; rheumatologic)
Eating Disorders	Cognitive-Behavioral Therapy (bulimia; binge eating)
	Family-Based Treatment (anorexia; bulimia)
	Interpersonal Psychotherapy (bulimia; binge eating)
Weight Management	Behavioral Weight Management
Insomnia Disorder	Cognitive-Behavioral Therapy
	Paradoxical Intention
	Relaxation Training
	Sleep Restriction Therapy
	Stimulus Control Therapy
Substance and Alcohol Use Disorders	Behavioral Couples Therapy (alcohol)
	MI, MET, and MET+CBT (mixed substances)
	Seeking Safety (mixed substance)
Borderline Personality Disorder	Dialectical Behavior Therapy
Relationship Distress	Emotionally Focused Couples Therapy

Note: This list was created in 2023 and influenced by several pages from the website for the Society of Clinical Psychology (SCP) and several systematic reviews (marked with [1] in the References section). On the SCP website, well-established treatments are described as having "Strong Research Support" under the 1998 EST criteria. MI = Motivational Interviewing; MET; Motivation Enhancement treatment; CBT = Cognitive-Behavioral Therapy.

You may notice that a good majority of the treatments are variations of some broad treatment approaches, specifically behavioral and cognitive therapies. In particular, *cognitive-behavioral therapy* (CBT) was used to describe a broad treatment approach even though CBT varies based on the specific disorder, behavior, or condition it is being used to treat. We should note that in the past, a purple hat therapy and a harmful treatment have been identified as being empirically supported – they are discussed earlier in this book and in the book *Pseudoscience in Therapy* (Hupp & Santa Maria, 2023).

Overall, there are many well-established treatments for adults, and the list continues to grow. Considerably more information can be found on the website for the Society of Clinical Psychology (SCP, n.d.b.). If you'd like to get an even more up-to-date and comprehensive view of well-established treatments, you can do so there. That website uses the phrase "strong research support" to represent well-established treatments based on the Chambless and colleagues (1998) EST criteria. There you can also see additional treatments that are probably efficacious (i.e., modest research support).

Similarly, another APA Division, the Society of Clinical Child and Adolescent Psychology (SCCAP; Division 53) hosts a website that identifies well-established treatments for youth (SCCAP, n.d.). Articles from the *Journal of Clinical Child and Adolescent Psychology* are the primary resource the SCCAP uses to identify treatments, referred to on the website as "Level One: Works Well." Table 15.2 includes the well-established psychosocial treatments for children and adolescents at the time of this writing.

Table 15.2 Well-Established Psychosocial Treatments for Children and Adolescents

Disorder/Issue	Well-Established Treatments
Autism Spectrum Disorder	Applied Behavior Analysis
Attention-Deficit/ Hyperactivity disorder	Behavioral Parent Training
	Behavioral Classroom Management
	Behavioral Peer Interventions
	Organization Training
Schizophrenia	Multimodal Therapy
	Family-Focused Therapy
	Cognitive-Behavioral Therapy for Psychosis
Bipolar Disorders	Family Skill Building Plus Psychoeducation
Depressive Disorders	Cognitive-Behavioral Therapy (adolescents)
	Interpersonal Psychotherapy (adolescents)
Anxiety Disorders	Cognitive-Behavioral Therapy
	Education
	Exposure
	Modeling
Obsessive-Compulsive Disorder	Family-Focused Cognitive-Behavioral Therapy
Posttraumatic Stress Disorder	Trauma-Focused Cognitive-Behavioral Therapy
Disruptive Behavior	Parent Behavior Therapy (children)
	Combined Behavioral, Cognitive, and Family Therapies (adolescents)
Eating Disorders	Family-Based Treatment
Weight Management	Behavioral Treatment (children)
Bedwetting	Urine Alarm (children)
	Dry-Bed Training (children)
Poor Sleep	Cognitive-Behavioral Therapy for Insomnia
	Brief Behavioral Therapy
	Behavioral Interventions

(*Continued*)

Table 15.2 (Continued)

Disorder/Issue	Well-Established Treatments
Substance Use	Cognitive-Behavioral Therapy (adolescents) Motivational Enhancement Treatment with CBT (adolescents) Family-Based Treatment – Ecological (adolescents)
Self-Harm/Ideation	Dialectical Behavior Therapy (adolescents)

Note: This table was created in 2023 and influenced by several pages from the Society for Clinical Child and Adolescent Psychology (SCCAP) website and several systematic reviews (marked with [*2] in the References section). On the SCCAP website, well-established treatments are described as "Level One: Works Well."

Similar to treatments for adults, the majority of well-established treatments are variations of behavioral and cognitive therapies. Visit the Division 53 website for up-to-date and more comprehensive information (SCCAP, n.d.). When taken together, these lists of well-established treatments might look long at first glance, but keep in mind that there's hundreds of psychosocial treatments available, and most of them aren't included in these tables. It's also important to recognize that the whole process of identifying well-established treatments has had its share of controversy, both from proponents of treatments with modest research support (i.e., probably efficacious) that are not currently classified as well-established treatments (e.g., psychodynamic therapy; Shedler, 2010), and especially by proponents of treatments that have little to no research support.

Raising the Bar to Science-Based Therapy

Even proponents of the movement to identify efficacious treatments have critiqued the methods used, and so we'll now move toward a few additional topics worth considering. That is, the current system of identifying well-established treatments (Chambless et al., 1998) has several limitations:

- **Low Bar for Being Characterized as a Well-Established Treatment.** It only takes two well done studies – conducted by two different teams – for an intervention to meet the criteria for being a well-established treatment (Chambless et al., 1998). Overall, this is a fairly low bar for a treatment to meet these criteria, and this opens the door for interventions to be characterized as well-established treatments even when there may be good reasons for caution. This low bar is also related to all of the issues below.
- **Conflicting Evidence.** Sometimes a treatment might have mixed research support, with two well done studies demonstrating efficacy and several studies showing the treatment is ineffective and even potentially

harmful. Thus, technically the treatment meets the criteria for being a well-established treatment even though the big picture is more complicated (Tolin et al., 2015a).

- **Statistical Significance and Clinical Significance.** It's possible for a study to show that a treatment group gets statistically better even though most of the participants in the treatment group continue to have substantial clinical impairment (Ogles et al., 2001). That is, sometimes the gains are small even though they are technically statistically significant. Overall, a consideration of effect sizes and clinical significance is critical.
- **Symptom Reduction and Functional Outcomes.** It's also possible for a study to show improvement in symptom reduction (such as depressed mood) without also showing improvement in functional outcomes (such as social relationships); however, functional outcomes are also very important (Tolin et al., 2015a).
- **Efficacy and Effectiveness.** Treatments tested in *efficacy* trials are examined in optimal conditions with a controlled environment and a highly trained research team whereas *effectiveness* studies take place in a real-world setting with natural conditions (Chambless & Hollon, 1998). Effects seen in a real-world setting may deviate from the positive effects seen in controlled environments. Therefore, effectiveness studies provide an important layer of evidence when it comes to determining how well a treatment really works.
- **Cultural Humility and Demographic Considerations.** People of color are underrepresented in much of the research on well-established treatments. Thus, it's important to consider how these treatments might work, and potentially be adapted for, all ethnicities and races (Pina et al., 2019). Similarly, treatments can have different levels of effectiveness for other demographic variables such as gender and age.
- **Length of Treatment Gains.** A well-established treatment could be immediately effective but the positive gains could be just as quickly lost. Thus, it's also important to consider how long the treatment gains last once the treatment is discontinued (Tolin et al., 2015a).
- **Treatment Packages and Their Components.** Early attempts at identifying well-established treatments focused on treatment packages that often had several similar name-brand variations. That is, the core components across those treatment packages were largely the same. More recently there has been an attempt to identify more generic treatment packages while also identifying which components (or processes) are key contributors to the treatment's effects (Hupp et al., 2018).
- **Therapy Relationships.** When considering core components of treatments, it's also important to recognize common factors that cut across treatment modalities. In particular, there are several aspects of the therapeutic relationship that have been shown to influence how well a treatment works,

such as: a) empathy, b) emotional expression, c) affirmation/validation, d) congruence/genuineness and the real relationship, e) goal consensus and collaboration, f) collection of client feedback, g) therapeutic alliance, and h) repair of alliance ruptures (Norcross & Karpiak, 2024).

- **Consideration of Plausibility.** A treatment can be identified as well-established even though one or more of its components has been developed without a plausible theoretical rationale that is consistent with a scientific understanding of human development (Hupp et al., 2019). Sometimes a component of a treatment even contradicts the known laws of nature, raising a red flag about the treatment's legitimacy.

- **Purple Hat Components.** Implausible treatment components are especially problematic when used in unison with effective components. For example, a person could wear a purple hat while also participating in CBT for an anxiety disorder (see Rosen & Davison, 2003, and Chapter 9 of this book). If the person gets better, they (and their therapist) might assume that the purple hat was a key component (and perhaps *the key* component) in decreasing their symptoms. In fact, research would show that the new purple hat therapy works. However, if the added implausible component was removed, the treatment would be just as effective. Overall, the added purple hat component appears to be contributing to the treatment's efficacy but it is not adding anything other than confusion.

With the above critiques in mind, it's apparent that a new system for evaluating treatments is warranted. The new system need not replace the previous framework but can provide an additional way to consider what works. In an article titled "Why Evidence-Based Practice Isn't Enough: A Call for Science-Based Practice," Lilienfeld and colleagues (2018) make the case for ways in which the criteria for identifying well-established treatments fall short (see also David & Montgomery, 2011). Evident from the article's title, and following suit from the field of medicine, the authors call for the term *science-based* to be used to represent a more rigorous alternative to the current *evidence-based* (and *empirically supported*) framework of identifying treatments that work. In the article, Lilienfeld and colleagues endorse the new criteria set forth by Tolin and colleagues (2015a) that have come to be called the "Tolin criteria" and which exemplify *science-based therapy*. Table 15.3 presents the science-based Tolin criteria.

These science-based Tolin criteria address most of the critiques of the previous framework. That is, these newer criteria emphasize: a) systematic reviews covering a wide range of studies, b) consistency across these studies, c) clinically meaningful improvement in symptoms and functional

Table 15.3 The Science-Based Tolin Criteria for Psychosocial Treatments

Definition of "High-Quality" Evidence	1 **Breadth of Literature and Solid Research Design:** wide range of studies included in the analyses with no major limitations. 2 **Consistent Results:** little variation between studies. 3 **Confidence:** the summary estimate has a narrow confidence interval.
Criteria for a **Very Strong Recommendation** (must have all 4 of these)	1 **Symptom Improvement:** high-quality evidence that the treatment produces a clinically meaningful effect on symptoms of the disorder being treated. 2 **Functional Outcome Improvement:** high-quality evidence that the treatment produces a clinically meaningful effect on functional outcomes. 3 **Evidence of Lasting Effects:** high-quality evidence that the treatment produces a clinically meaningful effect on symptoms and/or functional outcomes at least 3 months after treatment discontinuation. 4 **Evidence of Effectiveness:** at least one well-conducted study has demonstrated effectiveness in nonresearch settings (and as part of the wide range of studies included in the review).
Criteria for **Strong Recommendation** (only need 1 of these)	1 **Symptom Improvement:** moderate- to high-quality evidence that the treatment produces a clinically meaningful effect on symptoms of the disorder being treated. 2 **Functional Outcome Improvement:** moderate- to high-quality evidence that the treatment produces a clinically meaningful effect on functional outcomes.

Note: This table was adapted from Tolin et al. (2015a) which was adapted from Guyatt et al. (2006).

outcomes, d) generalizability to non-research settings, and c) evidence of lasting effects.

The Society of Clinical Psychology has created a manual for how to do systematic reviews using the science-based Tolin criteria (Boness et al., 2021). At the time of this writing, only a few systematic reviews using these criteria have been conducted. First, Tolin and colleagues (2015b) provieded a "strong" (but not "very strong") recommendation for exposure and response prevention for obsessive-compulsive disorder. Boness and colleagues (2020) also gave cognitive-behavioral therapy for insomnia (CBT-I) a "strong" recommendation. Similarly, Pfund and colleagues (2022) evaluated contingency management for drug use disorders, and Boness and colleagues (2023) evaluated CBT for substance use disorders, and both reviews provided "strong" recommendations. Overall, it's clear that more research is needed before these treatments can reach the very strong recommendation, and much work needs to be done to evaluate other treatments for other disorders.

Summary and Conclusion

Many treatments have been identified as having strong research support, which has traditionally been determined by criteria set forth by a task force from the American Psychological Association. Most interventions characterized as well-established treatments are from the behavioral and cognitive therapies. However, the bar for determining if a treatment is "well-established" has traditionally been somewhat low. To meet these criteria, a treatment only needs two well-done studies (by two different teams) with little emphasis on functional outcomes, consistent results, effectiveness, or lasting effects. To be fair, the very notion of creating criteria for identifying efficacious treatments was quite an important innovation by the American Psychological Association.

Looking ahead, it's time to raise the bar. The new science-based Tolin criteria provide stricter criteria that represent consistent results across more studies and emphasize functional outcomes and lasting effects. Given that only a few treatments have been evaluated based on the Tolin criteria, the field of clinical psychology has a long way to go before fully realizing the aspirational goals of identifying science-based therapies with very strong research support for each challenging psychological issue. Fortunately, the journey has already started, providing optimism that clinical psychology can one day move beyond the pseudoscience that is often used. For more discussion about the science-based therapy framework, see the book *Science-Based Therapy* (Hupp & Tolin, 2024).

Stephen Hupp, PhD, is a licensed clinical psychologist and professor of psychology at Southern Illinois University Edwardsville. Along with Cara Santa Maria, he is co-editor of the book *Pseudoscience in Therapy: A Skeptical Field Guide.* He is also Editor of *Skeptical Inquirer: The Magazine for Science and Reason.*

Vyla Hupp is a psychology student at the University of Illinois.

References

[*2]Altman, M., & Wilfley, D. (2015). Evidence update on the treatment of over-weight and obesity in children and adolescents. *Journal of Clinical Child and Adolescent Psychology, 44*(4), 521–537. 10.1080/15374416.2014.963854

[*1]American Psychological Association (under development). *Clinical practice guideline (CPG) for the treatment of chronic musculoskeletal pain in adults.* Author.

[*1]American Psychological Association (2017). *Clinical practice guideline for the treatment of posttraumatic stress disorder (PTSD) in adults.* Author.

[*1]American Psychological Association (2019). *Clinical practice guideline for the treatment of depression across three age cohort.* Author.

APA Presidential Task Force on Evidence-Based Practice. (2006). Evidence-based practice in psychology. *The American Psychologist, 61*(4), 271–285.

APA Task Force on the Promotion and Dissemination of Psychological Procedures (1995). Training in and dissemination of empirically-validated psychological treatments: Report and recommendations. *The Clinical Psychologist, 48*(1), 3–23.

[*1]Beasley, C. C., & Ager, R. (2019). Emotionally focused couples therapy: A systematic review of its effectiveness over the past 19 years. *Journal of Evidence-Based Social Work, 16*(2), 144–159.

[*1]Bighelli, I., Rodolico, A., García-Mieres, H., Pitschel-Walz, G., Hansen, W. P., Schneider-Thoma, J., ... & Leucht, S. (2021). Psychosocial and psychological interventions for relapse prevention in schizophrenia: A systematic review and network meta-analysis. *The Lancet Psychiatry, 8*(11), 969–980.

Boness, C. L., Hershenberg, R., Grasso, D., Kaye, J., Mackintosh, M., Nason, E., Shah, A., & Raffa, D. (2021). *The society of clinical psychology's manual for the evaluation of psychological treatments using the Tolin criteria.* Society of Clinical Psychology.

Boness, C. L., Hershenberg, R., Kaye, J., Mackintosh, M. A., Grasso, D. J., Noser, A., & Raffa, S. D. (2020). An evaluation of cognitive behavioral therapy for insomnia: A systematic review and application of Tolin's Criteria for empirically supported treatments. *Clinical Psychology: Science and Practice, 27*(4), e12348.

Boness, C. L., Votaw, V., Schwebel, F. J., Moniz-Lewis, D. I., McHugh, R. K., & Witkiewitz, K. (2023). An evaluation of cognitive behavioral therapy for substance use: An application of Tolin's criteria for empirically supported treatments. *Clinical Psychology: Science and Practice.* [online first publication]

[*2]Brickman, H. M. & Fristad, M. A. (2022). Psychosocial treatments for bipolar disorder in children and adolescents. *Annual Review of Clinical Psychology, 18*, 291–327. 10.1146/annurev-clinpsy-072220-021237

[*1]Bulik, C. M., Berkman, N. D., Brownley, K. A., Sedway, J. A., & Lohr, K. N. (2007). Anorexia nervosa treatment: A systematic review of randomized controlled trials. *International Journal of Eating Disorders, 40*(4), 310–320.

[*1]Butler, A. C., Chapman, J. E., Forman, E. M., & Beck, A. T. (2006). The empirical status of cognitive-behavioral therapy: A review of meta-analyses. *Clinical Psychology Review, 26*(1), 17–31.

Chambless, D. L., Baker, M. J., Baucom, D. H., Beutler, L. E., Calhoun, K. S., et al. (1998). Update on empirically validated therapies, II. *The Clinical Psychologist, 51*(1), 3–16.

Chambless, D. L., & Hollon, S. D. (1998). Defining empirically supported therapies. *Journal of Consulting and Clinical Psychology, 66*(1), 7–18.

[*2]Comer, J. S., Hong, N., Poznanski, B., Silva, K., & Wilson, M. (2019). Evidence base update on the treatment of early childhood anxiety and related problems. *Journal of Clinical Child and Adolescent Psychology, 48*(1), 1–15, 10.1080/153 74416.2018.1534208

[*2]Datta, N., Matheson, B. E., Citron, K., Van Wye, E. M., & Lock, J. D. (2022). Evidence based update on psychosocial treatments for eating disorders in children and adolescents. *Journal of Clinical Child & Adolescent Psychology, 52*(2), 159–170. DOI: 10.1080/15374416.2022.2109650

David, D., & Montgomery, G. H. (2011). The scientific status of psychotherapies: A new evaluative framework for evidence-based psychosocial interventions. *Clinical Psychology: Science and Practice, 18*(2), 89–99.

[*2]Dorsey, S., McLaughlin, K. A., Kerns, S. E. U., Harrison, J. P., Lambert, H. K., Briggs, E. C., Cox, J. R., & Amaya-Jackson, L. (2016). Evidence base update for psychosocial treatments for children and adolescents exposed to traumatic events. *Journal of Clinical Child and Adolescent Psychology, 46*(3), 303–330. 10.1080/15374416.2016.1220309

[*1]Dutra, L., Stathopoulou, G., Basden, S. L., Leyro, T. M., Powers, M. B., & Otto, M. W. (2008). A meta-analytic review of psychosocial interventions for substance use disorders. *American Journal of Psychiatry, 165*(2), 179–187.

[*2]Evans, S., Owens, J., & Bunford, N. (2014). Evidence-based psychosocial treatments for children and adolescents with attention-deficit/hyperactivity disorder. *Journal of Clinical Child and Adolescent Psychology, 43*(4), 527–551. 10.1080/15374416.2013.850700

[*1]Ferrando, C., & Selai, C. (2021). A systematic review and meta-analysis on the effectiveness of exposure and response prevention therapy in the treatment of obsessive-compulsive disorder. *Journal of Obsessive-Compulsive and Related Disorders, 31*, e100684.

[*1]Franz, M. J., VanWormer, J. J., Crain, A. L., Boucher, J. L., Histon, T., Caplan, W., ... & Pronk, N. P. (2007). Weight-loss outcomes: A systematic review and meta-analysis of weight-loss clinical trials with a minimum 1-year follow-up. *Journal of the American Dietetic association, 107*(10), 1755–1767.

[*2]Freeman, J., Benito, K., Herren, J., Kemp, J., Sung, J., Georgiadis, C., Arora, A., Walther, M., & Garcia, A. (2018). Evidence base update of psychosocial treatments for pediatric obsessive-compulsive disorder: Evaluating, improving, and transporting what works. *Journal of Clinical Child and Adolescent Psychology, 47*(5), 669–698. 10.1080/15374416.2018.1496443

[*2]Fristad, M. A., & MacPherson, H. A. (2014). Evidence-based psychosocial treatments for child and adolescent bipolar spectrum disorders. *Journal of Clinical Child and Adolescent Psychology, 43*(3), 339–355. 10.1080/1537441 6.2013.822309

[*1]Gillespie, C., Murphy, M., & Joyce, M. (2022). Dialectical behavior therapy for individuals with borderline personality disorder: A systematic review of outcomes after one year of follow-up. *Journal of Personality Disorders*, 36(4), 431–454.

[*2]Glenn, C. R., Esposito, E. C., Porter, A. C., & Robinson, D. J. (2019). Evidence base update of psychosocial treatments for self-injurious thoughts and behaviors in youth. *Journal of Clinical Child & Adolescent Psychology*, 48(3), 357–392.

Guyatt, G., Gutterman, D., Baumann, M. H., Addrizzo-Harris, D., Hylek, E. M., Phillips, B., ... & Schünemann, H. (2006). Grading strength of recommendations and quality of evidence in clinical guidelines: Report from an American College of Chest Physicians task force. *Chest*, 129(1), 174–181.

[*2]Higa-McMillan, C. K., Francis, S. E., Rith-Najarian, L., & Chorpita, B. F. (2016). Evidence base update: 50 Years of research on treatment for child and adolescent anxiety. *Journal of Clinical Child and Adolescent Psychology*, 45(2), 91–113, 10.1080/15374416.2015.1046177

[*2]Hogue, A., Henderson, C. E., Becker, S. J., & Knight, D. K. (2018). Evidence base on outpatient behavioral treatments for adolescent substance use, 2014–2017: Outcomes, treatment delivery, and promising horizons. *Journal of Clinical Child and Adolescent Psychology*, 47(4), 499–526. 10.1080/1537441 6.2018.1466307

Hupp, S., Macphee, F. L., & Pelham, W. E. (2018). The science of psychotherapy with youth. In S. Hupp (Ed.), *Child and Adolescent Psychotherapy: Components of Evidence-Based Treatments for Youth and Their Parents* (pp. 1–11). Cambridge University Press.

Hupp, S., Mercer, J., Thyer, B. A., & Pignotti, M. (2019). Critical thinking about psychotherapy. In S. Hupp (Ed.), *Pseudoscience in Child and Adolescent Psychotherapy: A Skeptical Field Guide* (pp. 1–13). Cambridge University Press.

Hupp, S. & Santa Maria, C. (2023). *Pseudoscience in therapy: A skeptical field guide*. Cambridge University Press.

Hupp, S. & Tolin, D. (2024). *Science-based therapy: Components of evidence-based treatments*. Cambridge University Press.

[*2]Kaminski, J. & Claussen, A. (2017). Evidence based update for psychosocial treatments for disruptive behaviors in children. *Journal of Clinical Child and Adolescent Psychology*, 46(4), 477–499. 10.1080/15374416.2017.1310044

[*2]Lecomte, T., Abidi, S., Garcia-Ortega, I., Mian, I., Jackson, K., Jackson, K., & Norman, R. (2017). Canadian treatment guidelines on psychosocial treatment of schizophrenia in children and youth. *The Canadian Journal of Psychiatry*, 62(9), 648–655.

Lilienfeld, S. O., Lynn, S. J., & Bowden, S. C. (2018). Why evidence-based practice isn't enough: A call for science-based practice. *The Behavior Therapist*, 41(1), 42–47.

[*1]Linardon, J., Wade, T. D., De la Piedad Garcia, X., & Brennan, L. (2017). The efficacy of cognitive-behavioral therapy for eating disorders: A systematic review and meta-analysis. *Journal of Consulting and Clinical Psychology*, 85(11), 1080–1094.

*2McCart, M. R., Sheidow, A. J., & Jaramillo, J. (2022). Evidence-based update of psychosocial treatments for adolescents with disruptive behavior. *Journal of Clinical Child and Adolescent Psychology* (online first publication). DOI: 10.1 080/15374416.2022.2145566

Norcross, J. C., & Karpiak, C. P. (2024). Psychotherapy relationships. In S. Hupp & D. Tolin (Eds.), *Science-Based Therapy*. Cambridge University Press.

Ogles, B. M., Lunnen, K. M., & Bonesteel, K. (2001). Clinical significance: History, application, and current practice. *Clinical Psychology Review*, *21*(3), 421–446.

*1Olatunji, B. O., Cisler, J. M., & Deacon, B. J. (2010). Efficacy of cognitive behavioral therapy for anxiety disorders: A review of meta-analytic findings. *Psychiatric Clinics*, *33*(3), 557–577.

*1Powers, M. B., Vedel, E., & Emmelkamp, P. M. (2008). Behavioral couples therapy (BCT) for alcohol and drug use disorders: A meta-analysis. *Clinical Psychology Review*, *28*(6), 952–962.

Pfund, R. A., Ginley, M. K., Boness, C. L., Rash, C. J., Zajac, K., & Witkiewitz, K. (2022). Contingency management for drug use disorders: Meta-analysis and application of Tolin's criteria. *Clinical Psychology: Science and Practice*. [online first publication]

Pina, A. A., Polo, A. J., & Huey, S. J. (2019). Evidence-based psychosocial interventions for ethnic minority youth: The 10-year update. *Journal of Clinical Child & Adolescent Psychology*, *48*(2), 179–202.

*1Rabelo, J. L., Cruz, B. F., Ferreira, J. D. R., de Mattos Viana, B., & Barbosa, I. G. (2021). Psychoeducation in bipolar disorder: A systematic review. *World Journal of Psychiatry*, *11*(12), 1407–1424.

Rosen, G. M., & Davison, G. C. (2003). Psychology should list empirically supported principles of change (ESPs) and not credential trademarked therapies or other treatment packages. *Behavior Modification*, *27*(3), 300–312.

Shedler J. (2010). The efficacy of psychodynamic psychotherapy. *American Psychologist*, *65*, 98–109.

*2Shepard, J. A., Poler Jr., J. E., & Grabman, J. H. (2017). Evidence-based psychosocial treatments for pediatric elimination disorders. *Journal of Clinical Child and Adolescent Psychology*, *46*(6), 767–797. 10.1080/153784416.201 6.1247356

Silverman, W. K., & Hinshaw, S. P. (2008). The second special issue on evidence-based psychosocial treatments for children and adolescents: A 10-year update. *Journal of Clinical Child & Adolescent Psychology*, *37*(1), 1–7.

*1Simon, G. E., Ludman, E. J., Bauer, M. S., Unutzer, J., & Operskalski, B. (2006). Long-term effectiveness and cost of a systematic care program for bipolar disorder. *Archives of General Psychiatry*, *63*, 500–508.

*2Stoll, R. D., Pina, A. A., & Schleider, J. (2020). Brief, non-pharmacological, interventions for pediatric anxiety: Meta-analysis and evidence base status. *Journal of Clinical Child & Adolescent Psychology*, *49*(4), 435–459.

*2Smith, T., & Iadarola, S. (2015) Evidence base update for autism spectrum disorder. *Journal of Clinical Child & Adolescent Psychology*, *44*(6), 897–922. DOI: 10.1080/15374416.2015.1077448

Society of Clinical Child and Adolescent Psychology (n.d.). Retrieved from https:// effectivechildtherapy.org/concerns-symptoms-disorders/

Society of Clinical Psychology (n.d.a.). Psychological treatments. Retrieved from https://div12.org/treatments/

Society of Clinical Psychology (n.d.b.). Diagnoses. Retrieved from https://div12. org/diagnoses/

Tolin, D. F., McKay, D., Forman, E. M., Klonsky, E. D., & Thombs, B. D. (2015a). Empirically supported treatment: Recommendations for a new model. *Clinical Psychology: Science and Practice, 22*(4), 317–338.

Tolin, D. F., Melnyk, T., & Marx, B. (2015b). Exposure and response prevention for obsessive-compulsive disorder. chrome-extension://efaidnbmnnni-bpcajpcglclefindmkaj/https://www.div12.org/wp-content/uploads/2019/10/Treatment-Review-ERP-for-OCD.pdf

*[1]Van Straten, A., van der Zweerde, T., Kleiboer, A., Cuijpers, P., Morin, C. M., & Lancee, J. (2018). Cognitive and behavioral therapies in the treatment of insomnia: A meta-analysis. *Sleep Medicine Reviews, 38*, 3–16.

*[2]Weersing, V. R., Jeffreys, M., Do, M. C. T., Schwartz, K. T., & Bolano, C. (2017). Evidence base update of psychosocial treatments for child and adolescent depression. *Journal of Clinical Child & Adolescent Psychology, 46*(1), 11–43.

*[1]Young, Z., Moghaddam, N., & Tickle, A. (2020). The efficacy of cognitive behavioral therapy for adults with ADHD: A systematic review and meta-analysis of randomized controlled trials. *Journal of Attention Disorders, 24*(6), 875–888.

Index

psychotropic medications 109
purple hat therapies: binaural beat 117, 120–121; energy psychology 117, 119–120; evidence-based components 116–117; eye movement desensitization and reprocessing therapy (EMDR) 117–119, 121, 122; features of 121–122
putative energies 102–106, 108, 109

randomized controlled trials (RCTs) 7, 84, 95–97, 106, 119, 129, 131, 132, 195
RCTs *see* randomized controlled trials
reflexology 105, 155
Reiki 102, 105, 107, 109, 155, 160, 163
representativeness bias 69
retrieval 165, 168
risky behavior 147–148, 150
Rorschach Inkblot 45–54
Rorschach Performance Assessment System (R-PAS) 50, 51, 53
Rorschach, Hermann 45, 48
Rotter Locus of Control Scale 67
R-PAS *see* Rorschach Performance Assessment System
RTCs *see* randomized controlled trials
Rush, Benjamin 91

SCAM *see* So-called alternative medicine
SCCAP *see* Society of Clinical Child and Adolescent Psychology
science-based clinical psychology: raising bar to science-based therapy 199–203; well-established treatments in 195–199
science-based therapy 199–203, **202**
scientist practitioner 7
scientist-practitioner model 6–7
self-centered impulsivity 186
sensing/intuition (S/I) 64
sexually violent predator (SVP) 181, 182
sham placebo-controlled designs 117, 119

Shatz, Carla 166
shiatsu 156
simple parenting solutions 144
So-called alternative medicine (SCAM) 156–163; harm to patients 160–161; integrated medicine (IM) 161–163; medical ethics 157–160
Society of Clinical Child and Adolescent Psychology (SCCAP) 198
spinal manipulation 156
stage hypnosis 81–83
Stagner, Ross 65
Stenger, Victor 105
storage 165, 168
strained parent-teen relationships 148–149
Stubblefield, Anna 94
subluxations 154
substantial disturbances 146–147
SVP *see* sexually violent predator syndrome 36
Szondi, Léopold (Lipót) 58–61, 70
The Szondi Test 58–61

Tapas Acupressure Technique® 119
TBIs *see* traumatic brain injuries
temper tantrums 143–145
terrible twos 143–145, 149, 150
therapeutic touch 102, 105–107, 156
thinking/feeling (T/F)64–65
Thought Field Therapy 119
Tide Pod challenge 148
tire tack evidence 180
TMS *see* transcranial magnetic stimulation
traditional Chinese medicine 102, 156
transcranial magnetic stimulation (TMS) 166
traumatic brain injuries (TBIs) 167
trepanning 90, 91

U.S. Department of Health and Human Services 103

validation studies 52
validity coefficient 52
veritable energies 103

For Product Safety Concerns and Information please contact our EU
representative GPSR@taylorandfrancis.com Taylor & Francis Verlag GmbH,
Kaufingerstraße 24, 80331 München, Germany

Printed and bound by CPI Group (UK) Ltd, Croydon, CR0 4YY
08/06/2025
01897002-0007